ADVANCE PRAISE FOR
THE GREATEST AMERICAN

"Few scholars today know Benjamin Franklin as well, or as intimately, as Mark Skousen. That familiarity is on full display in *The Greatest American*. Skousen, a direct descendant of his subject, ranges nimbly across the remarkable breadth of Franklin's life, from his views on business and economics to education and, yes, sex. Along the way, he makes a compelling case not only for Franklin's greatness but also for his relevance today. He is the most modern of founders—and the most fun."

—Eric Weiner, author, *Ben and Me*,
and former foreign correspondent for NPR

"Mark Skousen lucidly, delightfully and successfully lays out the life of one the most extraordinary figures in American—and indeed world—history. Franklin personified and promoted the characteristics and culture that made America great, especially the drive for self-improvement and inventiveness. His genius for diplomacy was absolutely essential for the success of the American Revolution. The significance of his astonishing scientific achievements, insights, and research are only now being fully appreciated. One can only exclaim: What a man!"

—Steve Forbes, chairman and editor in chief,
Forbes magazine

"We can't bring back Ben Franklin. That's too bad, because America could use him now. Mark Skousen does the next best thing: channeling the spirit of Franklin in this lively and accessible book. Strangers to Franklin will marvel at all he accomplished. Even Franklin experts will benefit from reminders of the breadth of his contributions to American life."

—H. W. Brands, University of Texas at Austin

"If I could go back in time to meet with any world historical figure, even more than Aristotle, Galileo, Newton, Jefferson, or Darwin I would love nothing more than spending an evening dining and drinking with Benjamin Franklin, one of the most intellectually diverse thinkers and doers of all time, and who arguably did as much as anyone to create the modern world. Mark Skousen's new book—*The Greatest American*—more than lives up to supporting the subtitle descriptor of Franklin as *The World's Most Versatile Genius*. Indeed he was, and the world is richer for his eighty-four years on this planet. A gripping narrative that carries the reader from one chapter of Franklin's life to the next. Bravo!"

—Michael Shermer, *Publisher Skeptic* magazine, author
of *The Moral Arc*

"If anyone embodies the Renaissance man, it's Ben Franklin—printer, scientist, musician, inventor, author, activist, statesman, and diplomat. Mark Skousen delves into every facet of his remarkable life, including Franklin's surprisingly active love life into his eighties, in this lively and entertaining book. Highly recommended!"

—Alexander Green, chief investment strategist, The
Oxford Club, and author of *Beyond Wealth*

"Of all the Founding Fathers, Benjamin Franklin is my favorite. He was America's first conscious capitalist, achieving financial independence by meeting the needs and well-being of his customers. He then used his wealth to improve the community and played a crucial role in saving the country during its darkest hours. More than any other writer, Mark Skousen illustrates why Franklin has come to be regarded, both by citizens and historians, as the greatest American."

—John Mackey, cofounder of Whole Foods Market

The
Greatest
American

The
Greatest
American

by **MARK SKOUSEN**

A REPUBLIC BOOK
ISBN: 978-1-64572-100-0
ISBN (eBook): 978-1-64572-101-7

The Greatest American:
Benjamin Franklin, The World's Most Versatile Genius
© 2025 by Mark Skousen
All Rights Reserved

Cover Design by Jim Villaflores

No part of this book may be reproduced, stored in a retrieval system, or transmitted by any means without the written permission of the author and publisher.

This is a work of nonfiction. All people, locations, events, and situations are portrayed to the best of the author's memory.

Republic Book Publishers
Washington, VA
www.republicbookpublishers.com

Published in the United States of America
1 2 3 4 5 6 7 8 9 10
Printed in Canada

To my wife, Jo Ann, and to all the descendants
of Benjamin Franklin

"It is the man and woman united that make the complete
human being. Together they are more likely to succeed in
the world."
—Benjamin Franklin

CONTENTS

How Well Do You Know Ben Franklin? Take This Quiz! xiii

Introduction xvii

Twenty-Two Careers xix

A Short History of Franklin's Life xxi

Chapter 1: The Most Modern of the Founders 1

Part I: On Business
Chapter 2: The Father of American Capitalism 7
Chapter 3: On Becoming Rich 10
Chapter 4: On Being a Good Business Manager 13
Chapter 5: Advice on Running a Successful Business 16
Chapter 6: On Creating a Club of "Useful Knowledge and
      Influence" 20
Chapter 7: On Being an Entrepreneur 24
Chapter 8: In Defense of Moneymaking and the Commercial
      Society 27
Chapter 9: In Defense of the Rich 30
Chapter 10: Franklin as Self-Help Guru 34
Chapter 11: Modern-Day Franklin Fans: Buffett and Munger 37

Part II: On Personal Finance and Investing
Chapter 12: On Working Hard, Budgeting, and Thrift 43
Chapter 13: The Power of Compound Interest: Franklin's Proof ... 47
Chapter 14: On Successful Investing 51
Chapter 15: On Fast Money 54
Chapter 16: On Investing in Real Estate 57

Chapter 17: On Getting Out of Debt 61
Chapter 18: On Surviving a Financial Crisis...........................65
Chapter 19: Protecting Your Capital in Wartime 68
Chapter 20: On Doomsayers and Fear Mongering 71
Chapter 21: On Austerity..76
Chapter 22: On Writing a Last Will 80

Part III: On Science, Technology, and Medicine
Chapter 23: The Wonders of Science...85
Chapter 24: Thunder and Lightning: The Philadelphia
    Experiments 88
Chapter 25: What?! Franklin Never Took Out Any Patents on
    His Inventions? 93
Chapter 26: Magic Squares: Ben Franklin as Polymath............98
Chapter 27: On Diet, Exercise, and Medical Science.............102
Chapter 28: Retirement and the Secret to a Long Life 106

Part IV: On Economics and the Economy
Chapter 29: Benjamin Franklin: Adam Smith's Invisible
    Hand? 113
Chapter 30: On Achieving the American Dream....................121
Chapter 31: On the Benefits of Free Trade 127
Chapter 32: On Inequality...130
Chapter 33: On Today's Heavy Tax Burden 133
Chapter 34: On Political Economy 137
Chapter 35: The Virtue of Thrift Makes a Comeback............141
Chapter 36: How Franklin Saved the Post Office and Unified the
    Colonies..146
Chapter 37: The First Copper Penny 150
Chapter 38: On Paper Money and Inflation 154
Chapter 39: On Being an Optimist..156

Part V: On Politics
Chapter 40: On Politics..161
Chapter 41: On Racism 165

Chapter 42: On Nepotism and Helping Relatives 168
Chapter 43: On Government Abuse of Our Rights 171
Chapter 44: Franklin's Three Symbols of America..................174
Chapter 45: On Celebrating the 4th of July 177
Chapter 46: On the United States Constitution 180
Chapter 47: On America: A Rising or Setting Sun? 183
Chapter 48: On War and Peace 186
Chapter 49: Franklin's Single Change in the Declaration of
   Independence..190

Part VI: On International Relations and Travel
Chapter 50: On Being an International Man..........................197
Chapter 51: On Traveling Abroad and Vacations...................200
Chapter 52: On the Chinese 203

Part VII: On Personalities
Chapter 53: On Fame and Vanity..209
Chapter 54: Have You Read Franklin's Masterpiece?..............214
Chapter 55: Seven Discoveries in Completing Franklin's
   Autobiography 218
Chapter 56: On Making Enemies...222
Chapter 57: On John Adams..226
Chapter 58: On Thomas Jefferson 229
Chapter 59: On George Washington......................................232

Part VIII: On Culture and Personality
Chapter 60: On a Lifelong Education 237
Chapter 61: On Fundraising 242
Chapter 62: On the Importance of Good Humor
   and Laughter...248
Chapter 63: On Chess, Sports, and Other Games 254
Chapter 64: On Winning Friends and Influencing People......258
Chapter 65: On Knowledge, Books, and Success...................262
Chapter 66: Franklin Said What?! 265

Part IX: On Religion and Philosophy
Chapter 67: The Benefits of a Useful Religion 271
Chapter 68: Franklin, the Practical Philosopher 274
Chapter 69: On Giving and Charity 278
Chapter 70: Franklin's Version of the First Thanksgiving 282
Chapter 71: On Dying and the Afterlife...................................286
Chapter 72: Claimed by the Masons and the Mormons 290

Part X: Personal
Chapter 73: Franklin's 13 Virtues...297
Chapter 74: Man of Letters: On the Importance of Letter
     Writing 300
Chapter 75: On Enjoying the Holidays.....................................304
Chapter 76: On Famous Ancestors and the Family Tree 307
Chapter 77: On Love, Sex, and Marriage: Franklin's Hard-to-
     Govern Passions 311
Chapter 78: On Marriage and Family Life.................................322
Chapter 79: Are We in Moral Progress or Decline?.................325
Chapter 80: Franklin and His Critics 328

What Would Benjamin Franklin Say Today: A Warning
     to America 345
Index 351
Acknowledgments..376
About the Author...377

HOW WELL DO YOU KNOW BEN FRANKLIN? TAKE THIS QUIZ!

1. What was Franklin's favorite symbol of America found on the American eagle silver dollar? (Chapter 44)
   A. Lady Liberty
   B. Eagle
   C. Turkey
   D. Rising sun
   E. Rattlesnake

2. Which of the following founding fathers became a bitter enemy of Ben Franklin? (Chapter 57)
   A. John Adams
   B. George Washington
   C. Thomas Jefferson
   D. James Madison
   E. Alexander Hamilton

3. Did Franklin abandon his wife when he moved to London in 1757? (Chapter 80)

4. How many illegitimate children did Ben Franklin sire? (Chapter 77)

5. What was his favorite scripture in the Bible? (Chapter 9)

6. What caused Franklin to change his mind about religion and belief in a personal God? (Chapter 67)

THE GREATEST AMERICAN

7. Which of the following quotes did Ben Franklin actually say or write? (Circle all correct answers.) (Chapter 66)
   A. "Beer is proof that God loves us and wants us to be happy."
   B. "Tell me and I forget. Teach me and I remember. Involve me and I learn."
   C. "Those who would give up essential liberty, to purchase a little safety deserve neither liberty nor safety."
   D. "Nothing is certain in this life but death and taxes."
   E. "By failing to prepare, you are preparing to fail."

8. What single change did Franklin make in the Declaration of Independence? (Chapter 49)

9. What was Franklin's favorite game? (Chapter 63)

10. What invention did Franklin obtain a patent on? (Chapter 25)
    A. Franklin stove
    B. Lightning rod
    C. Bifocals
    D. Glass armonica
    E. None—he never applied for any patents.

11. How did Franklin convince Scottish philosopher and economist Adam Smith to take an unpopular position supporting American independence in his famous book *The Wealth of Nations*? (Chapter 29)

12. Which of the following commissioners to France was successful in raising money for the American cause during the War of Independence? (Chapter 61)
    A. Ben Franklin
    B. John Adams
    C. Arthur Lee
    D. Ralph Izard
    E. John Jay

13. Most people seldom change their mind about anything. But Franklin was an exception. Identify how he changed his views in the following areas:
    A. From religious heretic to an active Theist who believes that "God governs in the affairs of men" (Chapter 67)
    B. From slave owner to abolitionist (Chapter 41)
    C. From a philanderer to a devote family man (Chapter 77)
    D. From a doting father to disinheriting his son William (Chapter 56)
    E. From critic to diplomat (Chapter 64)
    F. From defender of the British empire to American rebel (Chapter 45)
    G. From workaholic to man of leisure (Chapter 12)

INTRODUCTION

Benjamin Franklin has been honored for many things: the first scientific American (Joyce Chaplin), the most celebrated American of any age (H. W. Brands), America's first humorist (Paul Johnson), and the father of American capitalism (Jack Bogle).

In his 2003 Franklin biography, Walter Isaacson calls him "America's best writer" and "the most fascinating of American founders." He concludes that Franklin was "the most accomplished American of his age and the most influential in inventing the type of society America would become."

Villanova Professor Paul Pasles identifies Franklin as "the most brilliant founding father," a "polymath," and an "Enlightenment superman… printer, scientist, inventor, author, philosopher, diplomat, and more." He granted his status as "the poster child for all-around genius, the last true renaissance man: jack-of-all-trades, and master of many."

Carl Van Doren began his famous 1938 biography by noting that Franklin "was—and is—unsurpassed by any man in the range of his natural gifts and of the important uses he put them to."

In his 2022 documentary, Ken Burns calls Franklin "the greatest American diplomat."

The title of this book is not my own. Back in 1950, in his book *The American Mind*, the historian Henry Steele Commager, called Benjamin Franklin the "greatest American." He praised Franklin's pragmatism, diplomacy, and practical wisdom, which made him a key figure in American history.

THE GREATEST AMERICAN

Michael Hart, author of *The 100: A Ranking of the Most Influential Persons in History*, who identified him as "the most versatile genius in all of history."

In 2005, AOL/Discovery Channel poll ranked Benjamin Franklin the fifth most admired citizen by Americans and tied with George Washington as America's favorite founding father. Of all the founders, he symbolized the "Age of Enlightenment."

TWENTY-TWO CAREERS

Franklin's many-sided genius can be measured by the variety of jobs he held during his long life. I came up twenty-two careers:

1. Printer
2. Postmaster
3. Diplomat/ambassador
4. Governor (Pennsylvania)
5. Author/essayist
6. Humorist
7. Inventor and entrepreneur
8. Scientist
9. Financial guru
10. Fundraiser
11. Military leader
12. Delegate/legislator/founding father
13. Clerk
14. Economist
15. Land speculator
16. Colonial agent
17. Club president
18. Musician
19. City planner
20. Justice of the peace
21. Banker
22. University founder

A SHORT HISTORY OF FRANKLIN'S LIFE

When he was born, there was no evidence of his genius. The youngest of ten sons of a Boston soap and candle maker, Benjamin Franklin was born January 17, 1706, in Puritan Boston and became apprenticed as a printer. At seventeen he ran away to Philadelphia, where he became a successful publisher of almanacs, pamphlets, and newspapers. He married his wife Deborah and had three children. His business pursuits were so profitable that he was able to retire in his early forties. He then became a gentleman of leisure, engaged in scientific pursuits and civil affairs.

For the next forty years, he devoted himself largely to politics, the military, and diplomacy, becoming the first postmaster general and representing the colonies on two missions to England. He received many honorary degrees for his experiments and writings about electricity and was referred to as "Dr. Franklin."

He repudiated the Stamp Act before the English parliament, then returned home to become a signer of the Declaration of Independence. His devoted Debbie had died two years earlier. In the fall of 1776, he became America's first ambassador, negotiating an alliance with France, where he became the toast of French society. France's resulting support of America in its war of independence from Great Britain may have been the deciding factor in achieving victory in 1781 at the Battle of Yorktown. After negotiating a peace treaty, Franklin returned home triumphantly in 1785

THE GREATEST AMERICAN

and inspired the delegates at the Constitutional Convention to adopt the Constitution before he died in 1790, surrounded by his daughter and grandchildren. By the end of his life, he was the best-known American of his age.

According to many historians, Ben Franklin was the wisest, most intellectual, and most self-reflective and self-improving of the founding fathers. As such, he was both honored and vilified. This book attempts to show why.

Note: Throughout the text, A stands for the Autobiography *by Benjamin Franklin (Regnery, 2006), and CA stands for* The Compleated Autobiography *by Benjamin Franklin (Regnery, 2006), edited by Mark and Jo Ann Skousen.*

CHAPTER 1

THE MOST MODERN OF THE FOUNDERS

*"I have sometimes almost wished it had
been my destiny to have been born two
or three centuries hence."*
—Ben Franklin (1788)

Benjamin Franklin was the oldest of the founding fathers—he was indeed a whole generation ahead of George Washington, John Adams, and Thomas Jefferson—and yet he was the most forward-looking of the group and the most of modern of the founders. He was a supporter of free-enterprise capitalism and globalization, a skeptic about organized religion, defender of the rights of minorities, a lover of modern gadgetry, and proponent of the sexual revolution.

According to French historian Bernard Faÿ, he was "the apostle of modern times." Of all the founders, he would be the one most comfortable living today. He would not be surprised by the tremendous advances in people's incomes and living standards. After the American Revolution, he predicted that "America will, with God's blessing, become a great and happy country." He was an optimist and a believer in progress and the American dream, the idea that every American could get ahead through industry, thrift,

THE GREATEST AMERICAN

and a good education. Franklin was, in many ways, the father of American capitalism. He would be pleased with the buzz of daily life in the marketplace and our major cities.

As an advocate of the "new" economics of "free trade" and liberal immigration policies, he embraced the benefits of globalization, the spread of democracy and representative government. "Our cause is the cause of all mankind. God grant that not only the love of liberty but a thorough knowledge of the rights of man may pervade all nations of the earth so that a philosopher may set his foot anywhere on its surface and say, this is my country!"

Throughout his adult life, he was mesmerized by scientific advances in transportation, medicine, and agriculture, and loved to hear about and even create his own new inventions. "I have sometimes almost wished it had been my destiny to have been born two or three centuries hence," he dreamed, "for inventions of improvement are prolific, and beget more of their kind. The present progress is rapid. Many of great importance, now unthought of, will before that period be procured. I mention one reason for such a wish, which is that if the art of physic [medicine] shall be improved in proportion with other arts, we may then be able to avoid diseases, and live as long as the patriarchs in Genesis."[1] Franklin would be the first to have a cell phone and a high-definition (HD) television.

His attitudes toward religion are very much in keeping with today's tolerant and skeptical views. He opposed any kind of requirement of a religious test on legislators, and believe in a "general toleration of all." He actually donated funds to all the various churches in Philadelphia. Of the three virtues, hope, faith, and charity, he regarded charity (good works) as the most important. He believed in God but had his doubts about the divinity of Jesus Christ.

---

1   Letter to John Lathrop, May 31, 1788, cited in *The Compleated Autobiography*, p. 376.

THE MOST MODERN OF THE FOUNDERS

His views were advanced for his age when it came to the treatment of minorities. He employed slaves as a printer and diplomat, but gradually shifted his views and, at the end of his career, owned no slaves and was a strong advocate for the abolition of slavery. He considered blacks equally capable as whites. He blamed most of the Indian disputes on the white population.

Franklin was a defender of women's rights and treated them as his equals. "Women, especially, flocked to see him, to speak to him for hours on end," commented his French friend Jean-Baptiste Le Roy. The savant of Philadelphia is no distant marble figure like the reserved Virginian George Washington or the prudish John Adams. Here was a red-blooded American Casanova who distained the mores of a sexually repressed Puritan age, enjoyed a strong libido, and was adored and memorialized by the fairer sex for his charm, storytelling, fame, and savoir faire; a thoroughly modern founding father who had few hang-ups.

As far as politics is concerned, there are many characteristics of today's government he might find agreeable and some disagreeable. He was not especially fond of the gold standard, and preferred paper money in commerce, though he feared too much inflation could be "mischievous" and that "the populace are apt to demand more than is necessary." He supported and invested in Robert Morris's Bank of North America, a precursor to Alexander Hamilton's Bank of the United States, America's first central bank.

Some features of modern-day America would appall Franklin. He would feel terribly uncomfortable with the size and burden of today's national debt, and America's leaders' failure to balance the budget. The sheer size of the federal government would depress him. He believed "a virtuous and laborious [industrious] people may be cheaply governed." He would dislike the engagement in foreign wars by the US military. "The system of America is [should be] commerce with all, and war with none."

THE GREATEST AMERICAN

Finally, he hated party politics. "There are two passions which have a powerful influence in the affairs of men, ambition and avarice, the love of power and the love of money.... And of what kind are the men that will strive for this profitable pre-eminence, thro' all the bustle of cabal, the heat of contention, the infinite mutual abuse of parties, tearing to pieces the best of characters? It will not be the wise and moderate, the lovers of peace and good order, the men fittest for the trust. It will be the bold and the violent, the men of strong passions and indefatigable activity in their selfish pursuits. These will trust themselves to this government and be their rulers" (*CA* [*The Compleated Autobiography by Benjamin Franklin*], p. 360).

PART I

ON BUSINESS

CHAPTER 2

THE FATHER OF AMERICAN CAPITALISM

"His reputation is greater than that of Newton, Frederick the Great or Voltaire, his character more revered than all of them. There is scarcely a coachman or a footman or scullery maid who does not consider him a friend of all mankind."
—*John Adams*

Ben Franklin's fame has far outlasted his passing in 1790. Today, his name is linked to twenty-nine counties (only Washington and Jefferson have more), numerous schools, parks, roads, bridges, mountains, lakes, and even Civil War battles. They've even named a crater on the moon after him.

Franklin is tied with George Washington for the number of US postage stamps with his image. His influence is felt on today's commemorative silver "eagle" dollar, which includes his favorite symbol of America, the rising sun. Perhaps above all, his portrait is on the one hundred dollar bill, the largest denomination of US currency and a constant reminder of the fame and brilliance of the father of the American Dream.

THE GREATEST AMERICAN

Franklin advocated many sound principles in his life, shared through *Poor Richard's Almanac* and *The Autobiography of Benjamin Franklin*, that have been adopted in many businesses and investment services around the globe. They include industry, thrift, prudence, punctuality, trust, innovation, and honesty, all platitudes we should adopt in our own lives. Let's look at some examples of the organizations around the country that have adopted Franklin's principles:

The Franklin Institute in Philadelphia is named in honor of America's first scientist. In 1824, the State of Pennsylvania founded the Franklin Institute to highlight the usefulness of his inventions. It is one of the oldest centers of science education in the country and is dedicated to educating the public and creating passion for science and technology.

In Boston, the Benjamin Franklin Institute of Technology (BFIT) started with a bequest from Benjamin Franklin and a gift from Andrew Carnegie. Since 1908, this non-profit college has offered an affordable education for generations of technical apprentices. BFIT focuses on real-world solutions in industry and developing good citizens and civic responsibility, all of which Franklin would applaud if he were alive today.

Franklin even has a connection to Sam Walton, the founder of Walmart. Based in Wisconsin, the Ben Franklin five-and-dime and craft stores were launched in 1927. They are a low-cost discount chain that take their cue from Franklin's famous (if misquoted) motto, "A penny saved is a penny earned." Walton got his start in retail operating a Ben Franklin store. Of course, his operations take a "low-cost" approach to retailing. Walmart's old motto, "Always Low Prices" and its new one "Save Money. Live Better" both reflect Franklin's approach to life.

Franklin's name and virtues also have been associated with the investment industry. The most famous is the mutual fund investment firm Franklin Templeton, which trades publicly with

ON BUSINESS

the ticker BEN (in honor of Franklin). It was founded by Rupert Johnson Sr., in New York in 1947. He named the company after Benjamin Franklin because, he said, the founder epitomized ideas of frugality and prudence when it came to saving and investing. The company's first line mutual funds, Franklin Custodian Funds, was a series of conservatively managed equity and bond funds designed to appeal to most investors. In 1992, Franklin Funds combined with John Templeton's mutual fund organization and moved to California. Today there are more than twenty-five million individual and institutional investors invested in their two-hundred-plus mutual funds, with more than $1.5 trillion under management.

Finally, there is FranklinCovey, which provides time management training and leadership programs for businesses and individuals, including most of the Fortune 500 companies. Franklin Quest was formed by Hyrum Smith in 1981, who introduced the first Franklin Day Planner. In 1997, he combined with Stephen R. Covey's Leadership Center to form FranklinCovey. Among other products, the company markets the Franklin Covey planning system, modeled in part on two classic bestsellers, Franklin's *Autobiography* and Covey's *7 Habits of Highly Effective People*.

Of course, my investment newsletter, *Forecasts & Strategies*, is inspired by Franklin's teachings. Every month I aspire to help my subscribers achieve financial freedom through prudent investing, careful saving, and smart spending strategies. As Franklin once wrote, "No man ever was glorious, who was not laborious." It's a sentiment I agree with—no one gets rich (or at least stays rich) by accident. Yet it's also important to always remember why we build our financial moat in the first place: "Wealth is not his that has it, but his that enjoys it."

CHAPTER 3

ON BECOMING RICH

"In short, the Way to Wealth depends chiefly on two words, Industry and Frugality. He that gets all he can honestly, and saves all he gets (necessary expenses excepted) will certainly become RICH."
—*Ben Franklin, "Advice to a Young Tradesman" (1748)*

Several years ago, I visited St. Kitts in the Caribbean for the Liberty Forum conference (my seventy-sixth country to visit). As I was standing in line to go through immigration, the man next to me said, "Are you Mark Skousen?" I said, "Yes," and he said, "I'm a lifetime subscriber, and you've made me a rich man. In fact, I've made more money from your newsletter than from my business as a trial lawyer!" He and his wife were coming to the Caribbean to stay at the vacation home they had bought with profits from my newsletter recommendations.

As an eighth-generation direct descendant of Ben Franklin, I'd like to think I follow his advice when it comes to being "healthy, wealthy, and wise."

In 1757, on his way to England, the financial guru decided to write down his thoughts about making money and becoming rich. The essay was published in the 1758 edition of *Poor Richard's Almanac* and became so popular that he made it into a separate pamphlet called "The Way to Wealth."

ON BUSINESS

According to the sage from Philadelphia, the key to financial success depends on applying three grand principles: industry, thrift, and prudence. Let's discuss each one.

First, industry. By that, Franklin means working hard and working successfully. Franklin worked hard at becoming the best printer in Philadelphia and the colonies. He would show up early to work and stay late. He bought the latest presses and tools from England to stay ahead of the competition. Most importantly, he leveraged his success by borrowing judiciously and franchising his printing business throughout the East Coast.

Second, thrift. Living frugally means living within your means and avoiding unnecessary waste by shopping around and limiting your needs. As Poor Richard says, "There's much revenue in economy." Furthermore, "no revenue is sufficient without economy." Millionaires have gone bankrupt because they spent too much. The only secure way to build wealth and keep it is to save every year and invest it wisely.

George Clason incorporated Franklin's wisdom when he told the story of Arkad in *The Richest Man in Babylon* in the 1920s. He wrote, "In old Babylon there once lived a certain very rich man named Arkad. Far and wide he was famous for his great wealth. Also was he famed for his liberality. He was generous with his charities. He was liberal in his own expenses. But nevertheless each year his wealth increased more rapidly than he spent it." How? By always saving at least 10 percent of his new income, no matter how much he earned. Save a lot, and save often. I've known middle-class investors who save 35 percent of their income regularly by controlling their expenses. As John Train wrote in *The Money Masters*, "most of the great investors are misers."

Third, prudence. How many successful people in business have destroyed all their hard-earned wealth practically overnight by investing in penny stocks, a pre-IPO private placement, or a highly speculative venture that wiped them out? I've seen it time

THE GREATEST AMERICAN

and time again. It's tragic. As Poor Richard says, "A fool and his money are soon parted."

Franklin was willing to take risks, but never overdid it. He was always well diversified in rental properties, government bonds, bank stocks, and bank accounts in three countries. In the good times, he saved money and invested wisely, so that when the bad times came, he was able to weather the storm. In 1772, there was a banking crisis in London, but Franklin survived by having his funds in two conservative banking houses that withstood the bank run. "Being out of debt myself my credit could not be shaken by any run upon me," Franklin wrote home (*CA*, p. 75).

At the end of his life, Franklin mused, "The years roll round and the last will come; when I would rather it have said, *He lived usefully*, than, *He died rich*" (*CA*, p. 392). He ended up as both.

You can too if you play your cards right.

CHAPTER 4

ON BEING A GOOD BUSINESS MANAGER

"It is incredible the quantity of good that may be done in a country by a single man who will make a business of it, and not suffer himself to be diverted from that purpose by different avocations, studies and amusements"
—Benjamin Franklin (CA, p. 293).

"Franklin became a scientist and a patriot because his success as a business manager allowed him to retire at age 42 and pursue other interests."
—Blaine McCormick, Baylor University

Ben Franklin is many things—diplomat, inventor, patriot—but he was able to achieve all this because he was first and foremost a successful printer. (After all, his famous epitaph begins, "The body of B. Franklin, Printer.")

As noted earlier, Franklin is often called the founding father of American capitalism. In his will, he left £1,000 ($5,000) to the City of Boston to be used one hundred years later to help tradesmen improve their skills. By then the $5,000 investment had reached $420,000, from which the Franklin Institute of Technology was created as an evenings-only trade school. Andrew Carnegie matched the funds (a concept invented by Franklin) to create an endowment. Carnegie, like other industrial giants of the nineteenth century, was a Franklin admirer, as was banker Thomas Mellon. Mellon printed a thousand copies of Franklin's *Autobiography* to give to young people. Warren Buffett and Charlie Munger, long-time managers of the now famous Berkshire Hathaway investment company, are fans of the founding father, especially Franklin's emphasis on the power of compound interest. Buffett and Munger are known to be long-term investors. (See chapter 11.)

What can we learn from Franklin as a business leader?

Blaine McCormick, a professor of management at Baylor University, has devoted considerable study to Franklin's life and management skills. He's even rewritten the man's *Autobiography* in modern English, in a book called *Ben Franklin, America's Original Entrepreneur: Franklin's Autobiography for Modern Times* (Entrepreneur Press, 2005). I arranged for my mother, a direct descendant of Franklin, to give copies of the new version to all her children and grandchildren on the three hundredth anniversary of Franklin's birth. What a great legacy.

In 2000, Professor McCormick joined the host of experts writing about famous heroes and their management skills. He wrote a delightful little book called *Ben Franklin's 12 Rules of Management* (Entrepreneur Press, 2000). Here are the twelve rules:

1. Finish better than your beginnings.
2. All education is self-education.
3. Seek first to manage yourself, then to manage others.
4. Influence is more important than victory.
5. Work hard and watch your costs.
6. Everybody wants to appear reasonable.
7. Create your own set of values to guide your actions.
8. Incentive is everything.
9. Create solutions for seemingly impossible problems.
10. Become a revolutionary for experimentation and change.
11. Sometimes it's better to do 1,001 small things right than only one large thing right.
12. Deliberately cultivate your reputation and legacy.

ON BUSINESS

Let me highlight some of Franklin's virtues in business. One was that he was always staying ahead of his competition in the printing business. He was in constant contact with printers in London and ordering new type or presses. He was a regular reader, staying abreast of the latest inventions. He started the Junto, like today's Rotary Club, a social network of merchants to find out what others were doing. He called it a "club for mutual improvement."

He worked long hours and made sure the public knew it. Poor Richard said, "A good example is the best sermon," and Franklin did his best to practice this principle. He tried to do something good every day. He played games like chess that would improve his skills as a negotiator and competitor. He befriended competitors and politicians but avoiding directly contradicting them in their opinions. He made a point of listening to others, rather than always doing the talking. He believed that one must "Have a feedback system." He developed a positive attitude toward his enemies: "Love your enemies, for they tell you your faults." He tried to be accessible to all, not just the big wigs. Franklin was willing to talk to anyone, from the king of France to the local plumber. Industry and frugality were keys to Franklin's success—always spend less than you earn, be cost conscious, and use debt productively and prudently. "Beware of little expenses; A small leak will sink a great ship." Never put yourself into a bad negotiating position by being too heavily in debt. "Necessity never made a good bargain." And remember: "There is much revenue in economy, and no revenue is sufficient without economy…. A man's industry and frugality will pay his debts and get him forward in the world…. Business not well managed ruins one faster than no business." Be optimistic. Nobody likes a constant complainer. And most importantly, be known for your honesty. Reputation is everything in business.

Amen.

CHAPTER 5

ADVICE ON RUNNING A SUCCESSFUL BUSINESS

"Drive thy business! Let not it drive you."
—*Poor Richard's Almanac*

In 2004, the hit film *National Treasure*, starring Nicolas Cage, thrilled audiences with the possibility that our country's founders buried a remarkable amount of wealth available to anyone willing to decipher the clues telling of its whereabouts. The movie portrayed Benjamin Franklin as central to the scheme via his clever inventions and hints in his "Silence Dogood" letters. Rather than conspire to hide wealth from others, the real Benjamin Franklin left a roadmap to wealth that thousands have followed.

In his "Advice to a Young Tradesman" Franklin emphasized three grand keys to financial success: industry, frugality, and prudence.

Through his life and writings, Franklin did more than anyone else to lay the groundwork for wealth creation in our emerging nation. Before he became a patriot, founding father, or an internationally renowned scientist, Benjamin Franklin was a businessman. In fact, the vast majority of his political activities were funded by

ON BUSINESS

his business earnings. He chronicled much of his business story in his *Autobiography*, thus creating the first "rags to riches" story in American history. Business luminaries from Andrew Carnegie and Thomas Mellon to Berkshire Hathaway's Warren Buffett and Charlie Munger have sworn by Franklin's good counsel.

Most people know Franklin via his maxims from *Poor Richard's Almanac*. Franklin's almanacs were the bestselling reference works in the colonies and the advice contained in their pages served to educate a nation of craftsmen, farmers, and shopkeepers as to how to succeed in business. Advice like, "Early to bed and early to rise, makes a man healthy, wealthy, and wise," and "Hope of gain lessens pain," though basic, were also colonial America's business school. Although many flock to supposed business classics like Sun Tzu's *The Art of War*, those who live and work in a free-market economy would benefit far more from Franklin's writings.

Franklin used his autobiography and maxims to promote such virtues as honesty, hard work, thrift, doing good to others, and the power of a good reputation. He more often than not utilizes the power of reward in getting others to cooperate rather than relying on the power of punishment. As such, Franklin is an ideal role model for modern American entrepreneurs who constantly manage the tension to compete and cooperate in any given business situation. He counsels us to protect our interests and guard against foolish risks while at the same time helping others to succeed. Rather than counsel us to dominate the game per Niccolo Machiavelli or Sun Tzu, Franklin shows us how to lift the boats of those around us—as well as our own.

PRACTICAL BUSINESS STRATEGIES

Ben Franklin is famous for giving advice to aspiring entrepreneurs on ways to create and maintain a profitable business. "The Way to Wealth" and the *Autobiography* are inspiring "how-to" sources filled with Franklin's maxims and proverbs on how to get ahead in business.

THE GREATEST AMERICAN

Franklin developed a successful printing house in Philadelphia by constantly experimenting with new products and services, expanding his customer base, adding partners and franchises throughout the colonies, and applying for government contracts to print the local currency and deliver mail. He made a point of pushing his wheelbarrow in public so potential customers would recognize his virtues.

Here are eleven rules Franklin lived by in pursuing profits:

1. Hard work and patience pay off in the end. "Energy and persistence conquer all things."
2. Be cost conscious, be frugal, and manage your time. "Doth thou love life? Then do not squander time, for that's the stuff life is made of."
3. Live moderately. "Great spenders are bad lenders."
4. A job worth doing is a job worth doing well. "Haste makes waste."
5. Take the long road to success. "Patience in market is worth pounds in a year."
6. Always put business relationships on paper, especially among friends, to avoid future potential disagreements. "When a friend deals with a friend, let the bargain be clear and well penned, that they may continue to be friends to the end."
7. Master your business and keep up to date. "The used key is always bright."
8. Develop good contacts with everyone in your business, including government officials. Good relationships will help you obtain bargains with suppliers. (As mentioned earlier, Franklin established an organization called the Junto to get to know fellow tradesmen, which helped him immensely in expanding his business. You would be wise to join the Rotary Club or other local business and investment organizations.)

ON BUSINESS

9. Establish a "character of integrity" in business. Never underestimate the power of a good reputation. Never speak ill of others if you can help it. "Love your enemies, for they tell you your faults." Make a point of developing friendships, especially with influential people who may speak ill of you.
10. Seek to work and counsel with the most reliable and experienced business partners. Be alert to devious men and swindlers. "Don't judge men's wealth or piety by their Sunday appearance."
11. Be humble. "Success has ruined many a man."

Use Franklin's eleven principles to build surplus wealth and a retirement income from your business. Remember, your business or full-time job is typically the greatest source of wealth during your lifetime.

CHAPTER 6

ON CREATING A CLUB OF "USEFUL KNOWLEDGE AND INFLUENCE"

"I had formed most of my ingenious acquaintances into a club of mutual improvement, which we called the JUNTO."
—Benjamin Franklin (A [The Autobiography of Benjamin Franklin], p. 71)

In 1727, at the youthful age of twenty-one, Ben Franklin organized a club of "mutual improvement" called the Junto. Not unlike the Apostles at Cambridge University in the twentieth century, the secretive group was limited to twelve individuals and was by invitation only to "avoid improper persons."

Known initially as the "Leather Apron Club," members were largely merchants, mechanics, accountants, and pragmatic businessmen—all older than Franklin—who had broad interests in literature, poetry, science, mathematics, law, and public affairs. The club met Friday nights, first in an alehouse (tavern) and later in a house. The evening meetings were organized around a series of questions that Franklin devised, covering a range of intellectual,

ON BUSINESS

personal, business, and community topics. The list of questions included the following:

1. Have you met with any thing in the author you last read, remarkable, or suitable to be communicated to the Junto? particularly in history, morality, poetry, physics, travels, mechanic arts, or other parts of knowledge?
2. What new story have you lately heard agreeable for telling in conversation?
3. Has any citizen in your knowledge failed in his business lately, and what have you heard of the cause?
4. Have you lately heard of any citizen's thriving well, and by what means?
5. Have you lately heard how any present rich man, here or elsewhere, got his estate?
6. Do you know of any fellow citizen, who has lately done a worthy action, deserving praise and imitation? or who has committed an error proper for us to be warned against and avoid?
7. What unhappy effects of intemperance have you lately observed or heard? of imprudence? of passion? or of any other vice or folly?
8. What happy effects of temperance? of prudence? of moderation? or of any other virtue?
9. Have you or any of your acquaintance been lately sick or wounded? If so, what remedies were used, and what were their effects?
10. Who do you know that are shortly going [on] voyages or journeys, if one should have occasion to send by them?
11. Do you think of anything at present, in which the Junto may be serviceable to mankind? to their country, to their friends, or to themselves?
12. Hath any deserving stranger arrived in town since last meeting, that you heard of? and what have you heard or

THE GREATEST AMERICAN

observed of his character or merits? and whether think you, it lies in the power of the Junto to oblige him, or encourage him as he deserves?

13. Do you know of any deserving young beginner lately set up, whom it lies in the power of the Junto any way to encourage?

14. Have you lately observed any defect in the laws, of which it would be proper to move the legislature an amendment? Or do you know of any beneficial law that is wanting?

15. Have you lately observed any encroachment on the just liberties of the people?

16. Hath any body attacked your reputation lately? and what can the Junto do towards securing it?

17. Is there any man whose friendship you want, and which the Junto, or any of them, can procure for you?

18. Have you lately heard any member's character attacked, and how have you defended it?

In addition, members were expected to exchange knowledge of business affairs and to present papers on "any point of morals, politics, or natural philosophy," which would then be discussed. They were encouraged to have open minds, to avoid "fixed opinions" and "direct contradictions," nor should they engage in polemics, heated arguments, or fights. "Our debates were...to be conducted in the sincere spirit of inquiry after truth, without fondness for dispute, or desire of victory." Small fines were imposed if things got out of hand.

Out of the influential association came the idea of a subscription library, a volunteer fire department, an academy of youth, improved security (night watchmen), and even an experiment in printing paper money to stimulate local trade. As Philadelphia's premier printer, Franklin got the contract. It wasn't long before

ON BUSINESS

Franklin became the clerk of the Pennsylvania General Assembly—all because of his connections with members of the Junto.

Not surprisingly, the club became well known and everyone who was somebody in Philadelphia wanted to join. Franklin suggested franchising the Junto rather than expanding it, and within a few years, five or six other clubs got started with various names such as "The Vine," "The Union," and "The Band." Franklin wrote in his *Autobiography*, "The several clubs, [reflecting] the sentiments of the Junto, increased...our influence in public affairs, and our power of doing good" (*A*, p. 123).

Later in life, after several old friends had died, he looked back with fondness on the club. "Death begins to make breaches in the little Junto of old friends," he reminisced. "I find I love company, chat, a laugh, a glass, and even a song, as well as ever; and at the same time relish better than I used to do the grave observations and wise sentences of old men's conversations" (*CA*, pp. 17–18).

Want more detail? Check out the book *The Society of Useful Knowledge: How Benjamin Franklin and Friends Brought the Enlightenment to America*, by Jonathan Lyons (Bloomsbury Press, 2013).

CHAPTER 7

ON BEING AN ENTREPRENEUR

"He that would catch fish must venture his bait."
—*Poor Richard's Almanac*

Years ago, I gave a talk at the Kansas City Public Library on Benjamin Franklin and entrepreneurship. You can watch it on C-SPAN's *Book TV* show.[2]

Before my lecture, a spokesman for the Kauffman Foundation discussed the importance of entrepreneurship—innovation, creation of new businesses, products and processes, and risk-taking—the kind of activity Franklin flourished in as a printer, inventor, and public servant.

"Entrepreneur" comes from the French word meaning to "undertake." It was first used by Richard Cantillon, who used it to describe a speculator who pays a certain price for a product to resell it at an uncertain price, and Jean-Baptiste Say, who used it to mean an economic agent (business owner or capitalist) who brings together the right amount of land, labor, and capital to produce goods and services at a profit.

---

2   Go to C-SPAN's website (www.c-span.org) and search for "Lessons from Ben Franklin." Video dated December 22, 2012.

ON BUSINESS

Franklin lived after Cantillon and before Say but was caught up in the spirit of the French laissez-faire school as the American ambassador in Paris from 1776 to 1785. At the time, Franklin was taken with the "new" political economy of the French physiocrats Marquis de Condorcet, Jean-Baptiste Colbert, and A. R. J. Turgot. Franklin wrote favorably about these economists and how the government could best serve and promote commerce: "*Laissez nous faire*: Let us alone.... *Pas trop gouverner*: Not to govern too strictly." He joined them in arguing the classically liberal views in favor of competition, free trade, and lifting restraints on business.

Franklin was probably the most prominent example of successful entrepreneurship in America and wrote about his techniques in his *Autobiography*. He was innovative in all areas of his life—business, science, charities, and public causes.

He began his career as an apprentice under his older brother James in Boston. But he learned early in life that he hated working for others, especially his brother. He sought independence and at the age of seventeen ran away to Philadelphia, where he began working for printer Samuel Keimer. His wanderlust took him to London in 1725–26 where he was a journeyman printer. Upon returning to Philadelphia, he began his own printing business and purchased the *Pennsylvania Gazette* in 1729.

In his booklet, "The Way to Wealth," he preached diligence and hard work as an important key to success. Franklin himself often worked past 11 p.m. to get a job done, and if necessary, he would stay overnight to redo it. The townspeople took notice of his extra efforts, and Franklin's growing reputation lured customers away from his rivals.

He believed in the importance of public relations. Walter Isaacson calls Franklin "the country's first unabashed public relations expert." The publisher extraordinaire worked at his reputation and "took care not only to be in reality industrious and frugal, but to avoid all appearances of the contrary." Franklin wrote, "I dressed plainly; I was seen at no places of idle diversion; I never

THE GREATEST AMERICAN

went out a-fishing or shooting;...and to show that I was not above my business, I sometimes brought home the paper I purchased at the stores, thro' the streets on a wheelbarrow."

He was constantly searching for ways to improve his printing business, and always made a point of purchasing the latest equipment from London. Networking was critical to his success. He organized weekly meetings of a small group of other tradesmen and artisans called a Junto. At their weekly meetings, they asked how they "may be serviceable to mankind? to their country, to their friends, or to themselves?" They were constantly sending business each other's way.

He also franchised his printing business throughout the colonies, thus multiplying his wealth. He was so successful that he was able to retire in 1748, at the age of forty-two, and devoted the rest of his life to civic duties and science.

As a scientist and technologist, Franklin favored practical inventions: the more efficient Franklin stove, the lightning rod, the odometer, the bifocals, and daylight savings time, for example. He even discovered the Gulf Stream in the Atlantic Ocean. Other famous inventors, such as Thomas A. Edison and Alexander Graham Bell, followed in Franklin's footsteps by trying to find ways to help people live better.

Franklin was also a social entrepreneur, creating new organizations and clubs that benefited society. These included the Junto, the Library Company, the American Philosophical Society, the Academy for Education of Youth (now the University of Pennsylvania), the first fire insurance company, and the City Hospital.

Regarding the hospital, he came up with the idea of matching funds and working closely with the government to achieve his goals. He wrote in his *Autobiography*, "And I do not remember any of my political maneuvers, the success of which gave me at the time more pleasure, or...after thinking of it, I more easily excused myself for having made some use of cunning" (*A*, p. 149).

CHAPTER 8

IN DEFENSE OF MONEYMAKING AND THE COMMERCIAL SOCIETY

"He that has a trade has an office of profit and honor."
—*Poor Richard's Almanac (1756)*

You don't normally think of Franklin as a philosopher, but in *101 Great Philosophers*, Madsen Pirie, cofounder of the Adam Smith Institute in England, identifies this prominent founding father as one of the top "makers of modern thought."

What was Franklin's contribution to political philosophy? It was his defense of merchants, manufacturers, and money lenders—that is, the commercial society of moneymaking.

The classical view, held by the Greeks to the scholastics, and even by Thomas Jefferson, is that the ideal citizen should be independent of moneygrubbing. Aristotle and later the Romans believed that a good citizen should be a gentleman farmer who values leisure and agrarian simplicity. Producing goods was fine, but the trade and distribution of goods were suspicious. The public should beware of the money changers—they were surely unethical.

Moneymaking may be a necessary evil, but never a positive good, they said.

Franklin was one of the first thinkers who promulgated the modern view that moneymaking was not only necessary but beneficial to society. The successful Yankee merchant (him included) was shrewd, prudent, industrious, thrifty, and educated. Even speculators and money changers served a useful, productive purpose.

In *The Political Philosophy of Benjamin Franklin*, Lorraine Smith Pangle, professor of political philosophy at the University of Texas at Austin, put it best when she wrote that Franklin's form of wealth seeking "contributes to the common good of society, generating employment, enhancing security, multiplying pleasures, and drawing energies away from deadly religious quarrels and military adventurism into more constructive channels."[3]

Franklin adopted the views of the French philosopher Charles Montesquieu and the Scottish economist Adam Smith that asserted the commercial society moderates the passions of greed, fraud, and deception by teaching self-discipline, industry, frugality, education and training, and deferring gratification. Just as marriage moderates lust, so do the marketplace and competition discourage (but not eliminate) fraudulent and deceptive business practices. As Adam Smith wrote in *The Wealth of Nations* (1776), it is the fear of losing customers "which restrains his frauds and corrects his negligence."

The worldly philosopher of Philadelphia warned against businessmen who only seek money for money's sake and become parsimonious Scrooges. He believed wealth should be used for higher purposes—in pursuit of happiness, as Thomas Jefferson stated in the Declaration of Independence, for himself, family, friends, and the community.

---

3 Lorraine Smith Pangle, *The Political Philosophy of Benjamin Franklin* (Baltimore: Johns Hopkins University Press, 2007), pp. 18–19.

ON BUSINESS

Financial success leads to leisure time, and that liberty should be used to improve mankind through volunteer work, civil service, and social networking through clubs, churches, and foundations. Franklin practiced what he preached when he retired from his printing business. He didn't become a gentleman who retired to his farm and counted his money. (To use a modern-day example, he didn't just retire and play golf all day.) He loaned his money out to friends and business partners, and he spent a great deal of time supporting good causes in the community and making contributions in science and technology (such as his electrical experiments, which made him famous).

He didn't care much for the poor laws and other forms of public charity, but he was a strong supporter of private charities and good causes. He was a tireless advocate of civil associations over government programs. He supported volunteer organizations, including the Library Company, newspapers, the City Watch, the Union Fire Company, the Negro School of Philadelphia, and the Pennsylvania militia, a private alternative to defense.

He wrote of these private initiatives: "I have always thought that one man of tolerable abilities may work great changes and accomplish great affairs among mankind."

CHAPTER 9

IN DEFENSE OF THE RICH

"Nothing but money is sweeter than honey."
—*Poor Richard's Almanac (1735)*

As noted earlier, Benjamin Franklin was, in many ways, the most modern of the founding fathers. He rejected John and Abigail Adams' puritanical views about sex. He voted against a state religion and Sunday blue laws. Unlike George Washington, he gave up holding on to slaves and supported the abolitionists' cause. And, in contrast to his friend Thomas Jefferson, he liked big cities and big banks.

His key contribution to philosophy was his defense of commercial society and the benefits of business and moneymaking. It was rare indeed to find a political leader in his day who defended independent merchants, manufacturers, speculators, and money lenders—in short, the risk-taking wealthy entrepreneur.

The classical view, shared by the Greeks to the scholastics, is that the ideal ruler would be a landowner and the farmer, independent of commercial life and moneygrubbing. Jefferson held this classical view and favored the rural class as more honest and happier.

ON BUSINESS

Franklin rejected the idea that commerce and moneymaking was a necessary evil; rather it was a positive good. As Poor Richard said, "He that has a trade has an office of profit and honor." His favorite proverb in the Bible was "See thou a man diligent in his business? He shall stand before kings" (Proverbs 22:28). And he did!

Franklin praised the virtues of the Yankee merchant class—shrewd, prudent, industrious, thrifty, and educated. The trinity of good business was industry, thrift, and prudence. The *Autobiography*, published posthumously, tells largely how he created and used his wealth for good. It influenced millions of Americans, both young and old, who wanted to succeed in life, from Andrew Carnegie and Thomas Mellon in the nineteenth century to Warren Buffett and Charlie Munger in the twentieth century.

The great sociologist Max Weber praised Franklin for his defense of wealth-seeking activities. In accumulating wealth, Franklin practiced and advocated the Protestant ethic of discipline, hard work, and moral turpitude, and funneling emotional aggression into profitable business activities. As John Maynard Keynes said centuries later, "Better that a man should tyrannize over his bank account than over his fellow citizens."

Becoming wealthy allows you to have leisure time and to pursue higher interests: In Franklin's case, science and inventions, art and literature, book reading, joining clubs, civil service, and traveling.

He encouraged his fellow men of fortune to support private charities and good public causes. He personally supported many private charities and churches and was a major supporter of volunteer efforts and free associations, "the most fundamental civic expressions of liberty."[4] He believed that the successful businessman had an obligation to help out and not just use his gains for personal use.

He preferred private over public charities. He noted that rich Englishmen adopted the poor laws. "The poor laws were not made

---

4   Pangle, *Political Philosophy*, p. 127.

by the poor," he wrote. "The legislators were men of fortune. By that act they voluntarily subjected their own estates and the estates of others to the payment of a tax for the maintenance of the poor. Besides this tax, they had, by donation and subscription, erected numerous schools for educating gratis the children of the poor; they erected hospitals at an immense expense for the reception and cure of the sick, the lame, the wounded, and the insane poor, for lying-in women, and deserted children. They also continually contributed toward making up losses occasioned by fire, by storms, or by floods, etc. Surely there should be some gratitude due for some many instances of goodness!" (*CA*, p. 57).

Franklin loved city life, the bigger the better. His favorite cities were London and Paris, and when he returned to Philadelphia, he missed the hustle and bustle of the metropolitan lifestyle. In 1762, after spending several years as a colonial agent in London, he found his hometown "thinner of people, owing perhaps to my being so long accustomed to the bustling crowded streets of London" (*CA*, p. 22).

He wanted to do everything possible to expand the marketplace and grow. Franklin has often been called the "Father of America's Growth Machine." To encourage commerce, he favored free trade and laissez-faire—leave us alone—along the lines of Adam Smith and his "system of natural liberty" found in *The Wealth of Nations*. Unlike Jefferson, he was an advocate of the commercial banking system and of "plentiful" money supply and low interest rates. He owned stock in the Bank of North America in Philadelphia and would have undoubtedly supported Alexander Hamilton's plan for a national bank if he had lived to see it.

He made great contributions as an inventor, scientist, writer, and founding father, but he also offered valuable advice on money matters. His is one of the greatest success stories in American history, and much of his success in philanthropy, community, and public office came from his experience and capabilities in the fi-

ON BUSINESS

nancial world. According to *The Wealthy 100*, Franklin died one of the one hundred wealthiest Americans of all time. When he died, his estate was worth perhaps $50,000 or more, a fortune in those days and in today's dollars.

Why pay attention to Ben Franklin? His is the first "rags to riches" story in America. Throughout all his experiences, failures, and victories, he built a fortune that was never in jeopardy. By time he died in 1790 at the remarkable age of eighty-four, he was a self-made man, one of the richest in American history.

CHAPTER 10

FRANKLIN AS SELF-HELP GURU

When you browse the "self-help" section of a bookstore, remember that the first self-help guru was Benjamin Franklin, as told in his famous *Autobiography*. He was the first "Horatio Alger" in American life to pull himself out of poverty and become a big success.

Recently I read a biography of Dale Carnegie, *Self-Help Messiah: Dale Carnegie and Success in Modern America* by Steven Watts, and years ago I read Carnegie's bestseller, *How to Win Friends and Influence People*. It was written during the Great Depression, a time when people were down and out and needed an uplifting voice.

Like Franklin, Carnegie was born poor and tried his hand at numerous occupations—acting, used car salesman, teacher—before striking it rich with writing and public speaking. He practically became a millionaire overnight with his book.

Carnegie had no relation to his wealthy namesake, Andrew Carnegie, but like the steel magnate, Dale Carnegie was a big fan of Benjamin Franklin's *Autobiography*.

In *How to Win Friends*, Carnegie wrote, "Benjamin Franklin, tactless in his youth, became so diplomatic, so adroit at handling people, that he was made American Ambassador to France. The

ON BUSINESS

secret of his success? 'I will speak ill of no man,' he [Franklin] said, '...and speak all good I know of everybody.'"

Carnegie commented, "Any fool can criticize, condemn and complain—and most fools do. But it takes character and self-control to be understanding and forgiving. 'A great man shows greatness,' said [Scottish historian and author Thomas] Carlyle, 'by the ways he treats little men.'"

Carnegie recounts the story from the *Autobiography* where Franklin was able to befriend an enemy. In 1736, he was chosen to be clerk of the Pennsylvania General Assembly. A new member of the assembly favored another candidate and was angry that Franklin got the job. Franklin wrote:

> I therefore did not like the opposition of this new member, who was a gentleman of fortune and education, with talents that were likely to give him, in time, great influence in the House, which, indeed, afterwards happened. I did not, however, aim at gaining his favor by paying any servile respect to him, but, after some time, took this other method. Having heard that he had in his library a certain very scarce and curious book, I wrote a note to him, expressing my desire of perusing that book, and requesting he would do *me* the favor of lending it to *me* for a few days. He sent it immediately, and I returned it in about a week with another note, expressing strongly my sense of the favor.
>
> When we next met in the House, he spoke to me (which he had never done before), and with great civility; and he ever after manifested a readiness to serve me on all occasions, so that we became great friends, and our friendship continued to his death.

THE GREATEST AMERICAN

This is another instance of the truth of an old maxim that I learned, which says, "He that has once done you a kindness will be more ready to do you another, than he whom you yourself have obliged." And it shows how much more profitable it is prudently to remove, than to resent, return, and continue inimical proceedings.

It reminds me of Poor Richard's saying, "Tart words make no friends: a spoonful of honey will catch more flies than a gallon of vinegar."

Franklin's entire life was devoted to helping others solve problems. His scientific experiments were always meant to improve the daily lives of citizens—the Franklin stove, the lightning rod, the bifocals. In the *Autobiography*, Franklin lists thirteen virtues he believed were vital for success. He tracked his progress on a daily basis, and noted how often he failed—his "errata" in life. Carnegie did the same thing and did his best to live up to his teachings. He even kept a file of "Damned Fool Things I Have Done." Franklin would have been proud.

CHAPTER 11

MODERN-DAY FRANKLIN FANS: BUFFETT AND MUNGER

"Success has a thousand fathers, failure is an orphan."
—*Poor Richard's Almanac*

I witnessed the truth of the above Ben Franklin aphorism when my son and I traveled to Omaha, Nebraska, on May 2, 2015, to attend the fiftieth anniversary shareholders meeting of Berkshire Hathaway, known as the "Woodstock of Capitalism." A record crowd of fifty thousand showed up, and we barely found a seat at the CenturyLink Center.

There, we spent several hours taking in the wit and wisdom of Berkshire's founding chairman Warren Buffett, the world's most successful investors, and his late partner Charlie Munger. Together, they've succeeded in building an investment company like no other—$1,000 invested in Berkshire Hathaway stock in 1964, when Buffett took over a textile company, would be worth over $30 million today. That's an annualized return of over 18 percent in fifty years.

THE GREATEST AMERICAN

Today, they've invested in more than eighty businesses with a market value of over a trillion dollars, including GEICO, Coca-Cola, See's Candies, and Apple, among others. Taking into account employees and shareholders, Berkshire directly affects more than one million people. Dozens of books have been written about Buffett and his system of investing. In my own book *The Maxims of Wall Street*, I quote him more than any other guru, although Franklin comes close.

Not surprisingly, both Berkshire partners are fans of the founding father of American capitalism. Like Franklin, they have lived long lives, and now they have outlived Franklin. (Buffett is over ninety; Munger died in December, 2023, before turning one hundred. Franklin died when he was eighty-four.) Munger, in particular, idolized Franklin for his wide range of knowledge. A collection of Munger's lectures and public commentary was actually called *Poor Charlie's Almanack*. Like Munger, Franklin was self-educated and a wise observer of human nature. A thirst for learning and knowledge of human psychology are often attributes of successful investors.

Both Buffett and Munger took full advantage of the power of compound interest that Franklin wisely promoted. "Money begets money," as the old proverb goes. Franklin put it to use when he bequeathed £1,000 each to Boston and Philadelphia to last two hundred years, earning interest upon interest.

The managers of Berkshire Hathaway have adopted the same strategy with great success. Most investment companies pay out their profits in dividends, but Berkshire has never paid a dividend. Rather, it reinvests profits. Their policy is to "buy wonderful companies at fair prices, rather than buy fair companies at wonderful prices." Today, Berkshire Hathaway is sitting on over $325 billion in cash, looking for more businesses to buy. "We are swimming all the time," Munger said. "Let the tide take care of itself."

ON BUSINESS

They are also fans of Franklin's three virtues: industry, thrift, and prudence. As Munger said, "If you don't know how to save, I can't help you." Big savers inevitably become wealthy, he said.

Buffett is fond of collecting great quotes, and Franklin is one of his favorites. In his 2000 annual Berkshire letter, he quoted Franklin, "A small leak can sink a great ship." Berkshire is always watching its expenses and limits the number of employees it hires.

Like Franklin, Buffett and Munger are optimists about the future of America. "We have an incredible economic system that unleashes the American spirit. We have a wonderful future ahead of us," Buffett said. Many doomsayers are predicting the collapse of the US dollar. But Buffett disagrees: "The dollar will be the world's currency 50 years from now." He expects rising inflation and interest rates. Munger, meanwhile, did express concern about "the Federal Reserve printing too much money," and wasting it rather than spending it on much-needed infrastructure.

Both Buffett and Munger consider *The Wealth of Nations* by Adam Smith to be one of their favorite books on sound economics. Munger has commented that Adam Smith can teach us about "the productive power of the capitalist system." Franklin was of the same mind. He was a fan of the "new economics" of laissez-faire and free trade.

At one point in the meeting, Munger, in a response to the question, "What matters most to you?" replied, "Your main duty is to become as rational as you can possibly be. Rationality is a moral duty. Berkshire is sort of a temple of rationality." Meanwhile, Buffett said what matters most to him is that Berkshire does well. "If Berkshire wasn't building something that was continuously getting better, I wouldn't be happy."

Franklin would likely readily agree to such sentiments. "Yes, self-evident."

PART II

ON PERSONAL FINANCE AND INVESTING

CHAPTER 12

ON WORKING HARD, BUDGETING, AND THRIFT

Franklin's investment philosophy is twofold: to help you make a lot of money through intelligence and hard work and then to help you build a nest egg by prudently watching your expenses and successfully investing your savings.

Making a lot of money isn't a guarantee of financial independence. You have to learn to control your expenditures, manage your debts, and avoid bad investments. As Franklin stated, "No revenue is sufficient without economy." Millionaires have been known to go into bankruptcy because they failed to control their spending. As Poor Richard commented, "The Indies have not made Spain rich, because her outgoes are greater than her incomes."

Franklin summed it up beautifully when he published "The Way to Wealth" in 1758. After stressing the importance of working hard, he turned his attention to frugality—to save regularly and to live within your means. "If you would be wealthy, think of saving, as well as of getting."

He wrote, "Away then with your expensive follies, and you will not then have so much cause to complain of hard times, heavy

THE GREATEST AMERICAN

taxes, and chargeable families; for *Women and wine, game and deceit, Make the wealth small and the wants great.*"

Franklin warned of keeping up with the Joneses and the tendency to buy unnecessary "fineries and knick-knacks." As Poor Richard says, "Beware of little expenses; *A small leak will sink a great ship.*"

He cautioned, "*Buy what thou hast no need of, and ere long thou shalt sell thy necessaries.*"

When he was a young boy of five or so, he used his allowance to buy a whistle for ten pennies and proudly displayed it to his family, making a great deal of noise that annoyed his parents. When his siblings found out he had paid ten pennies for the whistle, they laughed to scorn. "So you give ten pennies for a whistle worth but two!" He never forgot that lesson in the value of money. (He retells the story in *CA*, pp. 206–207).

Franklin often disciplined himself in his business and personal affairs. In his *Autobiography* he criticized a competitor, Mr. David Harry, who he said "was very proud, dressed like a gentleman, lived expensively, took much diversion and pleasure abroad, ran in debt, and neglected his business." Franklin and his wife, on the other hand, were proud of the fact that they "kept no idle servants, our table was plain and simple, our furniture of the cheapest."

Then he mentioned how his wife Deborah had surprised him one morning with a china bowl and silver spoon at breakfast. "She thought her husband deserved a silver spoon and China bowl as well as any of his neighbors," he wrote. But he felt guilty about it.

In 1779, when he was ambassador to France, Franklin wrote a letter to his daughter Sally, castigating her for buying frivolous clothing for a ball:

"I could scarce believe my eyes in reading forward, that 'there never was so much dressing and pleasure going on,' and that you yourself wanted black pins and feathers from France, to appear, I suppose, in the mode! As I am always preaching that doctrine

ON PERSONAL FINANCE AND INVESTING

[frugality during wartimes], I cannot in conscience or in decency encourage the contrary, by my example, in furnishing my children with foolish modes and luxuries. I therefore send all the articles you desire that are useful and necessary, and omit the rest.... I must avoid giving you an opportunity of doing that with either lace or feathers. If you wear your cambric ruffles as I do, and take care not to mend the holes, they will come in time to be lace; and feathers, my dear girl, may be had in America from every cock's tail" (*CA*, pp. 198–199).

His critics later complained about his parsimony. Mark Twain said that Franklin took all the joy out of life, especially for boys growing up. D. H. Lawrence complained that Franklin reminded him of a man who is always buying a "cheap insurance policy." Shouldn't there be some sort of balance between being miserly and spendthrift?

I prefer the middle-of-the-road approach of George Clason in his classic story *The Richest Man in Babylon*. As noted in chapter 4, the rich man Arkad was rich and generous—but not too generous. He was liberal in his expenditures and charities, but nevertheless became wealthier every year. How? By always saving at least 10 percent of his new income, no matter how much he earned. The more he earned, the more he spent, but he never spent more than his annual income.

Only in his late seventies did Franklin learn to enjoy the material pleasures of life and "wasting" time playing games. In 1785, he wrote a friend about playing cards in the evenings. "I have indeed now and then a little compunction in reflecting that I spend time so idly: but another reflection comes to relieve me, whispering, 'You know the soul is immortal; why then should you be such a niggard of a little time when you have a whole eternity before you?' So being easily convinced, and, like other reasonable creatures, satisfied with a small reason, when it is in favor of doing what I have

THE GREATEST AMERICAN

a mind to do, I shuffle the cards again, and begin another game" (*CA*, pp. 351–352).

If Poor Richard were alive today, he would say, "Two of the hardest things to do is save when you're young, and spend when you're old."

CHAPTER 13

THE POWER OF COMPOUND INTEREST: FRANKLIN'S PROOF

"The money that makes money, makes more money."
—*Poor Richard's Almanac*

Ben Franklin is known as the father of thrift. His most famous saying is "A penny saved is a penny earned." (Poor Richard actually wrote, "A penny spar'd is twice got.")

This is the parsimonious side of saving—living within your means, sacrificing current consumption, and piling up cash in a bank account like Uncle Scrooge.

But there's also the positive benefits of saving—the thrill of investing your money and seeing it grow, either in a savings account at your local bank or earning dividends from publicly traded companies (the stock market).

As George Clason counseled in *The Richest Man in Babylon*, make your gold multiply. "Put each coin to laboring that it may reproduce its kind even as flocks of the field and help bring to thee income, or stream of wealth that shall flow constantly into thy purse."

THE GREATEST AMERICAN

The time value of money is known as compound interest, and it can multiply your wealth over time—especially when you start to save and invest early.

In 1785, the French mathematician Charles-Joseph Mathon de la Cour wrote a parody in which Franklin's "Poor Richard" could become the "Fortunate Richard" by leaving a small sum of money in his will to be used by his heirs after it collected interest for five hundred years.

Franklin wrote back to Monsieur de la Cour and said he loved the idea, which lead to his decision (noted earlier) to bequest £1,000 (approximately $5,000 at the time of his death) each to his native Boston and adopted Philadelphia on the condition that it earn interest for two hundred years.

In 1789, a year before he died, Franklin amended his will, stipulating that the funds should be used to make loans at 5 percent interest to young craftsmen under the age of twenty-five to help them set up their businesses. Franklin regarded "good apprentices" as those "most likely to make good citizens." The loans were to be given only to those craftsmen who were married, had completed their apprenticeships, and could obtain two cosigners to vouch for them.

After one hundred years, Franklin required that each city take 75 percent of the funds to be used for public works (bridges, roads, public buildings, and the like). They were to then continue loaning the money for another one hundred years. At the end of two hundred years (around 1990), each city would get about 25 percent of the money and their respective states would get the rest.

Had officials in Boston and Philadelphia followed through with Franklin's wishes successfully, they would each have had nearly $20 million at the end of the two hundred years. In reality, Boston only had about $5 million in its Franklin fund (having invested in savings accounts and an insurance company), and Philadelphia a little over $2 million (investing largely in mortgages) when the

ON PERSONAL FINANCE AND INVESTING

funds were dispersed in the early 1990s. Boston ultimately used the money to fund the Franklin Institute of Technology, while Philadelphia's funds are now used to assist recent graduates of Philadelphia high schools who wished to pursue careers in trades, crafts, and applied sciences.

Franklin's investment scheme goes to show you how difficult it is to invest and earn income on investments given the risks over a two-hundred-year period of American history—of war and peace, prosperity and depression, and bull and bear markets. Franklin himself worried about the risks, the "unforeseen difficulties that may arise." Still, turning $9,100 into $7 million is a testimony of the power of compound interest.

THE RULE OF 72

Franklin's funds earned approximately 3 percent per annum over the two-hundred-year period, not the 5 percent as he expected. Using the "Rule of 72," Franklin's fund doubled in value every twenty-four years at 3 percent interest return.

The Rule of 72, which some historians credit Franklin as its discoverer, is useful to determine how quickly your money doubles. You simply divide seventy-two by the rate you are earning on your money. If your money earns 3 percent a year, it will take twenty-four years for your money to double.

At 1 percent interest, it would take seventy-two years to double your money.

But if you invest in high-dividend paying stocks and earn an average 5 percent annual yield, it would take only fourteen years to double your money—not counting the capital appreciation of the stocks. But to take advantage of compound dividend yields, be sure to reinvest your dividends in stock.

One of the most powerful concepts in finance and investments is compound interest. It has a snowball effect on your investments. The longer you save or invest, the more compounding can bene-

THE GREATEST AMERICAN

fit you. Start today. As Poor Richard says, "Patience in market is worth pounds in a year." Or two hundred years!

Best source: *Benjamin Franklin's Last Bet: The Favorite Founder's Divisive Death, Enduring Afterlife, and Blueprint for American Prosperity* (Mariner Books, 2022).

CHAPTER 14

ON SUCCESSFUL INVESTING

"A fool and his money are soon parted."
—*Poor Richard's Almanac*

Ben Franklin is famous for giving advice to aspiring entrepreneurs on ways to create and maintain a profitable business. "The Way to Wealth" (published originally as part of his *Poor Richard's Almanac* in 1758) is an inspiring "how-to" pamphlet filled with Franklin's maxims and proverbs on how to build a successful enterprise.

What most people forget is that Franklin was also a successful investor after he retired from his printing business at the youthful age of forty-two.

At that time, 1748, he turned over his printing business to his partner David Hall, receiving an annual income for over twenty years afterwards. He never completely retired, however. He worked for the government as a postmaster, colonial agent, and minister to France. Nevertheless, over the years he built up a substantial fortune and relied on his savings and investment income to pursue a gentleman's career in science, politics, and community service.

Franklin built his investment retirement portfolio by saving, avoiding debt, placing well-collateralized loans (bonds), and investing in rental properties.

THE GREATEST AMERICAN

How did he manage his money?

First, Franklin ignored the doomsayers and profited from his prediction that America was destined to be a great prosperous nation. An incurable optimist, Franklin was always bullish on America, and life in general. As such, he was critical of the doomsayers and complainers: "I saw in the public papers of different states frequent complaints of hard times, deadness of trade, scarcity of money," he wrote in 1785. "It is always in the power of a small number to make a great glamour. But let us take a cool view of the general state of our affairs, and perhaps the prospect will appear less gloomy than has been imagined" (*CA*, pp. 332–333).

In his *Autobiography*, he told the story of an elderly man who repeatedly predicted economic depression and a real estate collapse in Philadelphia, and warned Franklin to sell his printing house and his real estate holdings. Franklin ignored his advice and prospered. Eventually, he said, "I had the pleasure of seeing him give five times as much for one [piece of land]" (*A*, p. 71).

Second, limit your speculative opportunities, so as not to jeopardize your entire portfolio with "sure deals." You are bound to be misled and overly optimistic about some speculations.

In 1769, Franklin joined with some partners/friends to seek a land grant of twenty million acres in the Ohio territory from the British Crown. He was told by his friends that the land grant was almost guaranteed. "We were daily amused with expectations that it would be completed at this or other time, but I saw no process made in it," he wrote a friend. His British agents frequently promised that the deal would take place "any day now," but five years later, nothing came of it. Ultimately, the partnership was never granted the land, and Franklin's investment went up in smoke.

Fortunately, Franklin's loss was small. He made the mistake of mixing money and friendship, but avoided the temptation to put too much money into a "sure deal."

Third, diversify your holdings and limit your risks. Franklin made it a point of having a wide variety of income sources, so that

ON PERSONAL FINANCE AND INVESTING

a loss in one would not destroy his entire portfolio. In addition to earning income from his role as minister and postmaster, he maintained seven or eight rental properties; earned interest-bearing bank accounts in Philadelphia, New York, London and Paris; invested in common stocks such as the Bank of North America, which paid a sizable dividend; and occasionally loaned funds at interest to individuals and institutions.

His sizable interest and rental income from bank accounts and real estate saved him from several severe financial setbacks during his years abroad. He recognized the cycle of boom and bust in life and prepared himself during the good times to survive the inevitable and unpredictable declines.

In 1767, while a colonial agent to England, his long partnership in the printing business ended. "A great source of my income was cut off," Franklin wrote, forcing him and his wife to become more frugal in their spending habits. He limited himself to a "single dish" when dining at home.

In 1772, there was a banking crisis in England, but Franklin survived unscathed. "I only hazard a little using my credit with the bank…. Being out of debt myself, my credit could not be shaken by any run upon me."

In 1774, Franklin suffered the most serious blow to his finances. As a result of the Hutchinson letters scandal (where he sent confidential letters among British officials to America, where they were published), Franklin was vilified in England and fired from his job as postmaster and colonial agent, which amounted to a loss of £1,800 a year in income. Frugal living in the good times and their sizable savings and income properties saved them from certain disaster.

CHAPTER 15

ON FAST MONEY

"Experience keeps a dear school,
yet fools will learn in no other."
—*Poor Richard's Almanac*

Making a quick buck is on everyone's mind. *Fast Money* is a popular TV show on CNBC airing twice a day, with five individuals giving their favorite stock tips at the end of the show. I even offer a trading service called "Fast Money Alert" using seasonal trading patterns to make money quickly.

What would Ben Franklin say about speculative fever and fast money?

First, Franklin believed that being an enterprising entrepreneur in business is your fastest way to financial success. In his short pamphlet, "The Way to Wealth," written in 1757 on his way to London, he said that "He who has a trade has an estate," and if you industriously work at your trade, you will be successful. "Diligence is the mother of good luck," he said.

Building a successful business is no easy task—we know that 90 percent of new businesses fail in the first couple of years. "There are no gains without pains," Poor Richard advised.

But if you look at the annual *Forbes* "400 Richest People in America" issue, the record is clear: the vast majority of fast money comes from creating a successful business that multiplies your

ON PERSONAL FINANCE AND INVESTING

wealth. There's always several dozen rags-to-riches stories in the 400 Richest issue, billionaires who made their fortune in a single generation.

Only a minority make it big by working for others. The best way to get rich slowly is to save regularly, watch your budget, and invest prudently. But back in Franklin's day, the stock market wasn't an alternative, only business was.

Franklin started from scratch when he arrived in Philadelphia as a teenager and became one of the richest Americans by establishing his own printing firm after working for other printers and learning the trade. He retired in his forties.

I recommend the same route Franklin took. The fastest way to make a fortune is by creating your own successful business. Learn skills from experts over you, and then strike out on your own when the time is ripe. You'll learn from your mistakes. "The used key is always bright."

The founder's three virtues in business were industry, thrift, and prudence. He always worked hard and long days. But more importantly, he worked smart, looking for opportunities to expand his printing business and always getting the best quality tools and equipment for his trade. Once he had developed a successful printing operation, he duplicated it by franchising his firm elsewhere throughout the colonies. Thus, he multiplied his wealth.

He was also careful not to be a spendthrift when he acquired surplus wealth. That was always a danger. The nouveau riche are always tempted to show off their newfound wealth by buying fancy clothes, a new car, and a house in an upper-class neighborhood—and often borrow money to finance their more expensive lifestyle. That's what gets the new rich into trouble. I'm always amazed at how many millionaires end up filing for bankruptcy by overextending themselves.

THE GREATEST AMERICAN

Ben Franklin had much to say on this topic. "There is much revenue in economy. And no revenue is sufficient without economy."

There's great wisdom in these two pieces of advice. If you live within your means and cut back on wasteful spending, it's like earning more money. Thus, "a penny saved [by budgeting] is a penny earned."

Moreover, if you don't live within your budget, you may never have enough money to live on. There is a natural tendency to spend whatever ready money is at hand or in the bank. You need to make it easy to save, and hard to spend those savings. Investing your savings in a tax-advantaged retirement program, such as a 401(k) or individual retirement account (IRA), is the best way to make sure you will never run out of money in your elderly years.

Speculative opportunities do arise from time to time. Franklin's favorite speculation was to buy a large parcel of the king's land in Ohio. He joined a group called the Grand Ohio Company for a grant of 2.4 million (!) acres of land in the Ohio territory. But year after year, "no progress was made in it," Franklin wrote. "The Ohio affair always seemed near a conclusion, but so difficult was it to get business forward in London, that as to our prospects for success, many things slip between cup and lip" (*CA*, p. 51). Indeed, it never came through and Franklin lost his investment.

Franklin's experience is not unlike today's "private placements," investing in private companies that plan to go public in the future. You buy "cheap" and wait for its IPO. It's anything but "fast money." It may take years before you get your money back, with a profit.

CHAPTER 16

ON INVESTING IN REAL ESTATE

*"Land is the most permanent estate and the
most likely to increase in value."*
—George Washington

Anyone who is earning more than he spends is automatically an investor. What did Benjamin Franklin do with his savings and wealth?

The stock market was only in its embryonic form in the eighteenth century. Occasionally shares in companies were available for purchase, such as the East India Company or commercial banks. Franklin did own some shares in Robert Morris's Bank of North America. But the stock exchanges in Europe largely consisted of government bonds.

Franklin also held funds in bank accounts in three countries—the United States, Britain, and France—where he collected interest payments of about 6 percent a year.

Another substantial source of investment income came from rental properties that he gradually accumulated. By the time he wrote his will in 1788, he owned a half dozen houses in Philadelphia.

THE GREATEST AMERICAN

Speculating in land was also an intriguing prospect in the colonies. Before and after the Revolutionary War, land was the investment of choice for Americans once they arrived from Europe—a choice that signified their faith and optimism in America's future. Historian Bernard Bailyn wrote, "Everyone with any ambition and capacity, it seems, on both sides of the Atlantic, sought some profit from what promised to be the greatest land boom in history. Plans were drawn up, revised, expanded, abandoned; companies formed overnight, sometimes quickly disappeared, sometimes grew into syndicates; and connections between American and British groups were universal, conceived of as a requirement for ultimate success."[5]

Washington was obsessed with the idea of amassing land in the West, tremendous amounts of it, putting it all under cultivation and bringing commerce and people there. He accumulated large tracts of land in Virginia and elsewhere. He wrote that "lands are permanent, rising fast in value, and will be very dear when our independency is established, and the importance of America better known." To the founders, land was a constant. As Washington scholar Glenn A. Phelps wrote, "It was not subject to the changing fortunes of paper money inflation, royal mercantile policies, the loss of political favor, or the decline of one's skills through age or poor health."[6] For leading Virginians, land was virtually a religion. The Reverend John Witherspoon even bought land. Patrick Henry biographer Henry Mayer wrote: "For Henry, as for the vast majority of his countrymen, land held the key to happiness and prosperity. Nine out of every ten Americans lived—and made their livings—on farms, and very few doubted the moral superiority of the agrarian way of life. To own land enough to feed and clothe the family and raise enough of a marketable crop to trade or sell

---

5 Bernard Bailyn, *Voyagers to the West: A Passage in the Peopling of America on the Eve of the Revolution* (New York: Alfred Knopf, 1986), p. 23.

6 Glenn A. Phelps, *George Washington and American Constitutionalism* (University Press of Kansas, 1993), pp. 7–8.

ON PERSONAL FINANCE AND INVESTING

for what the land could not yield seemed close enough to paradise for anyone."[7]

Franklin, like many of the founding fathers, was also a land speculator. Like Washington, Benjamin Franklin understood the importance of land to the American economy. Franklin wrote that "so vast is the territory of North-America that it will require many ages to settle it fully, and till it is fully settled, labor will never be cheap here, where no man continues long a laborer for others, but gets a plantation of his own, no man continues long a journeyman to a trade, but goes among those new settlers, and sets up for himself, etc."

Biographer Walter Isaacson noted that Franklin became "involved with a variety of partnerships, including ones called the Illinois Company and then the Indiana Company, that had failed to win support in London. In the summer of 1769, Franklin helped organize a consortium so powerful that he was convinced it would be able to outmaneuver Lord Hillsborough. The Grand Ohio Company, as it was named, included a collection of some of London's richest and most prominent names, most notably Thomas and Richard Walpole."[8]

In late 1760s, while a colonial agent in London, Franklin joined with some partners/friends to seek a land grant in the Ohio territory from the British Crown. He was told by his friends that the land grant was almost guaranteed. The Walpole speculators boldly request twenty million acres, one of the biggest land grabs in world history. Five years later, nothing came of it. Ultimately, the partnership was never granted the land, and Franklin's investment went up in smoke.

Wisely, Franklin never borrowed money to buy land and therefore avoided the risks of land speculation. Other founders weren't

---

7   Henry Mayer, *A Son of Thunder: Patrick Henry and the American Revolution* (Grove Press, 2001), p. 350.

8   Walter Isaacson, *Benjamin Franklin: An American Life* (New York: Simon & Schuster, 2004).

THE GREATEST AMERICAN

so lucky. Virginia's Henry Lee and Pennsylvania's Robert Morris and James Wilson ended up in prison because of their debts from speculation.

CHAPTER 17

ON GETTING OUT OF DEBT

*"If you would know the value of money, go try to borrow
some; for he that goes a-borrowing goes a-sorrowing."*
—*Poor Richard's Almanac*

Today, all the talk is about the growing federal deficit (over $2 trillion as of fiscal year 2024) and the national debt (over $36 trillion in 2025), on top of the fear of unfunded liabilities from Social Security, Medicare, and other entitlements.

For years, we Americans have lived the easy life made possible by credit cards and the consumer society. Now, it seems most Americans have found themselves in trouble and have been forced to retrench or even declare bankruptcy.

What would Franklin have to say?

First, it's important to emphasize that Franklin was not against debt per se. The line from Shakespeare's *Hamlet*, "Neither a borrower nor a lender be" was not for him. In fact, Franklin did borrow funds for business in his early years as a printer and enjoyed a huge income from lending money to friends and businesspeople after he retired.

Following his tri-principles of industry, thrift, and prudence, he suggested that going into debt was risky business, whether as a consumer, business, or a nation.

THE GREATEST AMERICAN

Undoubtedly, Franklin would castigate today's Americans for indulging in undersaving, overspending, and excessive consumer debt. In his famous work, "The Way to Wealth," he warned against going into debt for consumer expenditures. "But what madness must it be to run in *debt* for these superfluities!"

Borrowing money for creating or expanding a business is another matter and sometimes essential to get ahead. Franklin himself, though a man who preferred to be a creditor and saver rather than a borrower and consumer, saw the need to borrow funds to grow his printing business in the early years.

But every effort must be made to pay off one's debts in one's personal life and business, and to economize whenever possible. "No revenue is sufficient without economy," he wrote. "A man's industry and frugality will pay his debts and get him forward in the world.... Business not well managed ruins one faster than no business" (*CA*, pp. 148, 336).

We all know of millionaires who have gone bankrupt. Just because you have plenty of income and assets does not mean you can't run into financial trouble. Parkinson's Second Law, the expenditure rises to meet (and sometimes exceeds) income, occurs all too often. As Poor Richard warned, "A fool and his money are soon parted."

One of the most difficult things to do is to cut back when you have a setback in income. But retrenching is better than going into debt in order to maintain your lifestyle. When his printing partnership abruptly ended in 1767, Franklin made the difficult decision to cut back consumption (dining at home on only one "single dish") and urged his wife Deborah to do the same. It kept them out of trouble.

Franklin believed in managing one's budget carefully. Even though credit cards are a modern invention, he would no doubt consider them a dangerous source of wasteful and excessive spending.

ON PERSONAL FINANCE AND INVESTING

Remember these adages from *Poor Richard's Almanac*:

1. "Beware of small expenses; A small leak may sink a great ship."
2. "The honest man takes pains, and then enjoys pleasures; the knave takes pleasures and then suffers pain."
3. "Great spenders are bad lenders."
4. "Creditors have better memories than debtors."

Finally, Franklin opposed filing for bankruptcy, even in business. In his *Autobiography*, he recounted the story of Thomas Denham, a businessman who helped Franklin get started. "I must record one trait of this good man's character. He had formerly been in business at Bristol, but failed in debt to a number of people, compounded and went to America. There, by a close application of business as a merchant, he acquired a plentiful fortune in a few years. Returning to England in the ship with me, he invited his own creditors to an entertainment, at which he thanked them for the easy composition they had favored him with, and when they expected nothing but the treat, every man at the first remove, found under his plate an order on a banker for the full amount of the unpaid remainder with interest" (*A*, pp. 57–58).

Later in life, he developed a technique to influence others by lending money, not giving it away. When he was in Paris, he wrote a friend Benjamin Webb, who solicited his support for a cause back home: "'I do not pretend to *give* such a sum. I only *lend* it to you. When you shall return to your country with a good character, you cannot fail of getting into some business that will in time enable you to pay all your debts: In that case, when you meet with another honest man in similar distress, you must pay *me* by lending this sum to *him*; enjoining him to discharge the debt by a like operation when he shall be able and shall meet with such another opportunity. I hope it may thus go thro' many hands before it meets with a knave that will stop its progress.' This has been a trick of mine for doing a deal of good with a little money. I have not

THE GREATEST AMERICAN

been rich enough to afford *much* in good works and so I have been obliged to be cunning and make the most of a *little*" (*CA*, p. 313).

What about the national debt? Franklin saw the need for fiscal sanity at the personal and national level. Just as individuals should seek to discharge their debts, so the national government should have as a goal to pay off its obligations. He wrote, "Honesty in money matters is a virtue as justly as to be expected from a government as from an individual subject. Therefore, I am quite of the opinion that our independence is not quite complete till we have discharged our public debt" (*CA*, pp. 341–342).

Is anyone listening in Washington?

CHAPTER 18

ON SURVIVING A FINANCIAL CRISIS

*"Being out of debt myself, my credit could not
be shaken by any run against me."*
—*Ben Franklin (1772)*

Even the most prosperous nations are not immune to financial crises from time to time. In the United States, there have been at least a dozen downturns in the economy and several stock market crashes since the end of World War II.

What would Franklin's counsel be on dealing with a financial crisis?

Franklin himself lived through turbulent times. During his lifetime, he encountered severe financial panics, real estate crashes, runaway inflation, and revolutionary war. There was no Wall Street during Franklin's time, but even then it was difficult to preserve one's wealth. Many fortunes were destroyed, but somehow Doctor Franklin survived and prospered. How did he do it?

First, during the periods of peace and economic vibrancy, Franklin established good financial habits. He lived by his own three principles: industry, thrift, and prudence. "In prosperous fortunes, be modest and wise," he counseled in *Poor Richard's Almanac.* He and his faithful companion Deborah worked hard to make their printing business profitable, and then franchised it around the colonies to multiply their profits.

Second, the Franklins delayed personal consumption and saved regularly. In his *Autobiography*, the financial guru wrote that he lived and dressed "plainly." "We kept no idle servants, our table was plain and simple, our furniture of the cheapest." He expressed surprise one morning at the breakfast table to find a silver spoon in a china bowl. "They had been bought for me without my knowledge by my wife, and had cost her an enormous sum, but she thought her husband deserved a silver spoon and China bowl as well as any of his neighbors" (*A*, pp. 96–97). Such luxuries were the exception to the rule.

They avoided personal debt as much as possible and only borrowed funds to expand their printing business, and even then only "prudently." According to Franklin, "debt exposes a man to confinement, and a species of slavery to his creditors" (*A*, p. 115).

Thus, "frugality and industry freed me from my remaining debt, and produced affluence and independence," he wrote in his *Autobiography* (p. 101).

Third, Franklin invested his savings wisely: earning interest in various bank accounts (benefiting from compound interest), buying and managing rental properties in Philadelphia, and selectively loaning money to acquaintances.

Imagine if Franklin had spent all of his £1,800 every year on expensive furniture, dining in the finest restaurants, travel to exotic lands, and other consumption goods. Imagine if he had run up personal debts, thinking that his handsome annual income could easily cover the interest. How well would he have fared when he heard the news of his firing?

Like everyone, Franklin suffered during the war years from runaway inflation. He also had a meager salary during the nine years he served as America's ambassador to France. But his well-di-

ON PERSONAL FINANCE AND INVESTING

versified portfolio kept him well enough to die one of the richest men in America.

These are important lessons. You can be sure that the latest financial crisis won't be the last. Live by Franklin's rules (industry, frugality, prudence), and you won't be hurt.

CHAPTER 19

PROTECTING YOUR CAPITAL IN WARTIME

"There never was a good war, or a bad peace."
—Ben Franklin (1783)

When a militant group bombed innocent people in Paris, France, in November 2015, I was reminded of Benjamin Franklin's words in a letter to the British physician Sir Joseph Priestley in the summer of 1782 about the depravity of man during war, which causes a massive "quantity of pain, misery, and destruction."

War, according to Franklin, brought out the worst of mankind. "I am disgusted with them," he wrote, questioning whether they were worth saving by medical doctors like Dr. Priestley. "Men I find to be a sort of being very badly constructed, as they are generally more easily provoked than reconciled, more disposed to do mischief to each other than to make reparation, much more easily deceived than undeceived, and having more pride and even pleasure in killing than in begetting one another.... I cannot comprehend why cruel men should be permitted to destroy their fellow creatures" (*CA*, p. 271, 275).

He would be appalled to witness such carnage in Paris, the city of lights. "France is the civilest nation upon the earth," he wrote a friend in America. "It is really a generous nation, fond of glory and

ON PERSONAL FINANCE AND INVESTING

particularly that of protecting the oppressed. I advised our people in all parts of America to cultivate a friendship with the French people, and use every means to remove ancient prejudices" (*CA*, p. 161).

Franklin witnessed firsthand the effects of bloodshed in both the French and Indian War (1754–1763) and the War of Independence (1775–1783). "When princes make war by prohibiting commerce, each may hurt himself as much as his enemy. Traders, farmers and fishermen should never be interrupted or molested by their business, but should enjoy the protection of all in the time of war and peace. The source of wealth is land and industry, and the state must nourish both," he stated (*CA*, p. 300).

The terrorist attacks by Islamic extremists hurt the tourist trade. Today's France is heavily dependent on the tourism—7.5 percent of GDP, the highest of any European nation. Terrorist attacks don't do anyone any good.

The stock market is always hit in the short term when a military crisis occurs because of the fear it will do to trade and commerce.

Franklin was always in a position of financial security when war or a financial crisis hit. During periods of peace and prosperity, he avoided overspending. He lived by his own three grand principles: industry, thrift, and prudence. "In prosperous fortunes, be modest and wise," he counseled in *Poor Richard's Almanac*. He and his wife avoided personal debt as much as possible and used debt in business only "prudently."

He diversified his savings in secure, conservative investments, earning compound interest in various bank accounts, buying and managing income-producing rental properties, and selectively loaning out funds to friends and business partners.

In early 1974, while in London, relations between the colonies and the United Kingdom turned sour, and Franklin lost his job as postmaster general and colonial agent. He was suddenly cut off from his £1,800 a pound salary from the Crown, a prestigious sum. No wonder he hated war!

THE GREATEST AMERICAN

For most men, such a loss would have been devastating, but Franklin avoided the high life and always lived within his means and saved heavily. He was able to survive this debacle and went on to an illustrious career as a diplomat.

Like everyone, Franklin suffered during the war years from runaway inflation. He also collected a meager salary during the nine years he served as America's ambassador to France. Yet his long-term savings and investments kept him well-off enough to live the remainder of his life in relative wealth.

At the end of his life, he was sure that America made the right decision to declare independence, but he wished it could have been done without the sacrifice of so many lives and fortunes.

After signing the Treaty of Paris in 1783, finally ending the war with England, he sighed, "When will men be convinced that even successful wars do at length become misfortunes to those who unjustly commenced them, and who triumphed blindly in their success, not seeing all its consequences…. There is so little good gained, and so much mischief done generally by wars that I wish the imprudence of undertaking them was more evident to princes. For in my opinion *there never was a good war, or a bad peace*. What vast additions to the conveniences and comforts of living might mankind have acquired if the money spent in wars had been employed in works of public utility! What an extension of agriculture…what rivers rendered navigable…what bridges, aqueducts, new roads, and other public works, edifices and improvements rendering England a complete paradise…millions were spent in the great war doing mischief…and destroying the lives of so many thousands of working people who might have performed useful labor!" (*CA*, p. 302).

He hoped that the new United States of America would adopt this motto: "Commerce with every nation; war with none" (*CA*, p. 148).

At least half of Franklin's motto has been kept!

CHAPTER 20

ON DOOMSAYERS AND FEAR MONGERING

*"I saw in the public papers of different states frequent
complaints of hard times, deadness of trade, scarcity of
money, etc.... It is always in the power of a small number
to make a great clamour. But let us take a cool view of the
general state of our affairs, and perhaps the prospect will
appear less gloomy than has been imagined."*
—*Ben Franklin (1785)*

Whenever the stock market enters a correction, there's always a handful of Cassandras predicting a severe bear market ahead—or something even worse. They may forecast another stock market crash like the one we suffered from on October 19, 1987, when the Dow fell 22.5 percent in one day. It turned out to be my fortieth birthday, but few of my investment friends were celebrating. However, my subscribers were happy. Six weeks earlier, I had warned them that a crash was possible.

Yet, the market recovered quickly after the 1987 crash.

Over the years, I've collected doom-and-gloom predictions that have proven to be premature or simply wrong. "Dollar Collapse Inevitable by Fall of 2015," warned a former congressman and goldbug. A financial writer advised, "Batten down the hatch-

THE GREATEST AMERICAN

es!" Even Goldman Sachs, the prestigious New York investment banker, predicted an "earnings recession" and deflation ($20 a barrel oil) at that time.

Not to be outdone, Donald Trump, who was running for president in 2015, warned voters that the American dream was over.

Recently, I've received copies of books and special reports predicting a collapse of the dollar within six months, another stock market crash, and urged investors to get out of stocks and into gold. I added them to my collection of doomsayer books in my financial library that include such titles as *Crisis Investing, The Coming Deflation, How to Prosper During the Coming Bad Years* (published in 1979, the year before Ronald Reagan was elected and turned the country around), and *Wiped Out: How I Lost a Fortune in the Stock Market While the Averages Were Making New Highs*.

In Edinburgh, Scotland, there's a "Library of Mistakes" containing books making false predictions. I noticed several titles that were off base: *The Death of Inflation* (published in 1996) and *The Great Reckoning: How the World Will Change in the Great Depression of the 1990s*.

In 2011, a financial guru wrote a special booklet, "The End of America," predicting a collapse in the dollar and the stock market and recommended investors switch into gold.

Fortunately, a financial Armageddon was postponed. In fact, just the opposite occurred. King Dollar achieved new highs against the euro and the yen. The stock market roared ahead. Gold hit a new high at the time the bearish booklet was published and dropped by nearly 50 percent between 2011 and 2018. Those who followed the advice of this popular promotion were crushed financially, while missing out on one of the greatest bull markets in US history.

Franklin experienced similar bearish sentiments way back in the eighteenth century. He called them "croakers." He wrote in his *Autobiography*:

ON PERSONAL FINANCE AND INVESTING

There are croakers in every country, always boding its ruin. Such a one then lived in Philadelphia; a person of note, an elderly man, with a wise look and a very grave manner of speaking; his name was Samuel Mickle. This gentleman, a stranger to me, stopped one day at my door, and asked me if I was the young man who had lately opened a new printing-house. Being answered in the affirmative, he said he was sorry for me, because it was an expensive undertaking, and the expense would be lost; for Philadelphia was a sinking place, the people already half-bankrupts, or near being so; all appearances to the contrary, such as new buildings and the rise of rents, being to his certain knowledge fallacious; for they were, in fact, among the things that would soon ruin us. And he gave me such a detail of misfortunes now existing, or that were soon to exist, that he left me half melancholy.

Had I known him before I engaged in this business, probably I never should have done it. This man continued to live in this decaying place, and to declaim in the same strain, refusing for many years to buy a house there, because all was going to destruction; and at last I had the pleasure of seeing him give five times as much for one as he might have bought it for when he first began his croaking (*A*, pp. 70–71).

I know a similar case today. A longtime friend is a hard-money goldbug who watches Cassandras on cable TV and subscribes to newsletters constantly predicting disaster ahead. When the real estate market fell out of bed in 2007–08, it confirmed his worst suspicions. He sold his house and bought penny mining stocks.

Over the next several years, the real estate market recovered while his penny stocks fell to pennies. Now he wants to buy a house but is facing higher real estate prices and he has less money for a down payment.

J. P. Morgan warned, "He who is a bear on the United States will inevitably go broke."

And J. Paul Getty, one of America's first billionaires, warned, "Businessmen can profit handsomely if they will disregard the pessimistic auguries of self-appointed prophets of doom."[9]

Ben Franklin was a natural optimist who discounted doom-and-gloom predictions about America's future. "America will, with God's blessing, become a great and happy country," he predicted at the beginning of the new republic (*CA*, p. 301).

Near the end of Franklin's mission to France, Europe suffered a devastating winter in 1783–84. He wrote a friend, "We had a terrible winter in France.... Yet I was still alive, the sun started to return, the days to lengthen, the spring to come, the trees and gardens to regain their vendure, all nature to laugh, and to me, happiness" (*CA*, pp. 310–311).

Despite living through wars, depressions, bank crises, and personal hardships, the father of American capitalism survived and prospered. He developed multiple sources of income, including rental properties, saving accounts in three countries, and bank stock. He stayed out of debt most of his career, and always lived frugally and within his means.

While he loved to speculate on land deals, he never put too much of his wealth at risk. In 1772, while a colonial agent in London, he "was fortunate enough not to suffer in the general wreck of credit." He wrote a friend, "My two banking houses, Browns & Collinson, and Smith, Wright & Grey, stood firm, and they were the only people in the City in debt to me, so I lost

---

9   These and other quotations can be found in my book *The Maxims of Wall Street*, 10th ed. (Capital Press, 2020), available at www. skousenbooks.com.

ON PERSONAL FINANCE AND INVESTING

nothing by the failure of others; and being out of debt myself my credit could not be shaken by any run upon me: Out of debt, as the proverb says, was being out of danger. But I did hazard a little in using my credit with the bank to support that of a friend as far as £5000, for which I was secured by bills of the Bank of Douglas, Herod & Company, accepted by a good house; and therefore I call it only hazarding a little" (*CA*, pp. 74–75).

While he suffered occasional money problems, he died a wealthy man.

CHAPTER 21

ON AUSTERITY

"There is much revenue in economy."
—*Poor Richard's Almanac*

Several years ago, I appeared on John Stossel's show on Fox Business to discuss the growing debate, "Austerity vs. Stimulus: Which is the Best Way Out of the Great Recession?"

I debated Robert Kuttner, author of *Debtor's Prison: The Politics of Austerity Versus Possibility*, who contends that cutting back government spending will only cause more unemployment and misery. His champion was Daniel Defoe, the early eighteenth-century author of the classic novel, *Robinson Crusoe*. But Defoe was also a rake who went bankrupt, was in constant financial straits, and favored progressive changes in the harsh bankruptcy laws in Britain.

My hero is Benjamin Franklin, who was polls apart from Defoe when it came to sound financial strategies. Franklin was a firm defender of personal and fiscal austerity during depressed times. His principles of "industry, thrift, and prudence" served him well throughout an era of financial turbulence and war. He was never in jeopardy of filing for bankruptcy and died a wealthy man.

On a personal level, Franklin thought it essential to maintain good financial habits during the good times so that when the bad times came, he could survive without getting into trouble like his

ON PERSONAL FINANCE AND INVESTING

spendthrift neighbors. "In prosperous fortunes, be modest and wise," he counseled in *Poor Richard's Almanac*. The Franklins delayed personal consumption and saved regularly. He created his own rainy-day fund.

They avoided personal debt as much as possible and only borrowed funds to expand their printing business, and even then only "prudently." According to Franklin, "debt exposes a man to confinement, and a species of slavery to his creditors."

Thus, "frugality and industry freed me from my remaining debt, and produced affluence and independence," he wrote in his *Autobiography*.

When his printing partnership abruptly ended in 1767, Franklin made the difficult decision to cut back consumption and urged his wife to do the same. It kept them out of trouble.

In early 1774, Franklin became embroiled in the Hutchinson letters scandal and was dismissed from his position as postmaster general and colonial agent. For years, Franklin was used to earning a prestigious sum, a combined salary of £1,800 a year. (The average Brit was lucky to make £100 a year during this time.) Now, suddenly, he was without a job. For most men, such a loss would have been devastating, especially if they were used to living the high life.

Franklin did not spend all of his £1,800 every year but wisely set aside funds for a rainy day.

During the good times, he always lived within his means and saved heavily. He invested his saved funds in several rental properties back home and in bank deposits in conservative institutions in New York and London. During times of financial setbacks, he learned to cut back on his expenses. He believed that retrenching was better than going into debt in order to maintain his lifestyle. And he was well diversified.

Kuttner and other Keynesians believe that Franklin's personal philosophy of retrenchment during economic downturns should not apply to government. Belt-tightening and living within one's

77

means are "oversimplified" metaphors, he claims. "If you put an entire nation under a rigid austerity regime, its capacity for economic growth is crippled. Even creditors will eventually suffer from the distress and social chaos that follow." Only government can save the day by running up the national debt.

But Franklin was in the camp of the classical British economist and longtime acquaintance Adam Smith, who proclaimed in the exact center of his classic work *The Wealth of Nations*, "What is prudence in the conduct of every private family can scarce be folly in that of a great kingdom."[10]

Franklin saw the need for fiscal sanity at the personal and national level. Just as individuals should seek to discharge their debts, so should the national government have a goal to pay off its obligations. He wrote, "Honesty in money matters is a virtue as justly as to be expected from a government as from an individual subject. Therefore, I am quite of the opinion that our independence is not quite complete till we have discharged our public debt."

We must not ignore the benefits of austerity—eliminating waste in the private and public sector, rebuilding company balance sheets, improving labor and capital productivity, and warning government at all levels to avoid excessive "Great Society" welfare programs and deficits that got us into this mess in the first place. During the good times, governments need to build rainy-day funds so that cutbacks on essential government services are not necessary during the next downturn.

American economist Paul Krugman is fond of quoting his mentor, British economist John Maynard Keynes, who said in 1937, "The boom, not the slump, is the right time for austerity at the Treasury." But even during the good times, the Keynesians are afraid of running budget surpluses and encouraging high saving rates, fearing it might damper consumer demand.

---

10 Adam Smith, *The Wealth of Nations* (New York: Modern Library, 1966 [1776]), p. 424.

ON PERSONAL FINANCE AND INVESTING

The key to any recovery is to encourage the private sector, which represents the majority shareholders in the economy and the creator of new jobs. The Keynesians hope to jump-start business by running massive deficits and adopting more easy-money policies, thinking such spending policies will stimulate aggregate demand. But the truth is that government spending is often offset by private companies that cut back on private spending and build large cash positions in anticipation of higher taxes down the road and uncertain government policies, instead of investing funds in new projects and jobs. The crowding out problem is real.

My solution is more on the supply side: removing barriers to new production by cutting the corporate tax rate and curtailing new regulations (Obamacare, Dodd–Frank, Sarbanes–Oxley, EPA, IRS). By reducing the size of government, more money is made available to the private sector, which is more productive.

My favorite example of austerity is our neighbor to the north. In 1994, Canada faced a major fiscal crisis—out-of-control government spending reaching over 50 percent of GDP, skyrocketing deficits, a weak economy, and a sharply falling Canadian dollar (the *Wall Street Journal* called it the "northern peso.") Under the leadership of Prime Minister Jean Chrétien and finance minister Paul Martin, the Liberal Party decided "enough is enough," joined forces with the Conservative Party, and went on a three-year austerity plan, cutting back state spending and laying off federal workers. All the Keynesian economists in Canada opposed the plan, saying it would seriously curtail aggregate demand. Instead, they balanced the budget and then went on an eleven-year supply side tax cut program. Today the corporate tax rate is down to 15 percent. Government as a percentage of GDP fell below 42 percent, although it has recently been running deficits again. But Canada largely avoided the financial crisis of 2008. There's a lesson there for Americans.

CHAPTER 22

ON WRITING A LAST WILL

"The years roll round and the last will come; when I would rather it have said, He lived usefully, than, He died rich."
—*Ben Franklin (1750)*

Every January it is customary to make new year's resolutions. Why not make out a last will or update it? A 2019 study indicated that 55 percent of Americans die without a will. When a person dies intestate, the local court is required to create a will, and it may not go in accordance with the wishes of the deceased or heirs.

As a financial writer and business leader, Ben Franklin made sure he had a last will and testament, and in fact, he updated it several times before he died in 1790 at the age of eighty-four.

His will is a fascinating document—and quite controversial. He wrote his legal bequest in the summer of 1788 in Philadelphia at the age of eighty-two. He added a codicil, or addendum, a year later that would prove to be famously creative.

The first surprise came to his son William. He and his father used to be close but had become bitter enemies during the American Revolution. In earlier wills, the lion's share of Franklin's prop-

ON PERSONAL FINANCE AND INVESTING

erty had been earmarked for William. Now, they would go to his daughter Sally and her husband Richard Bache. Franklin left his son some worthless land in Nova Scotia, a few books and papers left in England, and the cancellation of his still outstanding debts to Franklin's estate—in essence, nothing. He added this final reproof, "The part he acted against me in the late war, which is of public notoriety, will account for my leaving him no more of an estate he endeavored to deprive me of" (*CA*, pp. 393–394). William never forgave him for this "shameful injustice," as he called it, and bitterly remarked that he would never set foot in America again.

Franklin's real estate holdings and household goods in Philadelphia, as well as some Ohio lands, were left to Sarah (also known as Sally) and Richard Bache. He gave Sarah alone the valuable miniature of Louis XVI that the king gave to Franklin as a parting gift; the ornament contained 408 diamonds, and Franklin gave it to his daughter on the condition that she would not remove or sell them. Alas, within a year of her father's death, the Baches sold the diamonds and traveled to Europe, a lifelong dream. (Personal note: I saw the Louis XVI miniature at the Franklin exhibit in Philadelphia in 2006, and sure enough, all the diamonds are missing.)

Next to the Baches, the biggest share of the estate went to William's son, Temple, who served as Franklin's secretary in France. Temple was assigned to be his literary heir. Franklin left him his library and all his manuscripts and papers, with the hope that Temple would finish his autobiography. Instead, he left for England and France, sired an illegitimate daughter, and never did complete Franklin's memoirs. (That task would finally be fulfilled in 2006 by yours truly with the publication of *The Compleated Autobiography* by Regnery Publishing.) The closest he came was in 1818, when he published four volumes of *Memoirs of the Life and Writings of Benjamin Franklin*.

THE GREATEST AMERICAN

Franklin left his other esteemed grandson Benny a thousand pounds' worth of printing equipment. He promptly began publishing the *Philadelphia Aurora*, which soon became the most notorious scandal sheet in the country. Benny attacked everyone, including George Washington and later John Adams when he was president, and the *Aurora* became, like his grandfather's *Gazette*, the largest circulating newspaper in the country. In 1798, he was arrested on the charge of libeling the president and exciting sedition. He was released on bail but caught yellow fever and died that summer at the age of only twenty-nine.

A year before dying, Franklin amended his will and made a bequest of £1,000 to his native Boston and his adopted Philadelphia. He wanted to see the incredible power of compounding at work. (See chapter 13 for details on how this worked out.)

PART III

ON SCIENCE, TECHNOLOGY, AND MEDICINE

CHAPTER 23

THE WONDERS OF SCIENCE

"I have sometimes almost wished it had been my destiny to have been born two or three centuries hence, for inventions of improvement are prolific, and beget more of their kind. The present progress is rapid."
—Ben Franklin (1788)

According to Harvard historian Joyce Chaplin, Ben Franklin was the "first scientific American." She goes so far as to claim that if it weren't for his inventions and scientific experiments in electricity, he would not have become an illustrious and effective statesman and diplomat. "He became a statesman because he had done science."

According to one list of the top one hundred scientists, he is one of the most "influential scientists who shaped the world."

Franklin's first love was not politics or even business. He was fascinated with all things "philosophical," the term used to describe science and technology in the eighteenth century. In fact, the reason he hated war so much was because it kept him from pursuing his career in science and corresponding with his ingenious friends in England.

THE GREATEST AMERICAN

After a successful career as a businessman, Franklin retired to become a "gentleman" devoted to public affairs and the pursuit of "useful" science. He was more interested in "applied" science than "theoretical" pursuits.

In 1742, he invented the Franklin stove "for the better warming of rooms and at the same time saving fuel."

In the late 1740s and early 1750s, he engaged in a series of experiments in electricity, including his famous kite experiment that demonstrated that lightning was electricity. His articles on the subject were published in Britain and France, for which he won the Royal Society's Copley Medal and honorary degrees from Harvard and Yale Colleges, William & Mary, and St. Andrews. From that time forward, he was known as "Doctor Franklin."

In 1752, he invented the lightning rod that protected homes from electrical storms. He also founded the first fire department in Pennsylvania. Upon returning home from France in 1786, he discovered that his own lightning rod had saved his home from destruction. "Thus the invention was of some use to the inventor."

Because of his invention of the lightning rod and his experiments in electricity, the French Finance Minister Anne-Robert-Jacques Turgot expressed the famous epigram of Franklin: "He stole the thunder from the heavens and the scepter from tyrants."

In 1766, Franklin was painted in a portrait as a man of science. He sits and reads, one hand holding a book, the other his chin. He is wearing his spectacles. A huge bust of Isaac Newton looms in the background, suggesting his intellectual heir.

In 1784, while ambassador to France, he came up with the idea of bifocals. "By this means, I wear my spectacles constantly, and I have only to move my eyes up or down as I want to see distinctly far or near, the proper glasses always being ready." (*CA*, pp. 320–321)

He found his new invention especially useful in France. "The glasses served me best at table to see what I ate, not being the best

ON SCIENCE, TECHNOLOGY, AND MEDICINE

to see the faces of those on the other side of the table who spoke to me; and when one's ears are not well accustomed to the sounds of a language, a sight of the movements in the features of him that speaks helps to explain, so that I understood French better by the help of my spectacles." (*CA*, p. 321)

In 1768, Franklin, who traversed the Atlantic Ocean eight times in his life, also was the first to discover and map the Gulf Stream that explained the longer passage of ships from England to America. By staying outside the Gulf Stream, ships traveling to America could save several days and arrive early. And ships traveling to England could pick up several days by staying within the Gulf Stream.

He also invented a crude odometer while inspecting post offices in America and may be the first to suggest daylight savings time.

Franklin was also interested in music and created a radically new arrangement of the "glass armonica" in 1761 while in England. This simple musical instrument was played by touching the edge of the spinning glass with dampened fingers. The armonica's beautiful tones appealed to many composers, including Mozart and Beethoven, although it is seldom played today.

Finally, Franklin was also keen on debunking myths and errors when it came to medicine and other natural sciences. "The sciences, which grow larger with the truth, have even more to gain by the suppression of an error." In 1785 in France, he was appointed one of the commissioners to investigate the "new art of healing" from "animal magnetism" sensationalized by the Viennese psychiatrist Franz Mesmer from Austria. He came to the conclusion that "the system of magnetism did not cure anything" (*CA*, pp. 321–322).

No doubt the multi-talented founding father would be fascinated by the variety and advancement of technology in the twenty-first century.

CHAPTER 24

THUNDER AND LIGHTNING: THE PHILADELPHIA EXPERIMENTS

*"I have, during some months past, had little
leisure for anything else."*
—Ben Franklin (1747)

*"His work on electricity was recognized as ushering
in a scientific revolution comparable to those wrought
by Newton in the previous century or by Watson
and Crick in ours."*
—Dudley Herschbach (Harvard professor of science and
1986 Nobel Prize winner)

What was it in Franklin's experiments in electricity that caught the attention of Europe's top scientists and resulted in his achieving fame as one of the top one hundred greatest scientists in the world? His achievements transformed the Pennsylvania printer into the best-known American in his time.

Prior to his experiments in electricity, Franklin had shown interest in the science of nature, resulting in the making of several

ON SCIENCE, TECHNOLOGY, AND MEDICINE

inventions, the most famous of which was the Franklin stove, a more efficient and cheaper way to heat people's homes.

When Franklin began his experiments, the science and understanding of electricity was in its infancy. In the 1740s there was the beginning of a craze of "electric shows" going around in Europe and the United States, where audiences were witness to sparks and electric shocks (even "electric kisses") among objects and individuals.

While visiting Boston in 1746, Franklin attended his first electric demonstration by a "Dr. Spence" and was so fascinated with the show that he wrote his British friend Peter Collinson, a man with widespread interest in all things scientific. Collinson sent him a glass tube known as a Leyden jar, a high-voltage container that stored twenty thousand to sixty thousand volts of electricity.

With this device, "I eagerly seized the opportunity of repeating what I had seen in Boston; and, by much practice, acquired great readiness in performing those, also, which we had an account from England, adding a number of new ones."

He also engaged in some parlor tricks or "electric parties," as they were called, performing the ringing of bells and making a spider dance and two people kiss. He even killed a turkey with his experiments, and he was once knocked out by a powerful shock.

At one point he connected a series of charging Leyden jars involving eleven panes of glass with thin lead plates glued to each side, which he called "an electric battery." He was the first to use the term "battery" to mean something that stored electric power.

Franklin had the free time and funds to experiment after he had sold his lucrative print shop to David Hall in 1948, and largely devoted the next five years to science. Having been a printer and a practical mechanic, he was able to advance the electrical experiments far more than his European counterparts. As French historian Bernard Faÿ noted, "He made excellent progress while his contemporaries of Europe were merely groping, for he was superior to them in two ways: he was a skillful manual workman and quick at seeing his way out of a fix."[11]

Static electricity had been known to exist for centuries but now scientists were keen on finding out exactly what was the nature of this invisible but powerful force that in small quantities could create sparks in an electric show, or so brutal that it could cook turkeys...and kill humans!

Galileo and Sir Isaac Newton explained the mystery of gravity throughout the universe. Now it was Franklin's turn to demonstrate that electricity was a single "fluid" that existed throughout the atmosphere, which under the right circumstances could display sparks and even lightning during a thunderstorm.

It was Franklin who originally proposed that this single fluid could develop both "positive" and "negative" electric charges between objects and humans. The French described two kinds of elasticity, "resinous" and "glazed," but Franklin's terminology won the day, as well as "plus" and "minus." As Franklin himself wrote in a letter to Collinson, "We say B is electrized *positively*; A *negatively*; or rather B is electrized *plus* and A *minus*." He also used the terms "condense" and "conductor."

Franklin concluded that the positive and negative charges must occur in equal amounts, known as the "conservation of charge" and "single fluid theory of electricity." As I. Bernard Cohen states, "Franklin's law of conservation of charge must be considered to be of the same fundamental importance to physical science as Newton's law of conservation of momentum."

Franklin made additional contributions, such as the distinction between insulators and conductors, the importance of electric grounding, and the concepts of capacitors and batteries. Biographer Carl Van Doren concluded, "He found electricity a curiosity and left it a science."

---

11 Bernard Faÿ, *Franklin: Apostle of Modern Times* (Boston: Little, Brown, and Company, 1929), p. 218.

ON SCIENCE, TECHNOLOGY, AND MEDICINE

"STEALING LIGHTNING FROM THE HEAVENS..."

At this time, there was a big debate whether lightning in the sky was electricity or not. The French even had a contest to see if there was a connection. But Franklin had an advantage. Thunderstorms were up to four times more common in the United States than Europe, and he took advantage of this situation by devising his famous kite experiment in June 1752.

It was held in Philadelphia in secret, and only observed by his son Billy, age twenty-two, at the time. Franklin was forty-six. Joseph Priestley wrote about the event fifteen years later.

He constructed a simple kite and attached a wire to the top to act like a lightning rod and at the bottom a hemp string. The last piece was the metal key. They launched the kite and waited. Just as they were about to give up, Franklin noticed loose threads of the hemp string standing erect. Ben moved his finger near the key and felt a spark.

Thus, he had proven that lightning was in fact electricity. Lightning and subsequent thunder were caused by the gradual separation of the negative and positive charges.

In 1751, Peter Collinson arranged for the publication of Franklin's letters on the subject in a treatise entitled *Experiments and Observations on Electricity*. The book was reissued in four more editions with additional material into 1774.

The response was electric. His fame grew dramatically from the colonies to Europe. Germany philosopher Immanuel Kant named him the "new Prometheus" for stealing the fire of heaven. Franklin was awarded the Royal Society's prestigious Copley Medal in 1753 and finally made a member of the Society in 1756. At the same time, he was awarded honorary master's degrees from Harvard and Yale, and William & Mary. In 1759, he received an honorary doctorate degree from the University of St. Andrews, making him officially "Dr. Franklin."

INVENTING THE LIGHTNING ROD

Ultimately, however, Franklin was a practical scientist, and this is where his fame grew. Fires caused by lightning storms were common in the United States, especially churches with their high steeples. Between 1755 and 1760, he devised the pointed lightning rod conductor to be placed at the top of churches, buildings, and homes, insulated to the ground and thus a reliable system to avoid fire. Pointed lightning rods became commonly used in the United States.

When he returned to Philadelphia after the War of Independence he found that his own house had been struck by lightning with no damage because of the lightning rod at the top. "So at length the invention has been of some use to the inventor, and afforded an additional pleasure to that of having seen it useful to others" (CA, p. 350).

In sum, he has the unique distinction of helping Americans heat their homes through the Franklin stove and protecting Americans from fire through the lightning rod!

CHAPTER 25

WHAT?! FRANKLIN NEVER TOOK OUT ANY PATENTS ON HIS INVENTIONS?

"As we enjoy great advantages from the invention of others, we should be glad of an opportunity to serve others by any invention of ours, and this we should do freely and generously."
—*Ben Franklin (1788)*

Benjamin Franklin was a natural born entrepreneur and innovator. His many inventions include the following:

— the Franklin stove
— lightning rod
— bifocals
— library chair
— swim fins
— street lighting
— glass armonica (musical instrument)
— wrote many articles and his *Autobiography*, including mapping of the Gulf Stream

— odometer
— urinary catheter
— long arm (to reach high bookshelves)

And yet he never applied for a patent for any of his inventions. Why?

THE CASE FOR INTELLECTUAL PROPERTY RIGHTS

A major debate among libertarians these days is the issue of intellectual property rights. When creating a new product or inventing a new technology or production process, most entrepreneurs rush to get their invention patented or trademarked. It's one of the first questions the investors on the TV show *Shark Tank* ask their budding entrepreneurs: "Do you have a patent on your invention?" They fear that if not some other knock-off artist will steal their invention and draw away profits.

After writing a book, you want to copyright it so that no other person can legally publish your work under another name. You put in long hours to create a unique work and want to receive the full value of your efforts. Then suddenly some foreign publisher pirates your book without your knowledge or permission, profiting from your hard work. You feel cheated, losing out on royalties.

If you have developed a unique style of artwork in paintings, sculptures, music, film, photography, or other expressions, should you not have the right to keep others from imitating your works or pirating them?

If you create a new lifesaving drug that costs millions to create and go through the FDA approval process, shouldn't you be able to recoup your costs before another competitor manufactures and sells a generic copy?

The traditional pro-property rights view has been enshrined in the Constitution. Clause 8 in Section 8 of Article I of the Constitution declares, "To promote the progress of science and useful arts, by securing for limited times to authors and inventors the exclusive right to their respective writings and discoveries."

ON SCIENCE, TECHNOLOGY, AND MEDICINE

THE CASE AGAINST PATENTS, TRADEMARKS AND COPY-RIGHT LAWS

Other libertarians argue that ideas as developed into new technologies and art should not be protected by law. They argue that trademarks, patents, and copyright law only create artificial monopolies that suppress technological advances and result in unnecessary legal defense proceedings that are costly and counterproductive. Their answer is to let the competitive market flourish, and everyone benefits in the long run. Patents and trademarks only restrict cooperation between entrepreneurs.

In his book, *How Innovation Works*, Lord Matt Ridley suggests that patent law often does more harm than good over time. He uses the example of James Watt and the steam engine he invented in the eighteenth century. He spent years suing companies that infringed on his patents. Ridley states, "Just how much Watt's litigiousness delayed the expansion of steam as a source of power in factories is a hotly contested issue, but the ending of the main patent in 1800 certainly coincided with a rapid expansion of experiments and applications of steam...." He concludes, "The evidence clearly shows that while intellectual property helps a little it also hinders and the net effect is to discourage innovation."[12]

Alex Tabarrok, a professor of economics at George Mason University, echoes the Laffer curve analogy, stating, "Beyond a certain point, stronger patents generate less innovation because they make it harder to share ideas and create barriers to entry."[13]

As to copyrighted works, Ridley points out that William Shakespeare never copyrighted his works. Pirated copies abound, and yet he still made money. Unauthorized use of books, music, film, and photography has exploded in the modern world, but has

---

12 Matt Ridley, *How Innovation Works* (New York: HarperCollins, 2020), pp. 24–25.

13 Quoted in Matt Ridley, "A Welcome Turn Away from Patents," *Wall Street Journal*, June 21, 2013.

THE GREATEST AMERICAN

not stopped the creation of new works. The big winners are monopoly publishers and universities who impose copyright fees to gain access on scientific studies and experiments. They hire the corporate lawyers who suit unauthorized users at the drop of a hat, all thanks for recently established laws and regulations.

WHAT WOULD FRANKLIN SAY?

Franklin's views in this regard are surprisingly liberal. After inventing the Franklin stove (which he sold at £5 apiece), the Pennsylvania governor offered him a lucrative patent. "But I declined it," he wrote in his *Autobiography.* "As we enjoy great advantages from the invention of others, we should be glad of an opportunity to serve others by any invention of ours, and this we should do freely and generously" (*A*, p. 141).

He never did bother to patent any of his inventions or register any copyright, although there were laws on the books both in the United States (in the Constitution) and in Europe that allowed him to do so. According to Franklin, an ironmaker in London borrowed from Franklin's designs and made a "little fortune" from a patent (*A*, p. 141), but he didn't mind.

Franklin believed that any disputes about his inventions could only "sour one's temper and disturb one's quiet" (*CA*, p. 178).

Of course, Franklin was a rich man and did not need the money to be gained from trademarks, patents, and copyrights. He also advocated that members of Congress should not be paid for their work as government officials, but that would mean only independently wealthy people would run the country.

Today, Elon Musk, CEO of Tesla Motors and SpaceX, has a similar attitude. He refuses to patent any of his innovations in electric cars or space exploration. In the spirit of Franklin, Musk favors open platforms and sharing of technology. His goal is simply to stay ahead of the competition. "I don't care about patents," Musk said in an interview. "Patents are for the weak." In his opinion, pat-

ON SCIENCE, TECHNOLOGY, AND MEDICINE

ents are "generally used as a blocking technique" that is designed to prevent others from innovating. "They're used like landmines in warfare," he said.

In sum, the search is still on to find the optimal level of patent, trademark, and copyright protection that encourages innovation without stifling it.

CHAPTER 26

MAGIC SQUARES: BEN FRANKLIN AS POLYMATH

*"It seems to me, that if statesmen had a little more arith-
metic, or were more accustomed to calculation, wars
would be much less frequent."*
—Benjamin Franklin (1787)

Several of Franklin's biographies claim that if he had one fault, it was his weakness in mathematics. Walter Isaacson claimed that math was a "scholastic deficit he never truly remedied." Indeed, Franklin Medal winner and mathematician Donald Knuth declared that Franklin was "a polymath who excelled at everything *except* mathematics."[14]

However, Villanova math professor Paul C. Pasles refutes this claim, citing Franklin's detailed accounts in his printing business, his essay on population growth, and his extensive development of magic squares and circles.

In Franklin's *Philadelphia Gazette* he stated, "...'tis well known that no business, commerce, trade or employment whatsoever,

---

14 Paul C. Pasles, *Benjamin Franklin's Numbers: An Unsung Mathematically Odyssey* (Princeton: Princeton University Press, 2021), p. 2.

ON SCIENCE, TECHNOLOGY, AND MEDICINE

even from the merchant to the shopkeeper, etc. can be managed and carried on without the assistance of numbers; for by these the trader computes the value of all sorts of goods that he dealeth in, does his business with ease and certainty, and informs himself how matters stand at any time with respect to men, money, or merchandize, to profit and loss, whether he goes forward or backward, grows richer or poorer.' Arithmetic 'is useful for all sorts and degrees of men, from the highest to the lowest.'"[15] He adds that geometry is indispensable to mariners, astronomers, geographers, and engineers.

In 1751, Franklin published an influential essay, *Observations Concerning the Increase of Mankind and the Peopling of Countries*, considered a landmark in demography, and one that was cited by Thomas Malthus in later editions of *An Essay on the Principle of Population*.

Based on a variety of factors in birth and death rates at the time, Franklin predicted that the population of the American colonies would "at least be doubled every twenty years" or at the outset every twenty-five years. Paul Pasles concludes, "His prognostications were remarkably accurate, especially when one considers that they were made in a time of great social upheaval, and that they belonged to a science that didn't properly exist yet." Pasles notes that in reviewing the census data from 1790 to 1850, the doubling of the US population occurred approximately every twenty-three years.

"The Malthusian notion that population may increase exponentially had been hinted at in Poor Richard's almanac, and stated outright in Franklin's *Observations*."[16]

Franklin's use of mathematics can be illustrated with his satire in a letter to the *Journal de Paris* in 1784, wherein he proposed a form of daylight savings time, whereby the French would be

15   Pasles, *Benjamin Franklin's Numbers*, p. 73.

16   Pasles, *Benjamin Franklin's Numbers*, 7.

THE GREATEST AMERICAN

aroused from their sleep when the sun came up, and thus save a great deal of money using less candlelight. He wrote:

> My love of economy induced me to muster up what little arithmetic I was master of, and to make some calculations.
>
> I took for the basis of my calculations the supposition that there are 100,000 families in Paris, and that these families consume in the night half a pound of candles per hour. Then estimating seven hours per day, and there being seven hours per night which we burn candles, the account gives us 128,100,000 hours spent at Paris by candle-light, which at half a pound of wax and tallow per hour, gives the weight of 64,075,000 pounds, which estimating the whole at the medium price of thirty sols the pound, makes the sum of 96,075,000 livres. An immense sum that the city of Paris might save each year, only by the economy of using sunshine instead of candles! (*CA*, p. 315)

MAGIC SQUARES

Finally, Franklin's playful experiment with magic squares and circles demonstrates his mathematical prowess. When he was a clerk in the Pennsylvania General Assembly, he said, "I was at length tired of sitting there to hear debates in which as clerk I could take no part, and which were often so unentertaining, that I was induced to amuse myself with making magic squares, or circles, or any thing to avoid weariness" (*A*, p. 145).

What are magic squares? As Franklin explained in a letter to a friend in 1752, "In my younger days, having some leisure...I had amused myself in making these kind of magic squares, and, at

ON SCIENCE, TECHNOLOGY, AND MEDICINE

length, had acquired such a knack at it, that I could fill the cells of any magic square, of reasonable size, as fast as I could write them, disposed in such a manner, as that the sums of every row, horizontal, perpendicular, or diagonal, should be equal" (*CA*, p. 32).

He went on to add, "But not being satisfied with these, which I looked on as common and easy things, I had imposed on myself more difficult tasks, and succeeded in making other magic squares, with a variety of properties, and much more curious" (*CA*, p. 32)

Here is one example that Franklin devised. Note that the numbers add up to thirty-four by row, horizonal, perpendicular, or diagonal. A Fibonacci number! (*CA*, p. 33)

16	3	2	13
5	10	11	8
9	6	7	12
4	15	14	1

Once he created a 16x16 magic square adding up 2,056.

Friends found Franklin's magic square creations "truly astonishing."

CHAPTER 27

ON DIET, EXERCISE, AND MEDICAL SCIENCE

"If you can get Dr. Inclination, Dr. Experience and Dr. Reason to hold a consultation together, they will give you the best advice that can be given."
—*Poor Richard's Almanac (1736)*

Ben Franklin was known as a polymath, with interests in politics, philosophy, history, mathematics, business, and science. He also lived to the ripe age of eighty-four at a time when the average lifespan was forty. He was the oldest member of the Continental Congress to sign the Declaration of Independence, having turned seventy in 1776.

Franklin had a lifelong interest in healthy living—hygiene, preventive medicine, exercise, illnesses and cures, medical devices and inventions, and institutions such as hospitals and assisted living facilities for the elderly. He was friends and had regular correspondence with physicians such as Benjamin Rush, Peter Collinson, John Fothergill, Jan Ingenhousz, and Joseph Priestley. A whole book has been written on *Doctor Franklin's Medicine* by Stanley Finger.

ON SCIENCE, TECHNOLOGY, AND MEDICINE

ON MEDICAL MALPRACTICE

Although he was not a physician or possessed a college degree in medicine, he had a surprising interest in all things medical. As a student of the Enlightenment, Franklin firmly believed in experiments and empirically testing therapies and medical devices. He was wary of "quack" medicines and practitioners. In 1784, while ambassador to France, he was asked by the French government to join a commission of experts to assess the benefits of "animal magnetism" of Professor Franz Mesmer. Franklin bluntly concluded, "The experiments we conduct on ourselves, including blindfold subjects, caused us to reject it absolutely as a cure of illness. We concluded that the system of magnetism did not cure anything; that both magnetism and his brilliant theory exist only in the imagination; and that a spectacle such as this seemed to transport us to the age and the reign of the fairies" (*CA*, p. 322).

On popular fads and superstitions, Franklin observed, "An error is always a spoiled yeast which ferments and eventually corrupts the substance in which it is introduced. But when this error leaves the empire of the sciences to spread among the multitude, and to divide and agitate minds when it presents a misleading way to heal the sick [referring to Mesmerism] whom it discourages from looking elsewhere for help, a good government has an interest in destroying it. The distribution of enlightenment is an excellent use of authority!" (*CA*, p. 321)

Franklin's positive contribution to health involved ways to enjoy a long and healthy life through personal hygiene, exercise, diet, preventive medicine, and realistic cures for illnesses and disease—a modern approach.

He was a firm believer in regular exercise. Sport was not as developed as it is today, and there's no evidence that he played golf or cricket, two games in their infancy in the eighteenth century. He loved to swim and even gave lessons in his youth. In his day, few people knew how to swim. Moreover, as historians Laurence

Brockliss and Colin Jones note, "frequent immersion in water was socially and medically frowned upon. Even aristocrats washed infrequently, for body odour was considered a protective cocoon and sexual stimulant."[17] As he became older, Franklin exercised by lifting weights and taking long walks. When he was a colonial agent in London, he made sure he took month-long vacations in the English countryside and Europe to enjoy fresh air and good health. "I depended chiefly on journeys into the country for the establishment of my health," he wrote a friend.

Franklin was well aware of the dangers of polluted air and lead poisoning. Franklin's stove was a practical invention that kept houses free of smoke. He was a strong advocate of open ventilation and improving air quality in homes, offices, shops, and hospitals. He urged officials to create a current of fresh air throughout hospitals and buildings to avoid foul air that might lead to dysentery and other diseases. (Benjamin Rush, a founder and physician, seconded his recommendation.)

HIS THEORY OF COLDS

His most controversial practice was his theory of colds. He believed in open windows even during cold weather, and often went so far as parading in the nude in the mornings with the windows open. "I rise early almost every morning, and sit in my chamber, without any clothes whatsoever, half an hour or an hour, according to the season, either reading or writing," he wrote. John Adams thought the "air bath" was a crazy idea.

He was always interested in the latest advances in medical science and technology. He advocated the relatively new procedure of inoculation against smallpox, which is all the more ironic after his four-year-old boy Franky died of the disease. It almost broke the heart of his parents. In 1772, he wrote, "now dead 36 years, whom

---

17   Laurence Brockliss and Colin Jones, *The Medical World of Early Modern France* (Clarendon Press, 1997), p. 788.

I have seldom since seen equaled in everything, and whom to this day I cannot think of without a sigh."[18]

THE GOUT, THE STONE AND OLD AGE

Despite living a long age, Franklin was never in perfect health and actually suffered from a number of illnesses. He kept a personal journal of his health problems, which included "scurff," a stubborn skin rash; painful gall stones lodged in his bladder; and gout (arthritis), due to overindulging and the love of meaty diets, heavy wines (port and Madeira), and rich French foods. Franklin was always looking for natural cures and possible surgery, but nothing worked.

In France, he was frequently covered with scurff, for which he sought professional help. He consulted a physician, who prescribed Belloste's pills, named after Dr. Augustin Belloste, who served as physician to the duchess of Savoy. The main ingredient of the pills was mercury, which had severe side effects, losing several of his teeth in the process. Fortunately, after a month, he stopped using the pills. Had he continued to ingest more mercury, he could have died before completing his mission.

Despite his ailments, he remained an optimist. "People who live long drink of the cup of life to the very bottom and must expect to meet with some of the usual dregs; and when I reflect on the number of terrible maladies human nature is subject to, I think myself favored in having only three incurable ones that have fallen to my share, viz., the gout, the stone, and old age; and that these have not yet deprived me of my natural cheerfulness, my delight in books and enjoyment of social conversation. There are many sorrows in this life, but we must not blame Providence inconsiderately, for there are many more pleasures. This is why I love life" (*CA*, p. 347).

---

18   Benjamin Franklin to Jane Mecom, January 13, 1772, in *The Papers of Benjamin Franklin, Vol. 19: January 1 through December 31, 1772*, ed. William B. Wilcox (New Haven: Yale University Press, 1975), 28–29.

CHAPTER 28

RETIREMENT AND THE SECRET TO A LONG LIFE

"Life, like a dramatic piece, should not only be conducted with regularity, but me thinks it should finish handsomely. Being now in the last acct, I begin to cast about for something fit to end with. Or if mine be more properly compared to an epigram, as some of its few lines are but barely tolerable, I am very desirous of concluding with a bright point."
—*Benjamin Franklin (July 2, 1756, at the age of fifty)*

"A long life may not be good enough, but a good life is long enough."
—*Poor Richard's Almanac*

With the debate over national healthcare being all the rage these days, I thought it appropriate to see Ben Franklin's advice on how to live a long and hearty life.

After all, Franklin outlived all of his contemporaries and was the oldest delegate to the Constitutional Convention in 1787. George Washington was a generation younger. Franklin was, indeed, the grandfather of the country.

ON SCIENCE, TECHNOLOGY, AND MEDICINE

How did he enjoy life so robustly until the ripe old age of eighty-four?

Franklin lived at a time when each individual was responsible for his own health. There was no Medicare, medical insurance, or Federal Drug Administration. The average lifespan was only forty years due to deadly diseases, epidemics, poor hygiene, and crank medical advice. In this age, Franklin was sort of a health nut, always warning against quack medical doctors (such as Dr. Mesmer, inventor of mesmerism) while alert to preventive care, the best remedies for ailments, and the latest breakthrough technologies in medicine, such as inoculation against smallpox. (One of his biggest regrets in life was losing his four-year-old boy, Franky, to smallpox.)

Among his many accomplishments, he founded the first major civilian hospital and medical school in the colonies.

His *Poor Richard's Almanac* offered many simple self-help tips, since medical doctors were scarce in those days. His almanac included such refrains as "To lengthen thy life, lessen thy meals," "Eat to live, not live to eat," and most famously, "Early to bed, early to rise, makes a man healthy, wealthy, and wise." (Few individuals practice this ancient advice anymore.)

But note: neither Franklin nor Poor Richard ever said, "Beer is living proof that God loves us and wants us to be happy." That's an internet creation. If he said anything along those lines, it would have been "wine" not "beer." (See chapter 66, "Franklin Said What?!")

And he was a fan of regular exercise. In his twenties, he taught people how to swim, and when he was a colonial agent in London, he insisted on taking month-long vacations to the countryside and Europe.

However, he was not immune to the dangerous practices of the day, such as bleeding patients. While in London as colonial agent, Franklin fell ill and was bled twice by his physician, who once drew eight ounces of blood from the back of his head and sixteen ounces the second time. Somehow he survived.

Franklin held his share of peculiar health crazes, including sleeping in the nude with the windows open and using electro-shock therapy.

Did Franklin believe in astrology? He printed horoscopes in his almanac, but that's because Franklin knew that astrology was popular among his readers. In fact, he sometimes poked fun of the absurd stargazers, such as the first edition in 1732 when he predicted the "inexorable death" of his chief competitor on October 17, 1733, "at the very instant" when Mars, the sun, and Mercury align.

GROWING OLD AND LIKING IT

In his elderly years, Franklin looked for ways to live longer and often offered advice as the friendly "Doctor Franklin." During the winter of 1785–86, for example, he wrote an essay "The Art of Procuring Pleasant Dreams," urging friends to exercise before, not after, eating meals. "If after exercise we feed sparingly, the digestion will be easy and good, the body lightsome, the temper cheerful, and all the animal functions performed agreeably. Sleep when it follows will be natural and undisturbed" (*CA*, p. 353).

He also advocated sleeping and early morning exercise with the windows open to fresh air. "With this view I would rise early almost every morning, and sit in my chamber, without any clothes whatever, half an hour or an hour, according to the season, either reading or writing. This practice was not in the least painful, but on the contrary, agreeable; and if I returned to bed afterwards, before I dressed myself, I made a supplement to my night's rest, of one or two hours of the most pleasing sleep that could be imagined" (*CA*, pp. 72–73).

He even took time to create another famous invention, bifocal lenses, that made life easier for the aged and the afflicted.

ON SCIENCE, TECHNOLOGY, AND MEDICINE

We should not conclude from all this that Franklin was the poster boy of healthy living. In fact, he was well-known for overindulging in the heavy dinners of the Europeans and Americans and for his love of wine and Madeira (which contains 50 percent more alcohol than ordinary table wines). In Paris, his wine cellar contained over one thousand bottles, and his dinner table overflowed with mutton, veal, beef, cheeses, butter, and pastries.

If there was a party going on in London or Paris, Franklin was the center of attention. "I find I love company, chat, a laugh, a glass, and even a song…and at the same time relish…the grave observations and wise sentences of old men's conversations" (and, I might add, young ladies' charms). (*CA*, p. 18)

But he paid for his ever-expanding social life with frequent bouts of gout (the swelling of the joints), kidney stones, a flaky skin condition (psoriasis), and lead poisoning (from being a printer and drinking too much wine). His large stones became so painful in the final years in America that Franklin used opium, which, he said, "afforded me some ease from time to time but then has taken away my appetite…and am become totally emaciated and little remains of me but a skeleton covered with a skin" (*CA*, pp. 381–382).

EVEN IN PAIN, FRANKLIN WAS UPBEAT

Still, he was always optimistic, even during periods of terrible pain. He noted once that a plethora of treatments—"I have been cupped, blooded, physicked, and at last blistered"—had the beneficial effect of losing weight. And once he wrote a satirical essay for Madame Brillon, "Dialogue Between the Gout and M. Franklin" (*CA*, pp. 219–222). His positive outlook made it easier for him to endure pain.

In sum, Franklin's message to us today would be to exercise regularly, eat and drink moderately, have a positive mental attitude

THE GREATEST AMERICAN

when facing illnesses, and make sure your social life is full of variety and new friendships.

Recommended book: *Doctor Franklin's Medicine* by Stanley Finger (University of Pennsylvania Press, 2006).

PART IV

ON ECONOMICS AND THE ECONOMY

CHAPTER 29

BENJAMIN FRANKLIN: ADAM SMITH'S INVISIBLE HAND?

*"Benjamin Franklin and Adam Smith are now
respectively depicted on the US $100 bill and
the Bank of England £20 note."*
—Tim Ogline

Adam Smith (1723–1790) is considered the father of free-market economics, and Benjamin Franklin (1706–1790) is considered the father of American capitalism. Two questions arise: did they know each other, and did they influence each other's views in politics, economics, and American independence?

In preparing to write this chapter, I came across an unusual book edited by Tim Ogline and published independently in 2018. The author combined Franklin's pamphlet, "The Way to Wealth" and an abridged version of Smith's *Wealth of Nations* into one volume (590 pages).

113

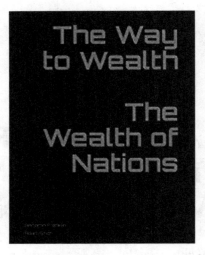

Ogline states, "This book is a compilation of two great texts of the 18th century that enabled many people to build and retain wealth. Benjamin Franklin and Adam Smith are now respectively depicted on the US $100 bill and the Bank of England £20 note."

DEBATE: HOW WELL DID THEY KNOW EACH OTHER?

Historians are divided on the closeness of the relationship that existed between Adam Smith and Benjamin Franklin, other than the fact that they crossed paths many times and both died in 1790.

Simon N. Patten, a longtime professor of economics and chair of the Wharton School at the University of Pennsylvania (founded by Benjamin Franklin), was convinced that Franklin and Adam Smith were "close friends and in frequent communication with each other," and that Smith's details of the American colonies and support for their independence was due to Franklin's influence.[19]

On the other hand, Geoffrey C. Kellow, political scientist at Carleton University in Canada, says just the opposite, that "they

19 Thomas D. Eliot, "The Relations Between Adam Smith and Benjamin Franklin Before 1776," *Political Science Quarterly*, 39, no. 1 (March 1924): 67.

ON ECONOMICS AND THE ECONOMY

were strangers." He states, "Franklin and Smith did know each other, barely. Their paths may have crossed though neither mentions contact with the other in their correspondence.... It is clear that they were not familiar with each other beyond the most casual acquaintance. They shared friends, most prominent among them David Hume, Henry Home (Lord Kames), and the Anglo-American publisher William Strahan, but there is no evidence that any significant friendship ever developed between the two men."[20]

He goes on to say, "Smith may have been inspired by Franklin but beyond that, in their daily lives, they shared little. In many ways the two men could not have been more different, one a lifelong bachelor who spent most of his life in the town of his birth and the company of his mother. The other was a legendary polymath, whose political and personal life spanned the Atlantic and the lion's share of the Enlightenment"[21] Of course, one could say the same about Adam Smith and David Hume—strange bedfellows.

Who's right?

It is true that there is no reference in any correspondence between the two that has survived, although both men lost correspondence during their lifetimes; Adam Smith was not much of a letter writer and had his papers burned at the time of his death in 1790.

Nevertheless, they clearly knew each other. Franklin and his son spent the summer of 1759 in Scotland and were introduced to the intellectual elite such as publisher William Strahan and physicians John Fothergill and John Pringle, all having close ties to Edinburgh. There Franklin received the honorary degree of doctor of laws at the University of St. Andrews. They stayed at the manor of Sir Alexander Dick, a renowned scientist and physician, and met with many members of the Scottish Enlightenment. Accord-

---

20   Geoffrey C. Kellow, "Benjamin Franklin and Adam Smith: Two Strangers and the Spirit of Capitalism," *History of Political Economy* 50, no. 2 (2018): 321–344.

21   Kellow, "Benjamin Franklin and Adam Smith," 325.

THE GREATEST AMERICAN

ing to Dr. Alexander Carlyle, Franklin and his son William were his guests at a dinner hosted by the clergyman and historian Dr. William Robertson, along with David Hume, Adam Smith, and jurist Lord Kames. Penn Professor Francis Thorpe makes a great deal out of this meeting: "The meeting of three such forces in the world by the communion of Franklin and Hume and Smith in their conversations in Edinburgh suggests a subject for philosophical examination."[22] Of course, at this time, Adam Smith was not as famous as Franklin. He had just published in April 1759 his *Theory of Moral Sentiments*, a topic that would greatly interest Franklin as a moral philosophy. The more famous book, *The Wealth of Nations*, wouldn't be published until 1776.[23]

Following up on the meeting, Smith wrote a letter to his publisher William Strahan on April 4, 1760, saying, "Remember me to the Franklins. I hope I shall have the grace to write to the youngest by next post to thank him in the name both of the College and of myself for his very agreeable present."[24]

In late August 1771, Franklin spent several months visiting Ireland and Scotland. He spent a few days at David Hume's house in Edinburgh, and while there, "He met with Adam Smith, who reportedly showed him some early chapters of the *Wealth of Nations* that he was then writing."[25]

---

22   Francis Newton Thorpe, "Benjamin Franklin and the University of Pennsylvania," *US Bureau of Education, Circular of Information*, no. 2, (1892): 104.

23   Carl Van Doren, *Benjamin Franklin* (New York: The Viking Press, 1938), 281–282.

24   Adam Smith to William Strahan, April 4, 1760, in *A Catalogue of the Library of Adam Smith,* ed. James Bonar (London: Macmillan and Co., 1894), facing page x.

25   Walter Isaacson, *Benjamin Franklin, An American Life* (New York: Simon and Schuster, 2004), 260–261. Isaacson's source is J. Bennett Nolan, *Benjamin Franklin in Scotland and Ireland: 1795 and 1771* (Philadelphia: University of Pennsylvania Press, 1956): "There is some disagreement about whether Adam Smith

ON ECONOMICS AND THE ECONOMY

On February 7, 1772, in a letter to Franklin from Edinburgh, David Hume reported that "the good wishes of all your brother philosophers in this place attend you heartily and sincerely, together with much regret that your business would not allow you to pass more time among them."[26]

Two years later, on February 13, 1774, Hume wrote Smith a letter when Smith was in London. At the time, Franklin was viciously attacked by the king's solicitor general Alexander Wedderburn in the "Cockpit" (a room in Whitehall Palace that was once used for cockfighting) for treason. Hume wrote, "Pray what strange accounts are these we hear of Franklin's conduct? I am very slow in believing that he has been guilty in the extreme degree that is pretended, tho' I always knew him to be a very factious man, and faction next to fanaticism is of all passions the most destructive of morality. I hear that Wedderburn's treatment of him before the council was most cruel without being in the least blamable. What a pity!" [27]

The Cockpit incident occurred during the two-year period when both Smith and Franklin lived and worked in London, Franklin as colonial agent and Smith to write and rewrite his magnum opus, *The Wealth of Nations*.

John Rae reports in the *Life of Adam Smith*, published in 1895 and one of the earliest Smith biographies, that much of *The Wealth of Nations* was probably written while he was in London in 1773–1776. Franklin was also in London in 1773 and stayed there until March 1775. In regards to this time, Rae quotes from Dr. John Fanning Watson, author of the *Annals of Philadelphia*, the follow-

---

showed Franklin chapters of the *Wealth of Nations*, published in 1776, but one of Smith's relatives said this was the case."

26   Benjamin Franklin, *The Works of Benjamin Franklin*, ed. John Bigelow, vol. 5, *1768–1772* (New York and London: The Knickerbocker Press, 1904), 325.

27   John Rae, *Life of Adam Smith* (London: Macmillan and Company, 1895), 267.

ing: "Dr. Franklin once told Dr. [James] Logan that the celebrated Adam Smith when writing his *Wealth of Nations* was in the habit of bringing chapter after chapter as he composed it to himself, Dr. [Richard] Price, and others of the literati; then patiently hear their observations and profit from their discussions and criticisms, sometimes submitting to write whole chapters anew, and even to reverse some of his propositions."[28]

ADAM SMITH PREDICTS AMERICA TO BECOME A GREAT NATION

Indeed, a large section of *The Wealth of Nations* discusses the American colonies in terms of trade policy, taxation, population, and economic growth, and almost always in a positive light, much to the dismay of the British elite. It is quite possible that the extensive pages devoted to the Americas were heavily influenced by Franklin's frequent commentaries to Smith while they were together in London. Smith even goes so far as to state that the American legislators "are employed in contriving a new form of government for an extensive empire, which, they flatter themselves, will become, and which, indeed, seems very likely to become, one of the greatest and most formidable that ever was in the world."[29] Smith's positive outlook for America mirrors Franklin's prediction that "America, with God's blessing, will become a great and happy country." Indeed, Smith went so far as to favor American independence, not a popular position in Great Britain at the time.

The final question is, to what extent can we find examples where Franklin's economic and political views showed up, directly or indirectly, in Smith's *Wealth of Nations*?

Both Smith and his close friend David Hume were strong advocates of free trade, and so was Benjamin Franklin. In response to reading one of David Hume's essays on free trade with the col-

28 Rae, *Life of Adam Smith*, 264–265.
29 Adam Smith, *The Wealth of Nations* (New York: Modern Library, 1965 [1776]), p. 588.

ON ECONOMICS AND THE ECONOMY

onies, Franklin said it would have "a good effect in promoting a certain interest too little thought of by selfish men...I mean the interest of humanity, or common good of mankind."[30]

"NO NATION WAS EVER RUINED BY TRADE"

Regarding trade with France, Franklin noted, "Our merchants complained in general of the embarrassments suffered by numerous internal demands of duties, searches, etc. that they were subjected to in France. In general I would only observe that commerce, consisting in a mutual exchange of the necessaries of conveniences of life, the more free and unrestrained it is, the more it flourishes; and the happier are all the nations concerned in it" (*CA*, p. 299).

He added, "It would be better if government meddled no further with trade and let it take its course. Most of the statutes, acts, edicts, and placards of Parliaments, princes, and states, for regulating, directly, and restraining of trade have either political blunders or jobs obtained by artful men for private advantage under the pretense of public good.... It is therefore wished that all commerce were as free between the nations of the world as it is between the several counties of England: so would all, by mutual communications, obtain more enjoyments. Those counties do not ruin one another by trade; neither would the nations. No nation was ever ruined by trade" (*CA*, p. 301).

In general, Franklin embraced the laissez-faire economics of Adam Smith. "When [Jean-Baptiste] Colbert assembled some wise old merchants of France and desired their advice and opinion how he could best serve and promote commerce, their answer, after consultation, was, in three words only, *Laissez nous faire*: 'Let us alone.' It is said by a very solid writer of the same nation, well

30   Benjamin Franklin letter to David Hume, May 19, 1762, in *The Papers of Benjamin Franklin, Vol. 10: January 1, 1762 through December 31, 1763*, ed. Leonard W. Labaree (New Haven: Yale University Press, 1958), 82–84; Quoted in Isaacson, *Benjamin Franklin*, 197.

THE GREATEST AMERICAN

advanced in the science of politics, who knows the full force of that maxim *Pas trop gouvener*. Not to govern too strictly, which perhaps would be of more use when applied to trade than in any other public concern" (*CA*, pp. 300–301).

No doubt Franklin would be sympathetic with Adam Smith's refrain, "Little else is required to carry a state to the highest level of opulence...but peace, easy taxes, and a tolerable administration of justice." Franklin himself wrote, "A virtuous and laborious [industrious] people may be cheaply governed" (*CA*, p. 189).

Franklin may have been more liberal when it came to a paper money standard in America, but he supported the Smithian virtues of thrift, balanced budgets, and peace whenever possible. He was famous for saying, "There never was a good war, or a bad peace" (*CA*, p. 302). On another occasion, he wrote, "The system of America is universal commerce with every nation; war with none" (*CA*, p. 148).

CHAPTER 30

ON ACHIEVING THE AMERICAN DREAM

"Franklin's most glorious invention is the American dream.... He pioneered the spirit of self-help in America."
—Jim Powell[31]

"Working people had plenty of employ and high pay for their labor. Everybody was well clothed and well lodged, and the poor provided for or assisted. And our commerce being no longer the monopoly of British merchants, we were well furnished with all the foreign commodities we needed, at much more reasonable rates than heretofore. These appeared to me as certain signs of public prosperity."
—Ben Franklin (1785)

In 2015, FreedomFest debated the question, "Is the American dream alive or dead?" Several economic historians, such as Gregory Clark (University of California at Davis), argue that it is dead, judging from the fall in entrepreneurship, productivity, and economic growth rates in the West, and the lack of social mobility. Alexander Green, author and chief investment strategist at the

---

31   Jim Powell, "Benjamin Franklin, the Man Who Invented the American Dream," *The Freeman* (New York: Foundation for Economic Education), April 1, 1997, https://fee.org/articles/benjamin-franklin-the-man-who-invented-the-american-dream/.

THE GREATEST AMERICAN

Oxford Club, countered that the American dream was alive and well, judging from the creation of new businesses, the number of new millionaires being created every year, and the bull market on Wall Street.

What do we mean by the American dream, and what did Ben Franklin have to say about it?

Since the founding of our nation, the American dream is that anyone, no matter what their background, race, religion, or gender, can pursue the Jeffersonian ideal of "life, liberty and the pursuit of happiness" by getting a fulfilling job, buying a home, rearing a good family, sending their kids to a good school, and having enough to retire comfortably someday. All you had to do was work hard and opportunities would arise in a free America.

The United States stood tall in declaring that any immigrant could come to America and pursue his own career path, and not be limited by his social class, religion, or race. Ours is a democratic meritocracy, not a European aristocracy. As Franklin wrote, "There were many in Europe who hoped for offices and public employments in America, who valued themselves and expected to be valued by us for their birth or quality, tho' I told them those bear no prices in our markets. In America, people do not inquire concerning a stranger, *What is he?* but *What can he do?*" (*CA*, p. 292)

The American dream also meant that people could develop skills and succeed without a formal education. They could learn on their own, just as Franklin did by borrowing books and reading (Franklin went to Latin school for a year). According to Franklin, the American dream was rooted in the ability to read and write. He sought to reduce America's low literacy rate by establishing the first public circulating library and the Junto.

Franklin's humble beginnings are described in considerable detail in his *Autobiography*, a true rags-to-riches story. The Franklin *Autobiography* has often been considered one of the most influential self-help or self-improvement books in history, along the lines

ON ECONOMICS AND THE ECONOMY

of Dale Carnegie's *How to Win Friends and Influence People* and Napoleon Hill's *Think and Grow Rich*.

In many ways, Ben Franklin is the epitome of the American dream, honest labor, and rugged individualism. According to historian Jim Powell, Franklin invented the idea of the American dream and progress for all as contained in his *Autobiography*.

He lived the classic rags-to-riches story. In 1723, at the age of seventeen, he ran away from his home in Boston. He arrived in Philadelphia penniless but in a few years had a thriving printing business that allowed him to be financially independent at the age of forty-two. In his "Advice to a Young Tradesman," he said that anyone could follow his example and become rich through his trinity of virtues, "industry, thrift and prudence."

He pioneered the spirit of self-help and self-reliance in America. After a few years of formal schooling, he taught himself French, German, Italian, Latin, and Spanish; he learned how to play the guitar, violin, and the harp. He traveled on his own to London as a young man and developed further skills as a printer. His popular annual almanacs were self-help personified. His *Autobiography* demonstrated his ability to express his views freely.

Instead of relying on the government, Franklin was a fan of private voluntary associations to create the first fire company, insurance agency, hospital, library, and academy. He promoted science and technology, being an inventor himself of practical products like the Franklin stove, the lightning rod, and bifocals. He was the first "commoner" to become a member of the British Royal Academy. He would be no fan of businesspeople who retired and played golf all day. He believed in being anxiously engaged in a good cause and was civic-minded throughout his "retirement" years.

His failure to control his "hard-to-be-governed" passions resulted in an illegitimate son named William. But he soon made up for this "errata" in his life by marrying his sweetheart Deborah

THE GREATEST AMERICAN

and creating a family by siring two more children. Ultimately, he had eight grandchildren who attended good schools and had successful careers. In his *Proposals Relating to the Education of Youth in Pennsylvania*, he recommended that the curriculum emphasize writing and speaking. He even said that blacks could achieve success through proper education (and he was one of the founders of the first Negro School of Philadelphia).

Affordable housing has always been part of the American dream. For most of his adult life, Franklin and his wife Deborah lived with his young family in smaller rented dwellings in Philadelphia. Mortgages were not typical in this era. However, in late 1762, Franklin returned from London and decided it was time to build a house of his own. Being financially independent, he financed the construction of a three-story, ten-room brick house set in the center of the courtyard off Market Street in Philadelphia. Although he returned to London and was not directly involved in its construction, he wrote frequently to his wife, who oversaw the building. She was given detailed instructions about its construction and embellishment.

When Franklin returned in 1775, his wife had died, and he continued to make improvements on his home, such as the completion of a music room. When he left for France to be ambassador, he left his daughter Sally and her husband and family to take care of the place.

He was gone another nine years, but upon returning home to Philadelphia in 1785, he once again attempted to build onto his property. Denied the opportunity to witness the building of the original house, he was now able to supervise every detail over the next five years, which he called his "amusement in old age."

He built an addition for his "growing family," including a long room for his library and scientific instruments, a dining room that could handle twenty-four persons, two bedchambers, and two garrets. His library room was ideal, allowing him to "write without

ON ECONOMICS AND THE ECONOMY

being disturbed by the noise of the children." Having a home of your own is truly an American dream, and Franklin fulfilled it in his lifetime.

And what about retirement? The American dream requires a comfortable, dependable retirement income. Franklin never did really retire. There was no government-mandated Social Security back then. Having enough to live on into retirement was an individual and family responsibility.

After he set aside his business interests to a partner, he was almost constantly involved in public duties as an assemblyman, a colonial agent, a delegate to Congress, the country's first ambassador (to France), the president of Pennsylvania, and a delegate to the Constitutional Convention in 1789. For these works, he earned an income, but always saved and invested enough funds to supplement his income and become financially independent. He did his best to avoid debt and own his houses outright. He earned income from several rental properties, from loans to friends, and from interest on bank accounts and government securities. As a result, he died a wealthy man and remained in good spirits most of his mature life.

Through his *Autobiography*, Franklin set the standard for the American dream, one that is imitated around the world. The *Autobiography* inspired many prominent Americans to achieve success, including James Harper, who launched the venerable publishing house now known as HarperCollins. Horace Greeley, a poor boy who became the editor of the *New York Tribune*, declared, "Of the men whom the world currently terms self-made—that is, who severally fought their life-battles without the aid of inherited wealth, or family honors, or educational advantages, perhaps our American Franklin stands highest in the civilized world's regard."

Franklin's *Autobiography* encouraged Thomas Mellon to leave his farm to become a banker. "I regard the reading of Franklin's *Autobiography* as the turning point of my life," he said. "Here was

THE GREATEST AMERICAN

Franklin, poorer than myself, who by industry, thrift and frugality had become learned and wise, and elevated to wealth and fame." The book also inspired steel entrepreneur Andrew Carnegie, and many others. Savings banks across America were named after Franklin. Today's Franklin Templeton group of mutual funds are based on the Franklin virtues.

As Jim Powell concludes, "Franklin championed personal responsibility, intellectual curiosity, honesty, persistence, and thrift—principles that have helped people everywhere lift themselves up. He nurtured an entrepreneurial culture which creates opportunity and hope through peaceful cooperation. He affirmed that by improving yourself and helping your neighbors you can make a free society succeed. His most glorious invention was—and is—the American dream."[32]

---

32 Jim Powell, *The Triumph of Liberty: A 2,000 History Told Through the Lives of Freedom's Greatest Champions* (Free Press, 2000).

CHAPTER 31

ON THE BENEFITS OF FREE TRADE

"The arrival of the CMA CGM Benjamin Franklin heralds a new era for trade. It sends a powerful message that our port stands among the world's greatest, and that we are prepared to continue growing and adapting to the demands of our global economy."
—LA Mayor Eric Garcetti

"No nation was ever ruined by trade."
—Ben Franklin

Benjamin Franklin would find it most agreeable to know that the world's largest cargo ship is named after him. The CMA CGM *Benjamin Franklin* is capable of carrying eighteen thousand twenty-foot shipping containers and is about a third larger than the biggest container ships (and nearly five times larger than the *Titanic*). It measures 1,300 ft. long, 177 ft. wide, and 197 ft. high. It stacks containers ten high.

Officially known as an Ultra Large Container Vessel, the gigantic commercial ship is truly international in scope. It is owned by a French shipping company, built in China, registered in London, and until now transports products from Asia to Northern Europe.

THE GREATEST AMERICAN

On December 26, 2015, the CMA CGM *Benjamin Franklin* arrived for the first time at the deepwater Port of Los Angeles to great fanfare. It had come from Korea and then returned to Shanghai, China, after visiting Oakland, California.

The twin ports of Los Angeles and adjacent Long Beach process about 40 percent of all the container ships that arrive in the United States, moving more than $290 billion US worth of goods in a year.

The ship's arrival was greeted by the mayor of Los Angeles, members of Congress, corporate officials, labor leaders, journalists, photographers, and TV stations. It was front-page news.

Franklin, being a technophile, would also be impressed with the vessel's power and technology. Her 78 ft. length engine room contains an advanced engine as powerful as 900 Ford Focus cars and her 21 knots thrust is equivalent to that of 11 Boeing 747-400 engines. The ship is also labor efficient. With a crew capacity of only twenty-seven members, the ship runs its own its waste recycle system, has a chef, and a swimming pool. (The *Titanic* had a crew of around 900.)

The small number of workers involved in this giant ship was a point of contention among union workers. In 2014, most West Coast ports were plagued by protests and shutdowns by workers' unions.

President Donald Trump and other Republicans have complained about the loss of jobs and manufacturing business to China and Mexico. They advocate protectionist measures, raising tariffs and protecting American jobs.

Franklin would stand for none of that. "It would be better if government meddled no further with trade and let it take its course," he wrote in a pamphlet in 1774. "Most of the statutes, acts, edicts, arets and placards of Parliaments, princes, and states, for regulating, directing, and restraining of trade have been either political blunders or jobs obtained by artful men for private advantages under the pretense of public good" (*CA*, p. 300).

128

ON ECONOMICS AND THE ECONOMY

Franklin advocated the French formula, "*Laissez nous faire*. Let us alone.... *Pas trop gouvener*. Not to govern too strictly" (*CA*, pp. 300–301).

He concluded, "It is therefore wished that all commerce were as free between all nations of the world as it is between the several counties of England: so would all, by mutual communication, obtain more enjoyments. Those counties do not ruin one another by trade; neither would the nations. *No nation was ever ruined by trade; even, seemingly, the most disadvantageous*" (*CA*, p. 301, emphasis added).

Franklin recognized the fact that opening up trade with foreign countries is a disruptive force, creating what Harvard Professor Clayton Christensen calls "creative disruption." Free trade closes some jobs and businesses, but it also creates others. On net balance, the nation as a whole is better off—consumers enjoy better and cheaper products, and workers find new and often better jobs. Studies have shown that the North American Free Trade Agreement between the US, Canada, and Mexico ultimately created more net jobs and income than before the agreement was reached.

After the War of Independence, he wrote a British friend, "Let us now forgive and forget. Let each country seeks its advancement in its own internal advantages of arts and agriculture, not in retarding or preventing the prosperity of the other" (*CA*, p. 301).

CHAPTER 32

ON INEQUALITY

*"The truth is, that though there are in that country
[America] few people so miserable as the poor of Europe,
there are also very few that in Europe would be called
rich; it is rather a general happy mediocrity that prevails."*
—*Ben Franklin (1784)*

Today there's a big debate going on about the growing gap between rich and poor, and what should be done about it. What did Benjamin Franklin have to say about inequality?

Franklin was a firm believer in democracy, the American hope that all citizens, rich and poor, could enjoy "life, liberty and the pursuit of happiness." He never liked to see a wide division between the rich and the poor.

In the early 1770s, while he was a colonial agent based in London, he took a series of trips with his son William through Scotland and Ireland. He discussed seeing small numbers of huge, vastly wealthy estates juxtaposed by overwhelmingly large numbers of destitute poor.

He wrote a friend in London, "I have lately made a tour thro' Ireland and Scotland. In these countries a small part of the society are landlords, great noblemen and gentlemen, extremely opulent, living in the highest affluence and magnificence."

ON ECONOMICS AND THE ECONOMY

In contrast, he continued, "The bulk of the people tenants, extremely poor, living in the most sordid wretchedness in dirty hovels of mud and straw, and clothed only in rags."

He advised his friend in London, "I assure you, that in the possession and enjoyment of the various comforts of life, compared to these people, every American Indian is a gentleman" (*CA*, p. 71).

Franklin noted how wealth was more equally divided in America. "I thought often of the happiness of New England, where every man is a freeholder, has a vote in public affairs, lives in a tidy warm house, has plenty of good food and fuel, with whole clothes from head to foot, the manufacture perhaps of his own family. Long may they continue in this situation!" (*CA*, p. 71).

Ten years later, after the American Revolution ended, Franklin wrote an essay advising Europeans who might want to immigrate to the newly established United States. He advised, "The truth is, that though there are in that country [America] few people so miserable as the poor of Europe, there are also very few that in Europe would be called rich; it is rather a general happy mediocrity that prevails. There are few great proprietors of the soil, and few tenants; most people cultivate their own lands, or follow some handicraft or merchandise; very few rich enough to live idly upon their rents or incomes, or to pay the high prices given in Europe for paintings, statues, architecture, and the other works of art, that are more curious than useful" (*CA*, pp. 335).

What to do about gross inequality in Europe? Franklin thought that free trade between countries would help. And he certainly believed in universal suffrage and basic education for all children.

What about taxing the rich and giving it to the poor? When in France, Franklin wrote a controversial letter to financier Robert Morris on Christmas Day, 1783, arguing that everyone needed to pay their fair share of taxes to pay for the revolution and social needs of the new country. It irked him that many colonists escaped paying taxes for the American cause. Because of tax evasion, he endorsed a second-best solution, the depreciation of the Continental currency (inflation) as an indirect way to force them to pay.

But Franklin believed above all that direct taxation on citizen's property was the most just way to pay for the war. He wrote: "All the property that is necessary to a man, for the conservation of the individual and the propagation of the species, is his natural right, which none can justly deprive him of: But all property superfluous to such purposes is the property of the public, who, by their laws, have created it, and who may therefore by other laws dispose of it, whenever the welfare of the public shall demand such disposition. He that does not like civil society on these terms, let him retire and live among savages. He can have no right to the benefits of society, who will not pay his club [dues] towards the support of it" (*CA*, p. 299).

Of course, the debate is over what constitutes "superfluous property" beyond just needs. Everyone has a different opinion on what is "fair" taxation and what constitutes "superfluous" wealth.

The debate continues to this day.

CHAPTER 33

ON TODAY'S HEAVY TAX BURDEN

"A virtuous and laborious [industrious] people
may be cheaply governed."
—Ben Franklin (CA, p. 189)

After compiling and editing *The Compleated Autobiography by Benjamin Franklin* in 2006, the three hundredth anniversary of Franklin's birth, I gave dozens of talks about Franklin around the country. In these talks, I mentioned a number of his famous sayings and told the audience that I found a few more statements of his that were profound but not well known. One was his statement made in a letter on July 1, 1778: "A virtuous and laborious [industrious] people may be cheaply governed."

The reaction of the audience was interesting. No matter whether I was talking to conservative Republicans or social Democrats, they all agreed that government was not cheap, but expensive.

We all agree that the government needs sufficient revenues to conduct basic policies—paying for national defense, the court system, the local police, and other essential duties. But do they need to take 30 percent to 50 percent of our income to do it? Has government gotten out of control?

THE GREATEST AMERICAN

In every election year, all the candidates debate taxes—should we increase taxes on the rich, cut taxes on the middle class and poor, adopt a flat tax, or what? The father of American capitalism had much to say on the subject.

Ben Franklin was no friend of the tax man. As a printer, he was opposed to the Stamp Tax that the British imposed on printed materials in 1765. But his opposition was more than simple commercial self-interest. He told the British ministers that they could have raised a great deal more money and less mischief if they had asked for "voluntary grants" from the colonies to the Crown. Franklin favored "persuasion" over "compulsive" taxation in paying for colonial government.

Eventually, Franklin at the old age of seventy became a revolutionary because Great Britain, a country he loved, and Parliament had so abused their powers that "total disunion" was inevitable. (He said so as early as 1771.)

Yet Franklin was no anarchist. He believed that every citizen should pay his fair share of government expense, during war or peace time. He was angry with William Penn and his descendants who exempted themselves from taxation as proprietors of Pennsylvania. He railed against American citizens who refused to support George Washington's troops during the War of Independence. "He can have no right to the benefits of society who will not pay his club dues towards the support of it," he wrote. At one point during the war, an exacerbated Franklin contended that runaway inflation during the war had one virtue—it forced the tax evaders to pay for the war through depreciation of the Continental currency!

During the Constitutional Convention in 1787, Franklin advocated a laissez-faire attitude toward government authority and its powers of taxation. He was in sympathy with the dictum often attributed to Thomas Jefferson, "Government governs best which governs least." The state has the power to tax but should tax lightly. He learned from the French, "*Laissez nous faire*: Let us alone.... *Pas trop gouverner*: Not to govern too strictly."

ON ECONOMICS AND THE ECONOMY

The financial founder disliked debt of all forms, public or private. Government must live within its means. "No revenue is sufficient without economy," he warned.

Franklin disliked showering favors on the rich, but he also opposed excessive taxation of the rich, who do much good in society. Regarding the poor laws in England, he wrote (worth repeating from chapter 9): "The poor laws were not made by the poor. The legislators were men of fortune. By that act they voluntarily subjected their own estates, and the estates of others, to the payment of a tax for the maintenance of the poor. Besides this tax, they had, by donation and subscription, erected numerous schools for educating gratis the children of the poor; they erected hospitals at an immense expense for the reception and cure of the sick, the lame, the wounded, and the insane poor, for lying-in women, and deserted children. They also continually contributed toward making up losses occasioned by fire, by storms, or by floods, etc. Surely there should be some gratitude due for some many instances of goodness!" (*CA*, p. 57).

Franklin was a free trader. He disliked relying too heavily on import duties to support government: "Most of the statutes, acts, edicts and placards of Parliaments, princes, and states, for regulating, directing, and restraining of trade have either political blunders or jobs obtained by artful men for private advantage under the pretense of public good. In general the more free and unrestrained commerce is, the more it flourishes. No nation was ever ruined by trade." (*CA*, p. 301)

Ultimately, he compromised his libertarian leanings and supported the Constitution, which created a much more powerful federal government than the Articles of Confederation. A year later, he wrote to a friend in France, "Thus, our new Constitution is now established, and has an appearance that promises permanency; but in this world nothing can be said to be certain except death and taxes" (*CA*, 381).

THE GREATEST AMERICAN

Franklin was, in many ways, resigned to paying taxes and living with a certain amount of distasteful bureaucracy. Franklin warned against spending too much time worrying about ways to avoid them. For some things were more taxing than government. In his popular pamphlet, "The Way to Wealth," he talked of greater issues: "Friends, the taxes are indeed very heavy, and if those laid on by the government were the only ones we had to pay, we might more easily discharge them; but we have many others, and much more grievous to some of us. *We are taxed twice as much by our idleness, three times as much by our pride, and four times as much by our folly*; and from these taxes the commissioners cannot ease or deliver us by allowing an abatement. However, let us hearken to good advice, and something may be done for us; 'God helps them that help themselves,' as Poor Richard says."

CHAPTER 34

ON POLITICAL ECONOMY

In January 2018, the American Economic Association's annual meeting was held in Philadelphia. In the spirit of Dr. Franklin, who entertained the delegates to the Constitutional Convention in the summer of 1787, I thought it appropriate to propose a session on "The Economics of Benjamin Franklin."

After all, economic historian Eric Roll wrote that "by common consent there is only one writer in [early American economic thought] who is worthy to be mentioned in the company of early political economists of Europe," and that was Benjamin Franklin. Roll believed that the founder "was as astute in economics as in other scientific matters."

The *Cambridge History of English and American Literature* names Franklin as the "only one prominent name in American economic discussion." It states, "His contributions represent the common-sense reactions of a powerful mind to the problems of the day, reinforced later on by general reflections suggested by the Physiocrats and Adam Smith."

The famous Philadelphian wrote widely on labor theory of value, wages, trade policy, population and immigration, finance,

THE GREATEST AMERICAN

banking and insurance, paper money and interest, agriculture and manufacturing, and taxation.

Franklin is frequently viewed as the father of American capitalism. He was fascinated with the buzz of daily life in the marketplace and in city life. In his annual *Poor Richard's Almanac*, especially his "Way to Wealth" pamphlet, he stressed the virtues of a commercial society. He was an optimist and a believer in progress and the American dream, the idea that every American could get ahead through industry, thrift, prudence, and a good education.

Franklin was sympathetic to the "new" economics (known back then as "political economy") of the day advocated by Adam Smith in his *Wealth of Nations* (published in 1776) and the French school known as the Physiocrats. They supported free trade and an unregulated market. Franklin wrote a friend in support of "*Laissez nous faire*: Let us alone.... *Pas trop gouverner*: Not to govern too strictly" (*CA*, pp. 300–301).

Regarding the radical idea of free trade, Franklin famously wrote, "No nation was ever ruined by trade." He added, "To lay duties on a commodity exported which our friends want is a knavish attempt to get something for nothing. The statesman who first invented it had the genius of a pickpocket. Most of the statutes, acts, edicts, and placards of parliaments, princes and states, for regulating, directing, and restraining of trade have either political blunders or jobs obtained by artful men for private advantage under the pretence of public good. In general the more free and unrestrained commerce is, the more it flourishes" (*CA*, p. 300).

In general, Franklin's foreign policy was simple: "The system of America is universal commerce with every nation; war with none" (*CA*, p. 148, written in 1778 during the American revolt against England).

Regarding government fiscal policy, he favored austerity and balanced budgets. He hated the idea of wasting money, either privately or publicly, and thought that cutting wasteful spending was

138

ON ECONOMICS AND THE ECONOMY

better than raising taxes. "No revenue is sufficient without economy." In general, he wrote a friend, "A virtuous and laborious [industrious] people may be cheaply governed." At the Constitutional Convention in 1787, he was much in sympathy with the dictum usually credited to Thomas Jefferson that "government governs best which governs least."[33]

His views on banking and monetary inflation were more liberal, however. In 1729, he wrote and published a pamphlet, *A Modest Enquiry into the Nature and Necessity of a Paper-Currency*, and won the contract with the Pennsylvania government to print paper money. This was the age of gold and silver as the primary money, and back in the eighteenth century, the British Crown prohibited the issuance of paper money in the colonies. Consequently, there was constantly talk of a shortage of coinage in Philadelphia and economic depression. Franklin hoped to remedy the situation by issuing paper money. "Paper money in moderate quantities has been found beneficial," he wrote. He was an early proponent of what we call today the "real bills doctrine" of providing sufficient credit to encourage commerce without going overboard.

During the American Revolution, he also saw an indirect benefit to depreciating the currency via inflation: It forced tax evaders to pay their fair share of the war! He wrote a friend, "This currency as we managed it was a wonderful machine. It performed its office when we issued it; it paid and clothed the troops, and provided victuals and ammunition; and when we were obliged to issue an excessive quantity, it paid itself by depreciation" (*CA*, p. 203).

However, after the war, he recognized that the paper-money inflation had its limits. "When more than the occasions of commerce require, it depreciates and is mischievous and the populous are apt to demand more than is necessary" (*CA*, p. 357).

---

33 Biographer Bernard *Faÿ says something similar in his book, Franklin: Apostle of Modern Times (Boston: Little, Brown, and Company, 1929), p. 504.*

THE GREATEST AMERICAN

Franklin was a great admirer of the Bank of England, and was a supporter of the Hamiltonian view of central banking and high finance. He was a shareholder of the Bank of North America.

In short, Benjamin Franklin would be in favor of what Peter Drucker calls "a powerful but limited government," though he would be aghast at the size and scope of big government today.

CHAPTER 35

THE VIRTUE OF THRIFT MAKES A COMEBACK

"If you know how to spend less than you get, you have the philosopher's stone."
—*Poor Richard's Almanac (1736)*.

Ben Franklin is famous for his adage, "a penny saved is a penny earned." In collecting quotations for his *Poor Richard's Almanac*, he would improve upon common sayings. One was an old proverb, "a penny spar'd is twice got." How is a penny spar'd (or saved) "twice got" (a penny earned)?

Assume you earn $100 a day. If you have $100 in your pocket and you spend it, you have to go out and do a day's work to get that $100 back. But with $100 in savings, you could take off a whole day of work and still enjoy a day's income by drawing upon your savings. In sum, saving is a source of earning power.

The more you save, the more earning power you build up. In addition, savings earns interest, which means more earning power and compounded returns. (Franklin was a big fan of compound interest.)

But in today's modern world, Franklin's virtue of thrift has come under attack. Since the 1930s, the British economist John Maynard Keynes and his followers have criticized Franklin and savings as a virtue. Most recently, Keynesians have warned consumers not to cut back on their spending during the financial crisis; it could make matters worse. "A penny saved is a penny lost," they contend because saving "leaks" out of the system and is not necessarily spent.

THE FALLACY OF "THE PARADOX OF THRIFT"

Starting with his first edition of his *Economics* textbook in 1948, MIT professor Paul Samuelson took delight in attacking the orthodox views of Adam Smith and Ben Franklin, which he called "the paradox of thrift." "Thriftiness during a recession can kill off income," he wrote. When people save more, they spend less on consumer goods, which in turn hurts business. According to Samuelson, Franklin's "old virtues may be modern sins."[34] Two other Keynesian economists, William J. Baumol and Alan S. Blinder, were bold enough to declare in a 1988 textbook, "While savings may pave the road to riches for an individual, if the nation as a whole decides to save more, the result may be a recession and poverty for all."[35]

Franklin would beg to differ. It pays to be economical at all times. During times of prosperity, businesses should build up retained earnings and consumers should save for a rainy day; during a downturn, it pays to avoid unnecessary expenses and to save. In fact, by prudently saving throughout the business cycle, well-managed businesses and conservative consumers will be in better shape to survive a recession and to invest when the economy bottoms. In fact, studies show that even during a recession, many business-

34   Paul A. Samuelson, *Economics* (New York: McGraw Hill, 1948), 270.

35   William J. Baumol and Alan Blinder, *Economics: Principles and Policy*, 4th ed. (New York: Harcourt Brace Jovanovich, 1988), 192.

ON ECONOMICS AND THE ECONOMY

es continue to upgrade their tools and equipment, and spend on R&D and new product development, which represents future consumption.

In 1757, on his way to London as a colonial agent, Franklin wrote what turned out to be his most popular pamphlet, "The Way to Wealth." He summarized his formula for financial success: "The way to wealth is as plain as the way to market. It depends chiefly on two words, industry and frugality; that is waste neither time nor money, but make the best use of both. Without industry and frugality nothing will do; with them, everything."

Franklin practiced what he preached, both as a businessman and consumer. In his *Autobiography*, published posthumously, he explained how he created his wealth—through hard work, creating his own business (publishing), constantly educating himself, adopting the latest innovations, and most importantly, saving and living within his means. He always lived frugally. (Frugality is listed as one of his thirteen virtues in his *Autobiography*.)

During the good times, he invested his saved funds in rental properties and bank deposits. During times of financial setbacks, he learned to cut back on his expenses. He believed that retrenching was better than going into debt in order to maintain his lifestyle. When his printing partnership abruptly ended in 1767, Franklin made the difficult decision to cut back consumption (he said he dined at home with only one "single dish") and urged his wife Deborah to do the same. It kept them out of trouble.

He constantly preached frugality in his *Poor Richard's Almanac* with such adages as:

1. "Beware of small expenses; a small leak may sink a great ship."
2. "The honest man takes pains, and then enjoys pleasures; the knave takes pleasures and then suffers pain."
3. "Women and wine, games and deceit, make the wealth small and the wants great."

THE GREATEST AMERICAN

4. "Creditors have better memories than debtors."
5. "No gains without pains."
6. "Ere you consult fancy, consult your purse."

Later in life, he counseled his son-in-law, "No revenue is sufficient without economy." He warned, "A man's industry and frugality will pay his debts and get him forward in the world.... Business not well managed ruins one faster than no business" (CA, pp. 148, 336). Undoubtedly, Franklin would castigate today's Americans for indulging in undersaving, overspending, and excessive consumer debt.

Throughout all his experiences, failures, and victories, he built a fortune that was never in jeopardy. By time he died in 1790 at the remarkable age of eighty-four, he was a self-made man, one of the richest in American history.

I urge you to follow Franklin's sage advice: Always spend less than you earn. Avoid getting too heavily into debt. Work hard to pay off your debts. Save monthly (at least 10 percent of your income). Your investment accounts will grow steadily if you invest your savings prudently and productively. Invest your savings either in your own business or in the successful businesses of others (via the stock market).

Manage your budget carefully. Live frugally within your means, and find ways to cut back on wasteful spending. Beware of credit cards, which make it easy to overspend. If you have trouble paying off your credit cards each month, use debit or charge cards that require payment in full each month.

Another good idea is to keep track of all your expenditures every day and compare your spending from month to month to see where you are wasting money. I tell students in my personal finance classes that every person I know wastes at least 10 percent on their income for needless expenditures. Writing down your expenditures daily is easy, and you will be surprised how much you can save.

ON ECONOMICS AND THE ECONOMY

If you do, you too will discover the philosopher's stone. As Kevin O. Leary, "Mr. Wonderful" on the television show *Shark Tank*, said, "Getting rich is easy if you follow three rules: spend less, save more, and invest the rest" ("Maxims of Wall Street," p. 24).

CHAPTER 36

HOW FRANKLIN SAVED THE POST OFFICE AND UNIFIED THE COLONIES

"In the fourth year of Franklin's administration, [the Post Office] paid a profit for the first time in its history."
—Thomas Fleming, *The Man Who Dared the Lightning* (1971)

"No one man before him had ever done so much to draw the scattered colonies together." —Carl Van Buren, Benjamin Franklin (1938)

Despite mammoth efforts to increase revenues and productivity, the US Postal Service has failed to make a profit in years. In fact, this year it's expected to run a deficit of nearly $10 billion. The difference is made up by the Treasury—that is, the American taxpayer.

Benjamin Franklin faced a similar challenge when he was made America's first postmaster general in 1753. Within four years, he reformed the Crown's mail service from an unreliable, expensive, and unprofitable service to an efficient, dependable, and rewarding operation. And in doing so, he helped make the thirteen colonies

ON ECONOMICS AND THE ECONOMY

come together as a nation. What was his secret, and what can we learn from his experience today?

First, some background: The colonial post office was run by the British Crown, which appointed local postmasters. The royal mail was expensive, slow, erratic, and limited to major towns. It was discriminatory—government officials like the Penns had the franking privilege (free mailing service). So did the local printers like Franklin, who was appointed postmaster of Philadelphia in 1737. Their newspapers could be circulated for free. And mailing letters was expensive, limiting its use to the wealthy, businessmen, and lawyers. Few colonists could afford to mail letters through the official royal mail. Finally, mail delivery was slow. A letter from Boston to Philadelphia might take six weeks to arrive. There was no centralized network to transport mail.

HOW FRANKLIN REFORMED THE ROYAL POST

How did Franklin transform the post office? First, he lobbied for the postmaster general job—and won it, because for sixteen years he had run the post office in Philadelphia. His experience paid off.

His first action was to make a grand tour of the postal service. Like a good manager, he felt it was essential to have first-hand knowledge of the mail system, and within a few months after his appointment, he went on a ten-week inspection tour of New England, from New Jersey to Massachusetts, to determine the problems facing the post office (poor roads, bad record keeping, and more). He talked face-to-face with riders and postmasters, responding to suggestions and improvements.

After his grand tour, Franklin immediately went to work. On the post roads, he had milestones erected to help riders pace themselves better. (These milestones still exist between Boston and New York.) After consulting with local postal workers, he suggested new roads, fords, and ferries to deliver the mail faster and more regularly. As a result, he was able to reduce the travel time for mail between Boston and Philadelphia from six weeks to three. Within a year, he had cut the delivery time of a letter between Philadelphia and New York to one day.

Franklin insisted on precise record keeping. When he started working for Andrew Bradford, who published Philadelphia's only newspaper, he noticed Bradford was irregular in his accounts. Drawing from this experience, he furnished a uniform system of accounts to all postmasters throughout the colonies and insisted that all postmasters keep precise accounts of their revenues and costs.

In his old newspaper, the *Pennsylvania Gazette*, he had for years printed the names of persons who had letters waiting for them, and introduced this practice in other post offices as well. Too often, letters were allowed to lie around or be read by friends. Franklin discontinued this practice in Philadelphia and imposed the same regulation in the rest of the colonies.

He also introduced home delivery and the penny post. If an individual failed to pick up a letter after their name was published in the newspaper, the letter would then be sent the next day for an additional fee. Franklin encouraged the same local delivery in other large towns. Unclaimed letters after three months were forwarded to the central office in Philadelphia. Thus, Franklin has another claim: inventor of the dead letter office!

Franklin also made the post office egalitarian. He reduced the price and expanded the service for all colonists, not just the wealthy or important people. He abolished the monopolistic practice of allowing local postmasters to distribute newspapers for free and opened the service to all papers for a small fee. Franklin was never one to maintain monopoly power. For example, he never trademarked any of his inventions. He thought they should be made available to everyone for their benefit, whether it be the Franklin stove, the lightning rod, or bifocals.

ON ECONOMICS AND THE ECONOMY

All these improvements in the postal system under Franklin cost money. It cost him and his partner, William Hunter, a great deal, and they incurred £900 over their first four years. But by the fourth year they collected more money in twelve months than they had in the previous thirty-six, earning a profit of £300 a year apiece. It remained profitable until the Revolutionary War broke out.

In three years, the colonial postal service was completely overhauled, and its new speed and reliability made it profitable and popular with the people. As biographer Carl Van Buren concluded, "No one man before him had ever done so much to draw the scattered colonies together."

It is entirely appropriate to remember Benjamin Franklin as the father of American capitalism. The post office has honored Franklin with his image on more stamps than any other person other than George Washington.

In celebration of Franklin's contribution to the postal service, I recommend that the post office issue a permanent one-cent stamp with his image on it and the words, "A penny saved is a penny earned."

CHAPTER 37

THE FIRST COPPER PENNY

"Mind your business."
—*Franklin's adage on the 1787 penny*

Inflation has finally caught up with the lowly penny. Like Australia, Sweden, and Canada, the US Treasury Department under Barack Obama announced that it may eliminate the penny from circulation. It hasn't happened yet, but it could. The new Department of Government Efficiency (DOGE) under Elon Musk reported that the US Mint produced over 4.5 billion pennies in 2024 at a cost of over $179 million. The new pennies look like copper, but since 1982 have been made primarily from zinc, and the cost is now 3 cents to produce each penny.

It is sad to think that in future generations, nobody will understand the significance of Ben Franklin's famous statement, "A penny saved is a penny earned." (Actually, he wrote originally, "A penny spar'd is twice got.") Nor will they throw pennies on his gravesite in Philadelphia.

Franklin has been linked with the penny for centuries. He was the designer of the first American penny in 1787. Known as the Fugio cent, it bears the image of a sun and sundial above Poor Richard's message "Mind Your Business." A chain with thirteen

ON ECONOMICS AND THE ECONOMY

links, each representing one of the original colonies, encircles the motto "We Are One" on the reverse.

In 1776, Franklin designed the Continental dollar, which was made out of bronze, due to the shortage of gold, silver, and paper money.

In 1779, while ambassador in Paris, Franklin corresponded with Edward Bridgen, a London merchant, about the purchase of copper metal to strike a copper penny in America. Americans were familiar with the English penny, but with independence on their minds, knew that they would need to create their own currency.

He wrote, "There has indeed been an Intention to strike *Copper* Coin that may not only be useful as small Change, but serve other Purposes." He proposed that coins contain important symbols and catchy phrases, such as "the Fear of the Lord is the Beginning of Wisdom…. Honesty is the best Policy…. He that by the Plow would thrive; himself must either lead or drive…keep thy Shop & thy Shop will keep thee…a *Penny* sav'd is a *Penny* got…. He that buys what he has no need of, will soon be forced to sell his Necessaries…and Early to bed & early to rise, will make a man healthy, wealthy & wise." These are all taken from *Poor Richard's Almanac*.

Alas, after more than two centuries, inflation has destroyed the penny. To be more precise, the constant inflation *since 1913* has destroyed the penny. The penny loses value every day from the small but discernible depreciation of our currency. Why? We gradually abandoned the classic gold standard starting in 1913, when the Federal Reserve was established; in 1933, Franklin Delano Roosevelt devalued the dollar and discontinued the gold standard domestically; and the last vestiges of the gold standard ended in 1971, when President Richard Nixon closed the gold window.

Before World War II, inflation wasn't a problem, except during war time (for example, the American Revolution, the War of 1812, the Civil War, and World War I). But during the Great Depression of the 1930s, we gradually weaned ourselves from the gold standard. Since the end of World War II, the cost of living has risen thirty-fold, or 3,000 percent! (See graph below.)

It's amazing the copper penny has lasted that long, given the

The Permanent Inflation Hypothesis:

The Declining Purchase Power of Money Since World War II

3,000 percent inflation.

Franklin wasn't against paper money, and thought a little inflation benefited trade. As the official government printer in Philadelphia, his company profited handsomely from the print job. But after witnessing the devastating depreciation of the Continental currency during the American Revolution, he came to believe that too much inflation was bad for America. He wrote, "Paper money in moderate quantities has been found beneficial; but when more than the occasions of commerce require, it depreciates and is mischievous and the populous are apt to demand more than is neces-

ON ECONOMICS AND THE ECONOMY

sary." He supported Article I, Section 10 of the US Constitution that required states to use only gold and silver as legal tender.

Since the US Postal Service started issuing stamps, Franklin has appeared many times on a one-cent stamp, and even once on a half-cent stamp issued during World War II. My, have things changed in eighty years.

In the previous chapter, I mentioned my proposal to the US Postal Service Citizens' Stamp Advisory Committee that they issue a permanent one-cent stamp with Franklin's image on it and his famous adage, "A penny saved is a penny earned." Sadly, if the penny goes the way of the dodo bird, my proposal will never come to pass.

CHAPTER 38

ON PAPER MONEY AND INFLATION

*"Paper money in moderate quantities has been found
beneficial; but when more than the occasions of commerce
require, it depreciates and is mischievous and the populous
are apt to demand more than is necessary."*
—Ben Franklin (1787)

What would founding father and financial guru Benjamin Franklin think of the Federal Reserve's pumping trillions of dollars into the US economy, so-called "quantitative easing" during the financial crisis in 2008–09?

Like fellow founders Alexander Hamilton and Robert Morris, Franklin was a cosmopolitan financier who supported modern-day banking and would have undoubtedly defended Hamilton's plan to create the first Bank of the United States. He owned shares in the Bank of North America.

Earlier in his career, Franklin campaigned for paper money in Pennsylvania at a time when hard money (gold and silver) was scarce. In the pamphlet he published in 1729, *The Nature and Necessity of a Paper-Currency*, he argued that it would "do much good by increasing the trade, employment, and number of inhabitants in the province" (*A*, p. 77).

ON ECONOMICS AND THE ECONOMY

However, after experiencing the runaway inflation of the American Revolution, when the phrase "not worth a Continental" became popular, Franklin recognized that inflation could get out of control and there could be too much of a good thing. "I now think there are limits beyond which the quantity may be hurtful," he wrote in his *Autobiography* (*A*, p. 78).

Indeed, Franklin warned that too much inflation could be "mischievous." That adjective could well apply to the Federal Reserve's schemes to adopt easy credit and reinflate the money supply whenever they're in a monetary crisis or economic collapse. The Fed engaged in a plot to artificially prop up the economy by keeping interest rates dangerously low and the money stock dangerously high, and suffered the consequences—a run on the dollar, soaring commodity prices, and a rush to buy the hard currencies, gold and silver.

CHAPTER 39

ON BEING AN OPTIMIST

"We had a terrible winter in France.... Yet I was still alive, the sun started to return, the days to lengthen, the spring to come, the trees and gardens to regain their verdure, all nature to laugh, and to me, happiness."
—*Ben Franklin (1784)*

Today it's easy to complain about America's condition: a spendthrift government, a sluggish economy, rising prices, and never-ending wars abroad. I recently returned from an investment conference where almost everyone was pessimistic about the future of America.

What would wise ol' Dr. Franklin say about these doomsayers?

Franklin was a born optimist, the Norman Vincent Peale of his day (remember Peale's classic book, *The Power of Positive Thinking?*). He was never depressed for long, even when he suffered serious personal setbacks. Sometimes he was frustrated by the never-ending War of Independence, which lasted for nine years, and the accompanying inflation, death, and ruined economy. But he was upbeat about the future. "America will, with God's blessing, become a great and happy country," he wrote, "and England, if she has at length gained wisdom, will have gained something more

ON ECONOMICS AND THE ECONOMY

valuable, and more essential to her prosperity, than all she has lost; and will still be a great and respectable nation" (*CA*, p. 301).

When Franklin returned to America after serving as America's first ambassador, the newspapers were full of negative news about the post-war economy. He observed, "I saw in the public papers of different states frequent complaints of hard times, deadness of trade, scarcity of money, etc." But he took a positive attitude. "It is always in the power of a small number to make a great clamour. But let us take a cool view of the general state of our affairs, and perhaps the prospect will appear less gloomy than has been imagined" (*CA*, p. 332). He was right. Once the government got its finances in order, the nascent American economy boomed in the 1790s.

Years earlier, Franklin learned to take a positive attitude about life, no matter how dire the short-term situation. In his *Autobiography*, he tells the story of the time (probably in the 1730s) when he was a young printer in Philadelphia and was approached by an elderly man "with a wise look and a very grave manner of speaking." The old man urged young Franklin to close down his printing house in anticipation of a terrible depression coming to Philadelphia. He warned Franklin that "Philadelphia was a sinking place," full of "half-bankrupts," and the elderly wise man had decided to avoid buying real estate in the city, for "all was going to destruction." In sum, "he gave me such a detail of misfortunes now exciting, or that were soon to exist, that he left me half melancholy" (*A*, p. 70).

Fortunately, Franklin ignored the old man's advice, and expanded his business and rental properties. Years later, he concluded: "At last I had the pleasure of seeing him give five times as much for one [house] as he might have bought for it when he first began his croaking" (*A*, p. 71).

Over the years, Franklin learned that there were two kinds of people: those who are upbeat and positive, and those who are neg-

THE GREATEST AMERICAN

ative and pessimistic. "There are croakers in every country, always boding its ruin," he observed in the *Autobiography*.

Later in life, he elaborated: "There are two sorts of people in the world, who with equal degrees of health and wealth, become the one happy, the other unhappy. Those who are to be happy fix their attention on the pleasant parts of conversation, and enjoy all with cheerfulness. Those who are to be unhappy think and speak only of the contraries. Hence they are continually discontented themselves, and by their remarks sour the pleasures of society, offend personally many people, and make themselves everywhere disagreeable" (*CA*, pp. 187–188).

Regarding the "disagreeable" economic and political situation facing America today, I suspect that Ben Franklin would be more in sympathy with these words of counsel from his contemporary friend, the economist Adam Smith, in *The Wealth of Nations* (1776): "The uniform, constant, and uninterrupted effort of every man to better his condition is frequently powerful enough to maintain the natural progress of things toward improvement, in spite both of the extravagance of government, and of the greatest errors of administration"[36]

The message is clear: Don't underestimate the future of America, despite our current problems.

---

36 Adam Smith, *The Wealth of Nations* (New York: Modern Library, 1965 [1776]), p. 326.

PART V

ON POLITICS

CHAPTER 40

ON POLITICS

"You can always employ your time better than in polemics."
—Ben Franklin (CA, p. 231)

What did Ben Franklin think of elections and partisan politics? Besides being a businessman, publisher, inventor, scientist, and man of letters, Franklin spent a good deal of his career as a statesman, legislator, and lobbyist. In fact, the final thirty-three years of his life were largely engaged in politics as a colonial agent in London, signer of the Declaration of Independence, first ambassador to France, and delegate to the Constitutional Convention.

"It is a singular thing in the history of mankind that a great people have had the opportunity of forming a government for themselves. We are making experiments in politics," he wrote during the Constitutional Convention in 1787 (CA, p. 370).

Yet, the longer he stayed in politics, the more he disliked it. He came to see adversarial political wrangling as dysfunctional and irrational, full of ambition and avarice. The battles in the Pennsylvania General Assembly, Congress, and Parliament created many enemies who held grudges against him until the day he died, and long afterward. He split over the subject of independence with his own son, William, who remained a loyalist to the bitter end. He lost friendships with British businessmen and scientists during the

American Revolution. He hated war and thought it should be the last option in political intrigue, not the first.

When he retired from his printing business in 1748, he quickly became involved in two areas of interest: his scientific studies and civic duties in Pennsylvania. He was a big supporter of what we would call today the voluntary "nongovernmental organizations" (NGOs), and helped organize the Library Company, the City Watch, the Union Fire Company, the Pennsylvania Academy (later the University of Pennsylvania), the American Philosophical Society (for natural scientific studies), the Pennsylvania militia (again voluntary and overtly democratic), and Pennsylvania Hospital, among other projects. He used his influence in the *Pennsylvania Gazette* to promote these good causes.

Inevitably, such philanthropic ventures involved the local government, and he was elected to the Pennsylvania assembly several times in the 1750s, though he avoided direct campaigning for the office. He famous motto was "Never ask, never refuse, and never resign an office," although he violated it several times in his political career.

"A REPUBLIC, IF YOU CAN KEEP IT"

He was a steadfast believer in democratic representation—"a republic, if you can keep it," as he told a young woman after signing the Constitution. For most of his career, he had immense faith in the common man who was moral and well educated. "A virtuous and laborious [industrious] people may be cheaply governed," he wrote. "The system of America is universal commerce with every nation; war with none" (*CA*, p. 148).

He was in the forefront of fights over taxation and American Indian squabbles with the Penns, the governors of Pennsylvania; he argued with the British over the Stamp Act and American independence; he tangled with John Adams, Arthur Lee, and other commissioners when he was ambassador to France.

ON POLITICS

Throughout it all, Franklin was the consummate diplomat and master politician. He was the only commissioner in France successful in raising funds and supplies for the American troops. He was the primary negotiator for the Treaty of Paris with England after the war and designed the Great Compromise during the Constitutional Convention of 1787.

His true mode was not to challenge enemies to battle but to try to win them over by persuasion. He learned the value of compromise after years of experience in business and dealmaking. He would often remain silent and not respond to personal attacks. Nevertheless, he lost many battles and created enemies along the way. He was often vilified by his countrymen, lost his position in the assembly, and was fired as postmaster general and colonial agent by the British before the American Revolution started.

When in France, he wrote, "I resolved to have no quarrel, and therefore have made it a constant rule to answer no angry, affronting or abusive letter, of which I have received many and long ones from Mr. Lee and Mr. Izard [fellow commissioners of France]. I never answered them, but treated the gentlemen with the same civility when we met as if no such letters existed. No revenge was necessary for me; I need only leave them to hiss, bite, sting and poison one another" (*CA*, p. 182).

SWITCHING SIDES: FROM HAMILTON TO JEFFERSON

At the end of his career, however, he became a bit more pessimistic about party politics and working for government. He wrote a friend, "I am of the opinion that almost any profession a man has been educated in is preferable to an office held at pleasure, as rendering him more independent, more a freeman and less subject to the caprices of superiors" (*CA*, p. 50).

On political factions, he warned, "There are two passions which have a powerful influence in the affairs of men, ambition and avarice, the love of power and the love of money.... And of

THE GREATEST AMERICAN

what kind are the men that will strive for this profitable pre-eminence, thro' all the bustle of cabal, the heat of contention, the infinite mutual abuse of parties, tearing to pieces the best of characters? It will not be the wise and moderate, the lovers of peace and good order, the men fittest for the trust. It will be the bold and the violent, the men of strong passions and indefatigable activity in their selfish pursuits. These will trust themselves to this government and be their rulers" (*CA*, pp. 360–361).

By the time he became involved in the Constitutional Convention in the summer of 1787, he appears to have shifted from a pro-government Hamiltonian to a laissez-faire Jeffersonian. According to historian Bernard Faÿ, "They [Congress] were directly opposed to Franklin's philosophy tendency, which might be summed up in this formula: the least government possible is the greatest good."[37]

---

37 Bernard *Faÿ, Franklin: Apostle of Modern Times (Boston: Little, Brown, and Company, 1929), p.* 504.

CHAPTER 41

ON RACISM

"This present age has been distinguished by a remarkable revolution. The human mind has felt its influence. Mankind begins at last to consider themselves as members of one family."
—*Ben Franklin (1788)*

As stated earlier, Ben Franklin was the most modern of the founders. There's no better example than his attitude toward race. He was ahead of his time in the eighteenth century when few American citizens and leaders questioned the institution of slavery. George Washington, Thomas Jefferson, and George Mason, all founding fathers from Virginia, opposed slavery, but never freed their slaves during their lifetimes. Mason called it a "pernicious" institution, despite owning two hundred slaves. Jefferson consistently opposed the practice, calling it a "moral depravity," a "hideous blot," and contrary to the laws of nature, yet allowed only a handful of slaves to go free in his will. Although Washington expressed personal opposition, he signed the first fugitive slave law in 1793, allowing slaveholders to recapture slaves in free states, and he promised emancipation only after his wife died.

John Adams never owned slaves and refused to hire slave labor throughout his career.

In Philadelphia, where Franklin resided, about 6 percent of the population were slaves. Franklin accepted ads for the slave

THE GREATEST AMERICAN

trade in the *Pennsylvania Gazette*, and personally owned a slave couple, but in 1751 sold them on pragmatic grounds—free blacks, he said, were more productive. But when he was made colonial agent in 1757, he took with him to London two black servants, Peter and King. King ran away, and no one knows what happened to Peter. For the rest of his life, Franklin no longer owned enslaved human beings.

In 1762–63, he returned to Philadelphia and on one occasion visited the local institution for blacks that he had helped finance. He wrote, "I visited the Negro School in Philadelphia and was on the whole much pleased, and from what I then saw, have conceived a higher opinion of the natural capacities of the black race, than I had ever before entertained. Their apprehension seems as quick, their memory as strong, and their docility in every respect equal to that of white children. You will wonder perhaps that I should ever doubt it, and I will not undertake to justify all my prejudices" (*CA*, pp. 25–26).

He did not get involved in the issue at the Constitutional Convention, where the delegates attempted to reduce the influence of slaveowners by designating blacks as representing three-fifths of the population in proportioning representation in the House, and agreed to ban the importation of slaves in 1808.

Franklin's conversion culminated in 1787, during the Constitutional Convention, when he became president of the Pennsylvania Society for Promoting the Abolition of Slavery. The main purpose of the Society was to free slaves and then to help them become good citizens. "The final purposes of our society are the suppression of the slave trade and the gradual abolition of slavery itself," he wrote a friend. "In the mean time we consider it as our indispensable duty to endeavor by all means in our power to alleviate the miseries of those unhappy people who are doomed to taste of the bitter cup of perpetual servitude" (*CA*, p. 382).

As president of the Society, Franklin gave "An Address to the Public" on November 9, 1789, declaring, "Slavery is such an atro-

ON POLITICS

cious debasement of human nature that its very extirpation, if not performed with solicitous care, may sometimes open a source of serious evils. The galling chains that bind his body do also fetter his intellectual faculties and impair the social affections of his heart."

When Congress met for the first time, Franklin presented a formal abolition petition to Congress in February 1790. Arguing that it was the duty of Congress to grant liberty "without distinction of color," he urged them to grant "liberty to those unhappy men, who alone, in this land of freedom, are degraded into perpetual bondage." But the opposition from the South was especially zealous. Congressman James Jackson of Georgia claimed the Bible sanctioned slavery, and without it, he said, nobody would do the hard and hot work on plantations.

In response, Franklin wrote his last great parody, written a month before he died. Published in the *Federal Gazette* as "Sidi Mehemet Ibrahim on the Slave Trade," the letter announced a petition by a purist Muslim sect asking for an end to the practice of capturing and enslaving European Christians to work in Algeria.

Imitating the speech by Congressman Jackson, the defenders of Christian slavery in Algeria responded, "If we forbear to make slaves of their people, who in this hot climate are to cultivate our lands?" An end to slavery of the "infidels" would cause land values to fall and rents to sink by half! And did not the Koran endorse slavery? In conclusion, the parody ran, "Let us then hear no more of this detestable proposition, the manumission of Christian slaves, the adoption of which would, by depreciating our lands and houses, and thereby depriving so many good citizens of their properties, create universal discontent, and provoke insurrections."

The author of the letter reported that the Algerian leader ultimately rejected the petition. Equally, Congress decided not to act on Franklin's abolition petition—and paid a heavy price seventy years later.

CHAPTER 42

ON NEPOTISM AND HELPING RELATIVES

"Ben Franklin was one of the greatest nepotists of the revolutionary era."
—*Adam Bellow, In Praise of Nepotism*

Whether owning a family business or running a company, there is always the temptation to play favoritism to family members and relatives by arranging for them to get a job or a contract. Is this a good idea? Most businesses prohibit or limit spouses and relatives from working together at a large company, for a variety of reasons.

Ben Franklin's experience is proof of the dangers of nepotism. He was a patron of his kin both near and far, largely to the fact that he had a small family himself, only William and Sarah, and thus felt inclined to become a guardian to many young relatives and friends in his lifetime. Through his own connections with friends in high places in Philadelphia, he became clerk of the Pennsylvania assembly in 1736 and procured a position as postmaster of Philadelphia in 1737. In 1753, he actively solicited the job of colonial postmaster general through friends in London and began a life of family patronage.

ON POLITICS

He first appointed his son William to take over his position as postmaster of Philadelphia and then the comptroller of whole colonial system. Billy, as he was affectionately called, accompanied his father to London in 1757, where he enrolled as a law student while his father was colonial agent. They frequently traveled together through England and Scotland.

Despite Franklin's homilies on the virtues of self-reliance, he worked hard to get his son a position of influence. In 1873, Ben arranged for his son to become the royal governor of New Jersey. It turned out to be his biggest mistake. William became an unwavering loyalist to the Crown even after the War of Independence started in 1776. When the British fired Franklin as postmaster, he asked his son to resign too as governor and join the rebellion. He refused. William ended up a prisoner and later moved to London, never to see his father again except at the end of Ben's life. "Nothing has hurt me so much and affected me with such keen sensations, as to find myself deserted in my old age by my only son," he wrote William. "And not only deserted, but to find [you] taking up arms against me in a cause where my good name, fortune and life were all at stake." He ended his letter, "This is a disagreeable subject. I drop it" (*CA*, p. 125). Franklin disinherited his son in his will.

Throughout his political career, he tried to help out his relatives. He arranged for Richard Bache, his son-in-law married to Sarah, to become the postmaster in Philadelphia during the war.

Being the youngest son in his family, he was particularly close to his youngest sister, Jane Mecom. Among Jane's many children, Franklin arranged for three of them to get jobs, one in the soap business, another in government, and a third as an apprentice. Her thirteen-year-old son, Benny, was the most promising, and Franklin arranged for him to become an apprentice to James Parker, a printer in New York. In 1742, Franklin bought Parker a press and four hundred pounds of type and set up a printing shop in New York in exchange for one-third of his profits.

THE GREATEST AMERICAN

But it turned out to be a disaster. As Jill Lepore tells the story in her delightful *Book of Ages: The Life and Opinions of Jane Franklin*, Benny turned out to be neither hard-working nor frugal, had gotten smallpox, and complained that his boss Parker was a cruel master who beat him. Benny tried to run away to sea, but was caught. To resolve the matter, Franklin decided to release Benny from his apprenticeship in New York and send the teenager to Antigua in the Caribbean islands to run his printing franchise (the previous printer had been run into debt and drank himself to death). "The island is reckoned one of the healthiest in the West Indies," he assured her. But Antigua was even worse than New York. It was a sugar factory run by absentee landlords and slaves, and the island was beset with hurricanes, disease, and pirates.

Yet he continued to help out his grandsons and nephews. William's son, Temple, and Sarah's son Benny accompanied Franklin to France in 1776 when he was made ambassador. Temple became his secretary, and later Benny set up shop as a printer in Philadelphia after the war and became the publisher of the strident newspaper, *The Aurora*. Franklin so soured on the idea of getting his grandsons positions in government that he encouraged them to go into business instead. He wrote, "I am of the opinion that almost any profession a man has been educated in is preferable to an office held at pleasure [government job], as rendering him more independent, more a freeman and less subject to the caprices of superiors. My grandson Benny being a very sensible and good lad, I had thoughts of fitting him for public business, but being now convinced that service is no inheritance. I determined to give him a trade that he may have somebody to depend on, and not be obliged to ask favors of office of anybody" (*CA*, p. 296).

Perhaps Franklin had learned his lesson the hard way.

A portrait of Franklin by Robert Feke c. 1746–1750, widely believed to be the earliest known painting of Franklin.

"Benjamin Franklin, Printer," by John Ward Dunsmore, c. 1928.

Franklin's bookshop in Philadelphia, 1745, by Jean Leon Gerome Ferris, c. 1910.

"The Way to Wealth," by Benjamin Franklin, 1758.

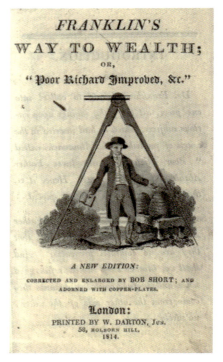

Poor Richard, 1733.
AN
Almanack
For the Year of Christ
1733,

Being the First after LEAP YEAR.

And makes since the Creation — Years
By the Account of the Eastern *Greeks*   7241
By the Latin Church, when ☉ ent. ♈   6932
By the Computation of *W.W.*   5742
By the *Roman* Chronology   5682
By the *Jewish* Rabbies.   5494

Wherein is contained

The Lunations, Eclipses, Judgment of the Weather, Spring Tides, Planets Motions & mutual Aspects, Sun and Moon's Rising and Setting, Length of Days, Time of High Water, Fairs, Courts, and observable Days.
Fitted to the Latitude of Forty Degrees, and a Meridian of Five Hours West from *London*, but may without sensible Error, serve all the adjacent Places, even from *Newfoundland* to *South-Carolina*.

By RICHARD SAUNDERS, Philom.

PHILADELPHIA:
Printed and sold by B. FRANKLIN, at the New Printing-Office near the Market.

The Philadelphia Experiments: Franklin's famous kite experiment demonstrating that lightning was electricity (Chapter 24)

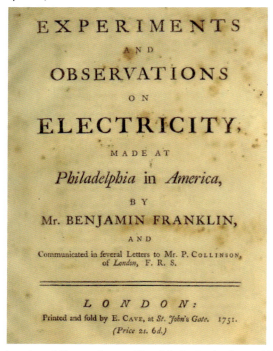

Title page of *Experiments and Observations on Electricity* by Benjamin Franklin, 1751 (Chapter 24)

Portrait of Adam Smith (1783–1790) (Chapter 29)

The first copper penny, designed by Benjamin Franklin in 1787 (Chapter 37)

A stamp issued in 1947 in honor of the centennial of stamp collecting, with portraits of George Washington and Benjamin Franklin (Chapter 59, p. 234)

Benjamin Franklin with his grandsons in Paris representing the American cause during the Revolutionary War. *Credit: North Wind Picture Archives / Alamy Stock Photo.*

The Rising Sun

The three symbols Franklin used to represent America: the rattlesnake, the turkey, and the rising sun (Chapter 44)

American eagle silver dollar (Chapter 44)

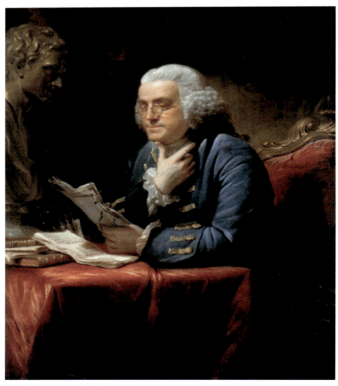

David Martin, *Benjamin Franklin*, 1767.

Howard Da Silva as Ben Franklin in the musical *1776* (Chapter 62)

When Charles Willson Peale (1741–1827) called upon Franklin uninvited in 1767, he accidentally witnessed the well-known Franklin kissing an unknown lady and secretly sketched the scandalous scene for future generations. Source: American Philosophical Society, www.amphilsoc.org/item-detail/diary-sketch.

The Signing of the Constitution, by Howard Chandler Christy. *Credit: Pictures Now / Alamy Stock Photo.*

Writing the Declaration of Independence, 1776 (Chapter 46)

Franklin's return to Philadelphia, 1785. *Credit: Niday Picture Library / Alamy Stock Photo.*

1706 — 1790

THE
AUTOBIOGRAPHY
of
Benjamin Franklin

TWYFORD, *at the Bishop of St. Asaph's,* 1771

DEAR SON: I have ever had pleasure in obtaining any little anecdotes of my ancestors. You may remember the inquiries I made among the remains of my relations when you were with me in England, and the journey I undertook for that purpose. Imagining it may be equally agreeable to you to know the circumstances of my life, many of which you are yet unacquainted with, and expecting the enjoyment of a week's uninterrupted leisure in my present country retirement, I sit down to write them for you. To which I have besides some other inducements. Having emerged from the poverty and obscurity in which I was born and bred, to a state of affluence and some degree of reputation in the

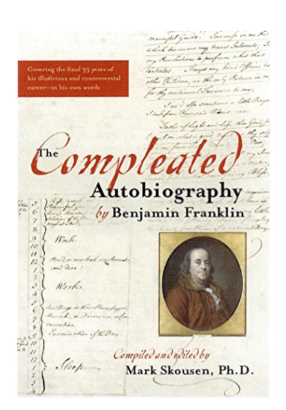

Portrait of Franklin wearing a Masonic apron and collar. "Franklin Opening the Lodge" by Kurz & Allison, 1896 (Chapter 72)

First president of the St. George Temple Wilford Woodruff's vision of the founding fathers requesting Temple Ordinances (Chapter 72)

FORM OF THE PAGES.

TEMPERANCE.

Eat not to dulness: drink not to elevation.

	Sun.	M.	T.	W.	Th.	F.	S.
Tem.							
Sil.	*	*		*		*	
Ord.	*	*	*		*	*	*
Res.		*				*	
Fru.		*				*	
Ind.			*				
Sinc.							
Jus.							
Mod.							
Clea.							
Tran.							
Chas.							
Hum.							

Franklin's 13 Virtues (Chapter 73)

"Ben's Belles," 1973. Series of story illustrations by Norman Rockwell from 1964 edition of *Poor Richards' Almanac* (Chapter 75)

Franklin courting his future wife, Deborah Read, 1852.

Benjamin Franklin, Alexander Hamilton, and others discussing the framing of the Constitution in Philadelphia, 1787. *Credit: North Wind Picture Archives / Alamy Stock Photo.*

CHAPTER 43

ON GOVERNMENT ABUSE OF OUR RIGHTS

"I am a mortal enemy to arbitrary government and un-limited power. I am naturally very jealous for the rights and liberties of my country and the least encroachment of those invaluable privileges is apt to make my blood boil."
—*Benjamin Franklin (1722)*

Having lived through the American Revolution, Ben Franklin experienced firsthand the abuse of individual rights. He witnessed British agents imposing taxes on American colonists without their consent, breaking into and searching their homes without permission, confiscating papers and other properties without due process of law. While in Paris as ambassador, British solders entered his home in Philadelphia and scattered his personal papers, never to be recovered.

The Bill of Rights was included in the original US Constitution to stop these travesties of justice once and for all. Franklin was a strong supporter of these rights, which included the Fourth Amendment. It states:

THE GREATEST AMERICAN

> The right of the people to be secure in their persons, houses, papers, and effects, against unreasonable searches and seizures, shall not be violated, and no warrants shall be issued, but upon probably cause, supported by oath or affirmation, and particularly describing the place to be searched, and the persons or things to be seized.

No doubt, Franklin would be appalled to see the abuses going on in our country today.

In 2014, the *New York Times* reported on another scandal by the federal tax authority, misnamed the Internal Revenue Service. It is not internal—the IRS even goes after citizens who live abroad; revenue is a polite word for forced taxation; and there is little "service" to an agency that puts you on hold for hours before answering questions.

The outrage involved the cash reporting requirements. In an effort to catch drug dealers and tax evaders, commercial banks, car dealers, and coin dealers are required to fill out a form to tell the IRS if anyone has handed over more than $10,000 in cash. The law also makes it illegal to "structure" deposits under $10,000 to avoid the reporting requirements, that is, making a series of deposits under the reporting level.

The *Times* told the story of power-hungry government agents who decided without any warrant or evidence of a crime to confiscate the bank accounts of small restaurant owners who regularly deposited less than $10,000 a day in their bank accounts. They did so on suspicion only, without charging anyone with a crime! It turned out that these were legitimate citizens who ran restaurants and other cash businesses. Not surprisingly, the IRS actions destroyed their businesses and their lives.

"How can this happen?" asked the owner of a small restaurant in Iowa. "Who takes your money before they prove that you've done anything wrong with it?"

ON POLITICS

In July 1776, Franklin and fifty-five other delegates to the Continental Congress issued the Declaration of Independence, a document that Franklin helped write, in which a list of grievances was recorded.

1. "He [the King of England] has erected a multitude of new offices, and sent hither swarms of officers to harass our people, and eat out their substance."

2. "For imposing taxes on us without our consent."

3. "For depriving us in many cases, of the benefits of trial by jury."

4. "In every stage of these oppressions we have petitioned for redress in the most humble terms: Our repeated petitions have been answered only by repeated injury."

Sometimes it sounds like it's time for another Declaration of Independence!

Fortunately, we still live in a democracy where citizens have a recourse to injustices and violations of their rights—either in the courts or by changing the law by the legislature.

Franklin was an optimist about the future of America, but even he warned of the dangers of an overweening state. "Hence as all history informs us, there has been in every state and kingdom a constant kind of warfare between the governing and the governed; the one striving to obtain more for its support, and the other to pay less. And this has alone occasioned great convulsions, actual civil wars, ending either in dethroning of the princes or enslaving of the people. Generally indeed the ruling power carries its point, and we see the revenues of princes constantly increasing, and we see that they are never satisfied, but always in want of more. I am apprehensive, therefore, perhaps too apprehensive, that the government of these states may in future times end in a monarchy, and a King will the sooner be set over us" (*CA*, p. 361).

Pray it never be.

173

CHAPTER 44

FRANKLIN'S THREE SYMBOLS OF AMERICA

"America will, with God's blessing, become a great and happy country."
—Benjamin Franklin (1783)

At various times over the years, Ben Franklin used three symbols to represent America: the rattlesnake, the turkey, and the rising sun.

THE RATTLESNAKE

In a letter published in the *Pennsylvania Journal* on December 27, 1775, Franklin wrote an anonymous letter under the pseudonym "An American Guesser," suggesting that the rattlesnake best represented the "temper and conduct" of American colonists. He noted that one of the drums he witnessed in a parade of soldiers had a rattlesnake painted on it, with the motto "Don't tread on me" under it.

In the letter, Franklin recounted "the worldly properties" of a snake: "I recollected that her eye excelled in brightness, that of any other animal, and that she has no eye-lids. She may therefore be

ON POLITICS

esteemed an emblem of vigilance. She never begins an attack, nor, when once engaged, ever surrenders: She is therefore an emblem of magnanimity and true courage.... Her weapons with which nature has furnished her, she conceals in the roof of her mouth, so that, to those who are unacquainted with her, she appears to be a most defenseless animal; and even when those weapons are shown and extended for her defense, they appear weak and contemptible; but their wounds however small, are decisive and fatal. Conscious of this, she never wounds 'till she has generously given notice, even to her enemy, and cautioned him against the danger of treading on her" (*CA*, pp. 112–113).

And regarding the rattles, he went on to observe that he "went back and counted them and found them just thirteen, exactly the number of the Colonies united in America," adding that "the ringing of thirteen together, is sufficient to alarm the boldest man living."

After this letter was printed, the rattlesnake quickly became a symbol of the colonists' cause, and after independence, has become known as the Gadsden Flag, a symbol of American patriotism and defiance of state power.

On January 26, 1784, while ambassador to France, Franklin wrote a letter to his daughter Sally in Philadelphia, expressing doubts about the bald eagle as the proper "representative of our country." He contended that the eagle is "a bird of bad moral character. He does not get his living honestly.... He is a rank coward: The little king bird not bigger than a sparrow attacks him boldly and drives him of the district."

He suggested that the turkey would have been a better choice. "For the truth the turkey is in comparison a much more respectable bird, and withal a true original native of America.... He is besides, though a little vain & silly, a bird of courage, and would not hesitate to attack a grenadier of the British guards who should presume to invade his farm yard with a red coat on" (*CA*, p. 313).

THE GREATEST AMERICAN

Finally, on September 17, 1787, the day the delegates signed the Constitution, James Madison reported that Franklin, the oldest member of the convention at the age of eighty-one, pointed to the president's chair. George Washington had used this chair for nearly three months. It had a half-sun painted on it. Franklin eloquently stated before all the representatives: "I have...often in the course of the session...looked at that...without being able to tell whether it was rising or setting. But now at length I have the happiness to know that it is a rising and not a setting sun" (*CA*, p. 368).

Today, Franklin's symbol of the rising sun can be found on the obverse (front) side of the American eagle silver dollar. Since 1985, when the Liberty Coin Act was passed and signed by President Ronald Reagan, over six hundred million of these silver dollars have been minted. I encourage all of you to buy one or more from a local or national coin dealer. Most collectors hide these beautiful coins in safe deposit boxes, but I recommend you give them as gifts for birthdays, graduations, anniversaries, and special rewards to employees, or anyone who does a special deed. I give an American silver dollar to each student who takes one of my classes at Chapman, as a way for them to remember my class. It includes the date they took my course. I tell them to keep it in their pockets or purses as a good luck piece, and to remember the importance of liberty and sound money.

CHAPTER 45

ON CELEBRATING THE 4TH OF JULY

"When I read in all the papers of the extravagant rejoicings every 4th of July, the day on which was signed the declaration of independence, thereby hazarding our lives and fortunes, I am convinced of the universal satisfaction of the people with the revolution and its grand principles."
—*Benjamin Franklin (1787)*

Benjamin Franklin and the other fifty-five founders were taking a great risk when they signed the Declaration of Independence in 1776. They didn't actually sign the document until a few months later, but July 4 was the day they dated the resolution and released it to the public. The Liberty Bell was rung on Monday, July 8, upon the first reading of the Declaration in Philadelphia. It was read on the same day before George Washington's troops arrived in New York to battle the British. The American Revolution was officially on!

At this time, John Adams wrote his wife Abigail, "It will be celebrated by succeeding generations as the great anniversary festival. It ought to be commemorated as the day of deliverance, by solemn acts of devotion to God Almighty. It ought to be solemnized with pomp and parade, with shows, games, sports, guns, bells, bonfires,

THE GREATEST AMERICAN

and illuminations, from one end of this continent to the other, from this time forward forever more."

How right he was. The following July 4, 1777, the American colonists celebrated the first anniversary of the Declaration of Independence, but it was not made an official holiday by Congress until 1870.

Franklin was the oldest founder to support the revolution and the Declaration of Independence. He was seventy years old. He was one of five members of the committee in charge of writing the Declaration. As far as we know, he made only one change to Thomas Jefferson's document. (See chapter 49, "Franklin's Single Change in the Declaration of Independence.")

In December 1775, he supported Thomas Paine's writing of the incendiary pamphlet *Common Sense*, and in July 1776, he had no qualms about pledging his life, fortune, and sacred honor to full independence. He firmly believed that "it is the natural right of men to quit, when they please, the society or the state, and the country in which they were born, and either join with another or form a new one as they may think proper" (*CA*, p. 120).

As early as 1771, while colonial agent in London, Franklin anticipated a separation of America and Britain. "I did not pretend the gift of prophecy, but I thought one could clearly see... the seeds sown of total disunion of the two countries" as a result of the Townshend Acts, which imposed heavy duties on American imports (*CA*, p. 65).

When the members of the Second Continental Congress gathered on August 2, 1776, to sign the Declaration, Franklin mused, "We must all hang together, or assuredly we shall all hang separately."

Indeed, many of the signers faced hardships and heavy losses during the Revolutionary War. Franklin himself paid a heavy price for his treasonous act. He largely gave up his pursuit of scientific discovery during the nine-year conflict; lost friendships in Britain

ON POLITICS

and Scotland, as well as in France with John Adams and the Lee brothers; lost much of his wealth; saw his papers at his home in Philadelphia destroyed by the British; and became bitter toward his son William (they never reconciled).

Yet he never doubted the new road America was taking. Two years into the revolution, while ambassador to France, he told a fellow commissioner, "The manner in which the whole of this business had been conducted was such a miracle in human affairs, that if I had not been in the midst of it, and seen all the movements, I could not have comprehended how it was effected. I had no doubt of our finally succeeding in this war by the blessing of God. This is the greatest revolution the world has ever seen" (*CA*, pp. 130, 132).

He knew America was making the right decision declaring its independence, and then, after winning the war, creating a new nation and a new constitution. "America will, with God's blessing, become a great and happy country" (*CA*, p. 301).

After the convention ended, as Franklin was leaving the Pennsylvania State House (now Independence Hall), Elizabeth Willing Powel, wife of the mayor and a prominent socialite, asked him, "Well, Doctor, what have we got, a republic or a monarchy?" He replied, "A republic, if you can keep it."

CHAPTER 46

ON THE UNITED STATES CONSTITUTION

"Thus I consent, Sir, to this Constitution because I expect no better, and because I am not sure that it is not the best."
—Ben Franklin (1787)

September 17 is Constitution Day in the United States, and schools across the country will be learning about the Constitution. Every September 17, members of Congress take turns and read the entire Constitution.

The United States has lived under the same government and Constitution now for nearly 240 years. The US Constitution, with its emphasis on checks and balances and on individual rights, has been imitated by over one hundred nations. While the Constitution increased the scope and role of the state compared to the Articles of Confederation, the aim of the Constitution was to limit the powers of government. As James Madison, the father of the Constitution, stated in Federalist Paper #45, "The powers delegated by the proposed Constitution to the federal government are few and defined.... If Congress can do whatever in their discretion can be done by money, and will promote the General Welfare, the Government is no longer a limited one, possessing enumerated powers, but an indefinite one."

Franklin, a member of the Pennsylvania delegation to the Constitutional Convention in the summer of 1787, was a firm believer in limiting the power of the state and minimizing the passions of avarice and ambition. He adopted the French phrase, "*Laissez nous faire*: Let us alone.... *Pas trop gouverner*: Not to govern too strictly" (*CA*, p. 300). He personally witnessed the excessive powers of the king and wished to severely limit his authority. "A virtuous and laborious people may be cheaply governed," he wrote. He disliked the idea of a single president running the country. "I am apprehensive...that the government of these states may in future times end in a monarchy, and a King will the sooner be set over us" (*CA*, p. 361).

He favored an efficient, democratically elected single legislature, the kind Pennsylvania had. He disliked a dual chamber of a House and a Senate, which he compared to a snake with two heads, the result being "lengthy disputes and delays and great expenses, and promote factions among the people and obstruct the public business." Limiting the Senate to two representatives might create an aristocracy, he said, "giving the rich a predominancy in government."

Franklin was not always consistent in his critique of the rich aristocracy running government. For example, he insisted that public officials be unpaid and thus independent of pecuniary interests, but that would have limited the legislature to wealthy citizens only. Fortunately, Congress ignored his views on this subject.

Nevertheless, being a businessman and diplomat, he understood the value of compromise. He worked behind the scenes to make it happen. At one point, he urged the convention to hire a clergyman to petition God to help the delegates come together in their disputes. His plea was ignored, however, for fear that the public would fret about a convention that required a minister to pray for them.

His diplomatic skills came in handy. During the debate over representation of the House and Senate, Franklin told the delegates, "A joiner, when he wants to fit two boards, takes off with his plane the uneven parts from each side, and thus they fit. Let us do the same." His views were incorporated into the Connecticut Compromise—letting the Senate be elected by the states and the House by population. "I have the happiness to report that a similar plan was eventually adopted," he wrote (*CA*, pp. 365–366).

"I CONSENT TO THIS CONSTITUTION BECAUSE THIS SYSTEM APPROACHES SO NEAR TO PERFECTION"

When it came time to sign the document, Franklin made a famous speech of reconciliation. He told the delegates, "It is a singular thing in the history of mankind that a great people have had the opportunity of forming a government for themselves. We are making experiment in politics. In these sentiments, I agree to this Constitution, with all its faults, if they are such.... When you assemble a number of men to have the advantage of their joint wisdom, you inevitably assemble with those men all their prejudices, their passions, their errors of opinion, their local interests, and their selfish views. From such an assembly can a perfect production be expected? It therefore astonishes me, Sir, to find this system approaching so near to perfection as it does" *CA*, p. 367).

"On the whole, Sir, I cannot help expressing a wish that every member of the convention who may still have objections to it would, with me, on this occasion doubt a little of his own infallibility, and, *to make manifest our unanimity* put his name to this instrument" (*CA*, p. 368).

As a result of Franklin's impassioned plea, thirty-nine members signed the document, among them George Washington, James Madison, and, of course, Benjamin Franklin.

CHAPTER 47

ON AMERICA: A RISING OR SETTING SUN?

"America will, with God's blessing, become a great and happy country."
—Ben Franklin (1783)

Today, many pundits are saying that the nineteenth century was dominated by the British empire and the twentieth century belonged to America, but the twenty-first century will be led by China. The economy of the United States is only growing at 2–3 percent a year, compared to 8–10 percent by China. According to these critics, the United States, encumbered by debt, an aging population, and stalled technology, is destined to decline into the sunset.

Would Franklin concur? Every Independence Day, I am reminded of the words of Benjamin Franklin, who was generally optimistic about the future of this great country and its government. Before the Philadelphia Constitution Society in 1785, he stated:

> I think myself happy in returning to live under the free constitution of this commonwealth, and

hope that we and our posterity may long enjoy it. The laws governing justice are well administered, and property is as secure as in any country on the globe. Our wilderness lands are daily being bought up by new settlers, and our settlements extend rapidly to the westward. When I read in all the papers of the extravagant rejoicings every 4th of July, the day on which was signed the declaration of independence, I am convinced of the universal satisfaction of the people with the revolution and its grand principles. Their unbound respect for all who were principally concerned in it, whether as warriors or statesmen, and the enthusiastic joy with which the day of the Declaration of Independence is everywhere annually celebrated are indisputable proofs of this truth (*CA*, p. 347).

At the end of the Constitutional Convention in September 1787, Franklin remarked, "Whilst the last members were signing the document, I looked toward the president's chair, at the back of which a sun happened to be painted, and observed to a few members near me, that I had often found it difficult to distinguish in their art a rising from a setting sun. I have, said I, often in the course of the session and in the vicissitudes of my hopes and fears over the issues, looked at that sun behind the president, without being able to tell whether it was rising or setting. But now at length I have the happiness to know that it is a rising and not a setting sun" (*CA*, p. 368).

What about the Fourth of July? What would Franklin think about America as we celebrate American independence?

No doubt the founding grandfather of our nation would be proud of the economic prowess and progress of the American economy over these many decades. But he and his fellow found-

ON POLITICS

ers would be shocked by the size and scope of government. For the federal government alone, the budget amounts to 25 percent of the economy (GDP); counting welfare transfers, government spending approaches more than 40 percent of GDP. As of 2024, the national debt exceeds $35 trillion, over $100,000 per citizen. See up to date figures at https://www.usdebtclock.org/.

Franklin was no doomsayer, but did express his concern about excessive government power in future generations. And he had no taste for fighting expensive foreign wars.

Fortunately, Franklin's worst fears have not been realized, and no doubt he would still see America as a "rising sun." But we must be eternally vigilant. Said Franklin, "Only a virtuous people are capable of freedom. As nations become corrupt and vicious, they have more need of masters. America is too enlightened to be enslaved" (*CA*, p. 369).

CHAPTER 48

ON WAR AND PEACE

"The system of America is universal commerce with every
nation; war with none."
—Benjamin Franklin (1778)

Given that the United States' past history involved many foreign conflicts, what was Franklin's attitude about war?

America won its freedom, but it was a bloody revolution that
cost fifty thousand lives and lasted nine years. It divided families,
destroyed friendships, and diminished the standard of living.

Similarly, Franklin was devoted to his son William. They had
done everything together, including traveling to England, and
clearly had a deep affection for each other. Franklin arranged for
his son to become the royal governor of New Jersey. But when the
war came, William insisted on remaining a loyalist. After suffering
through a long vicious war pursued by the British, which Franklin
carefully catalogued in his letters, journals, and even on proposed
coins and medallions, forgiveness was easier said than done. Franklin felt his bitterness was justified. In a letter, he lambasted his son
for "taking up arms against me in a cause where my good name,
fortune and life were all at stake." Perhaps the fact that William
refused to apologize for his fateful decision while insisting on a
"reconciliation" made it all the harder to forgive and forget.

ON POLITICS

The rift between father and son is one reason Franklin often said, "There never was a good war, or a bad peace." It destroyed forever a part of his being, his close relationship with his son. The war destroyed this familial bond, as well as his friendships with many other British and American confidants.

Another reason why Franklin detested war—all wars—is that it kept him from his first love: his scientific pursuits. He constantly complained in England and France how little time he had to correspond with fellow scientists and to pursue his own inventions. When the war was over, he immediately tried to pick up where he left off, working on several creative projects, such as the long arm to withdraw books from high up on a shelf. But he felt the war cut short his dreams of technological revolution, and his ability to discover and create new practical innovations. And so he spoke often of his wish to have been born in the next century or two.

Franklin wished that all wars would end after the revolution. His most famous statement, "There never was a good war, or a bad peace," suggests a certain distaste for battle, even when his side won. "When will men be convinced that even successful wars do at length become misfortunes to those who unjustly commenced them, and who triumphed blindly in their success, not seeing all its consequences. There is so little good gained, and so much mischief done generally by wars that I wish the imprudence of undertaking them was more evident to princes. For in my opinion there never was a good war, or a bad peace. What vast additions to the conveniences and comforts of living might mankind have acquired if the money spent in wars had been employed in works of public utility! What an extension of agriculture…what rivers rendered navigable…what bridges, aqueducts, new roads, and other public works, edifices and improvements, rendering England a complete paradise…millions were spent in the great war doing mischief… and destroying the lives of so many thousands of working people who might have performed useful labor!" (*CA*, p. 302).

THE GREATEST AMERICAN

Franklin preferred voluntary militias over standing armies as a prudent national or local defense against attackers. During the French and Indian War in the 1750s, Franklin was elected colonel in the Philadelphia militia, but declined to serve. Admitting to be the quintessential civilian, he had no taste for killing, no love of danger, and no desire to be a military hero. In fact, he loved liberty, reason, and gentle persuasion so much that he saw little need for military discipline, and instead suggested that good military leaders should lead by example, not by fear. "Alexander and Caesar received more faithful service, and performed greater actions by means of the love their solders bore them, than they could possibly have done, if instead of being beloved and respected they had been hated and feared by those they commanded," he wrote in his journal.[38]

Franklin even went so far in 1755 to undercut the rules of military law in the local militia by forbidding the military council to impose any fines or corporate penalties for disobeying the rules. He always opposed conscription or a draft on the grounds that cowards in arms do more harm than good. Needless to say, General George Washington did not agree on this issue and thought Franklin's military philosophy was naive. During the Revolutionary War, Washington complained about the limitations of a volunteer, democratic army and the trials associated with men who elected their own leaders and fought solely out of their patriotic duty and honor. He imposed severe punishment, even threatening execution at times, if soldiers failed to obey.

Franklin's views can be summed up in a sentence reminiscent of George Washington's farewell address, who in 1796 warned citizens, "The great rule of conduct for us, in regard to foreign nations, is, in extending our commercial relations, to have with them

---

38 Benjamin Franklin, "Journal of a Voyage," July 27, 1726. Quote in Pangle, *The Political Philosophy of Benjamin Franklin* (Baltimore: Johns Hopkins University Press), p. 116.

ON POLITICS

as little political connection as possible." Franklin said it better in 1778, nearly two decades earlier: "The system of America is universal commerce with every nation; war with none" (*CA*, p. 148).

CHAPTER 49

FRANKLIN'S SINGLE CHANGE IN THE DECLARATION OF INDEPENDENCE

Fill in the blank. Thomas Jefferson wrote the following in the Declaration of Independence: "We hold these truths to be

_____."

If you answered "self-evident," you are mistaken.

Jefferson actually wrote in the first draft, "We hold these truths to be sacred and undeniable."

In June 1776, Jefferson asked Franklin and several other members of the draft committee to peruse his first draft and suggest alterations. Franklin made only one significant change that we are aware of. With his left hand, he boldly struck out the words "sacred and undeniable" and replaced them with "self-evident."

We aren't sure why, but I surmise he made the change because "self-evidence" was a more scientific expression in the age of Enlightenment, a reflection of secular humanism so popular among Deists like Franklin—and Jefferson. Truths like "life, liberty and the pursuit of happiness" did not have to be proven. They were part of nature.

ON POLITICS

Jefferson approved of the change, and the published version came out with the famous lines, "We hold these truths to be self-evident, that all men are created equal, that they are endowed by their Creator with certain unalienable Rights, that among these are Life, Liberty and the pursuit of Happiness. That to secure these rights, Governments are instituted among Men, deriving their just powers from the consent of the governed, That whenever any Form of Government becomes destructive of these ends, it is the Right of the People to alter or to abolish it, and to institute new Government."

Franklin came to similar conclusions before 1776. He was a pragmatist who occasionally adhered to a natural rights doctrine. In 1775, he wrote, "It has always been my opinion that it is the natural right of men to quit, when they please, the society or state, and the country in which they were born, and either join with another or form a new one as they may think proper. The Saxons thought they had this right when they quitted Germany and established themselves in England" (*CA*, p. 120).

Many other changes and deletions were made to the Declaration by the full Continental Congress, such as the importation of slaves. Franklin was sitting next to Jefferson, saw how disturbed he was about the changes, and told him a story. "I told him that I had made it a rule, whenever in my power, to avoid becoming the draughtsman of papers to be reviewed by a public body. I took my lesson from an incident which I related to him. When I was a journeyman printer, one of my companions, an apprentice hatter, having served out his time, was about to open shop for himself. His first concern was to have a handsome signboard, with a proper inscription. He composed it in these words, 'John Thompson, Hatter, makes and sells hats for ready money,' with a figure of a hat subjoined; but he thought he would submit it to his friends for their amendments. The first he showed it to thought the word 'Hatter' tautologous, because followed by the words 'makes hats,'

THE GREATEST AMERICAN

which show he was a hatter. It was struck out. The next observed that the word 'makes' might as well be omitted, because his customers would not care who made the hats. If good and to their mind, they would buy, by whomsoever made. He struck it out. A third said he thought the words 'for ready money' were useless, as it was not the custom of the place to sell on credit. Everyone who purchased expected to pay. They were parted with, and the inscription now stood, 'John Thompson sells hats.' 'Sells hats!' says his next friend. Why nobody will expect you to give them away, what then is the use of that word? It was stricken out, and 'hats' followed it, the rather as there was one painted on the board. So the inscription was reduced ultimately to 'John Thompson' with the figure of a hat subjoined" (*CA*, pp. 121–122).

After the revolution, Franklin altered his religious views and shifted from being a Deist to becoming an active Theist. He told the members of the Constitutional Convention that he believed God intervened in the revolution to assure the American victory: "The manner in which the whole of this business had been conducted was such a miracle in human affairs, that if I had not been in the midst of it, and seen all the movements, I could not have comprehended how it was effected. I had no doubt of our finally succeeding in this war by the blessing of God. This is the greatest revolution the world has ever seen" (*CA*, p. 130).

He went on to say: "I have lived a long time; and the longer I live, the more convincing proofs I see of this truth, that God governs in the affairs of men! If it had not been for the justice of our cause, and the consequent interposition of Providence in which we had faith, we must have been ruined. If I had ever before been an atheist, I should now have been convinced of the being and government of a Deity. It is He who abases the proud and favors the humble! May we never forget his goodness to us, and may our future conduct manifest our gratitude" (*CA*, p. 365).

ON POLITICS

Given the change in his religious philosophy, I suspect that if he had it to do over again, Franklin would have kept Jefferson's more eloquent language in the first draft of the Declaration: "We hold these truths to be sacred and undeniable..."

PART VI

ON INTERNATIONAL RELATIONS AND TRAVEL

CHAPTER 50

ON BEING AN INTERNATIONAL MAN

"Why, Sir, you find no man, at all intellectual, who is willing to leave London. No, Sir, when a man is tired of London, he is tired of life; for there is in London all that life can afford."
—Samuel Johnson (1777)

Ben Franklin was above all the international man. More than any other founder, he spent a great deal of time traveling around the country and overseas, and corresponded with people from many foreign lands.

When he arrived in London as colonial agent for the Pennsylvania commonwealth, one of the first anonymous letters he wrote for a British newspaper was signed, "A Traveller."

But Franklin was exceptional in this regard. Most Americans did not travel. Franklin's wife Deborah never set foot outside of Pennsylvania (much to his regret). In the eighteenth century, the social and political order was strict, and most people stayed in one place all their lives. They never ventured into another colony, let alone a foreign country. As French historian Bernard Faÿ wrote, "The thousands of tiny civilizations which made up the universe of the eighteenth century existed side by side, isolated the one from

THE GREATEST AMERICAN

the other by differences in language and the difficulties of communication. They differed extremely; language, customs, polite manners, the style of wigs and coat tails—all these changed every thirty miles."[39]

There were few travelers, and not all were upstanding citizens. "There were few routes, few conveyances, few good boats, but many cutthroats, bad roads and real pirates," according to Faÿ.

But for the exceptional traveler who could escape such misfortunes, the change in venue and people was a delight, and a great learning experience. For curiosity seekers like Franklin, it was an adventure he always looked forward to, "drunk with the joy of being free and seeing the world," as Faÿ described it.

Franklin's first experience traveling was as a runaway. He left Boston at the age of seventeen to become a printer in Philadelphia. But he was never a hobo or "PT" (permanent traveler) like today. He moved around a lot, but always with a purpose in mind—to get a job, become educated, or to meet with authorities.

"Travelers tell fine tales" is a proverb of the eighteenth century, and Franklin lived up to the reputation. He wrote eloquently about his first voyage to England in 1724 at the age of eighteen in his *Autobiography*, and his efforts to succeed as a printer. When he returned in 1757 as colonial agent, he told the account of being shipwrecked: "When my son William and I arrived in England by ship in 1757, we narrowly escaped running ashore on the rocks.... The bell ringing for church, we went thither immediately, and with hearts full of gratitude, returned sincerely thanks to God for the mercies we had received: were I Roman Catholic, perhaps I should have vowed to build a chapel; but as I am not, I should build a lighthouse" (*CA*, p. 5).

During his years in London and Paris, he ventured into the countryside, and developed lifelong friendships in Scotland, France, Germany, and Italy. He wanted to visit the Middle East

---

39 Bernard *Faÿ*, *Franklin: Apostle of Modern Times* (New York: Little, Brown, and Company, 1929), p. 66.

ON INTERNATIONAL RELATIONS AND TRAVEL

and Asia, but circumstances discouraged him. He made up for it with correspondence. He was sent a Chinese gong from a correspondent in China.

Work often kept him from his travels, which he regretted. "Sometimes after long confinement at writing, with little exercise, I felt sudden pungent pains in the flesh of different parts of the body. A journey used to free me of them. I continued in health, notwithstanding the omission of my yearly journeys, which I was never able to take while in France, being confined necessarily by business" (*CA*, pp. 176–177).

Let that be a warning to all of you. In today's world, it much cheaper to travel. But many fail to do it because of work. I encourage you to plan on traveling regularly. It will be good for your health and spirits, as Franklin counseled.

When he didn't travel, Franklin was always corresponding. In addition to official correspondence to American and foreign officials, he wrote letters to several thousand individuals during his lifetime on business, political, scientific, and personal affairs. Most of these private letters have been lost, and those which have been preserved over the years have been published in *The Papers of Benjamin Franklin* by Yale University Press. These letters are open to the public and can be read at your leisure at https://franklinpapers.org/. These papers served as a basis of my completing Franklin's memoirs, published by Regnery in 2006 as *The Compleated Autobiography of Benjamin Franklin*.

CHAPTER 51

ON TRAVELING ABROAD AND VACATIONS

"I depend chiefly on journeys into the country for the establishment of my health and spirits."
—*Ben Franklin (1758)*

No matter where Franklin lived throughout his eighty-four years, he loved to travel. He was constantly on the road, or boarding a ship to travel abroad. He traversed the Atlantic Ocean eight times, more than any other founding father. By contrast, George Washington never did go to Europe, although he received an invitation from Franklin to do so.

Why did Franklin travel so much? It was a much-needed diversion from a grueling schedule of meetings and decision-making as a businessman, agent, and diplomat. During the debates over the Stamp Act in 1765–66, Franklin confessed that he was so "extremely busy, attending members of both Houses, informing, explaining, consulting, disputing, in a continual hurry from morning to night till the affair was happily ended" that it caused him to become ill. "I had been used to making a journey once a year," he said, for his "health and spirits." He finally got away and journeyed

ON INTERNATIONAL RELATIONS AND TRAVEL

to Germany with the queen's physician, Sir John Pringle, "where we drank the waters some days." He concluded, "As I was soon well, my hearty journey had perfectly answered its intention" (*CA*, pp. 45–46).

In his youth, Franklin was inclined "toward the sea," and wished to follow in the footsteps of his older brother Josiah, who became a seaman. "Living near the water, I was much in and about it, learnt early to swim well, and to manage boats; and when in a boat or canoe with other boys, I was commonly allowed to govern, especially in any case of difficulty."

However, his father declared against it, and eventually young Benjamin turned to apprenticing to become a printer. But he always had a wanderlust for travel. At the youthful age of seventeen, he quit his brother's printing business and traveled by sloop down to New York and over to Philadelphia. From there, as a successful printer and then as a postmaster, he visited a number of the original thirteen colonies.

As he became involved in public affairs, he traveled to the colonies of New York and Massachusetts and presented his Albany Plan of Union.

He changed locations more frequently when he became a colonial agent in 1757 and journeyed overseas to London. He had first taken a ship to England in 1724 at the tender age of eighteen, but only stayed for two years.

He hoped to take his wife Debby with him to London, but she refused. She had an "invincible aversion to crossing the seas." A homebody, she never did accompany her husband to either England or France, and they became estranged as husband and wife.

Franklin stayed in England for five years, 1757–62, and then again 1764–1775, at which time he served as colonial agent for Pennsylvania, Massachusetts, and New York. Based in London, he began his regular habit of traveling into the countryside of England and Scotland when Parliament was out of session. "I found

THE GREATEST AMERICAN

the journey advantageous to both my health and spirits," he wrote. He took his son William with him, and they visited their ancestral home and became acquainted with individuals of science and politics.

He became especially enamored with Scotland. After a tour to the Scottish Highlands, he wrote a friend, "On the whole, I must say, I think the time we spent there, was six weeks of the densest happiness I have met with in any part of my life" (*CA*, pp. 16).

After declaring independence, the United States sent Dr. Franklin to France to serve as America's first ambassador. He was seventy years old when he arrived in Paris in December 1776. Unfortunately, he was so busy he was not able to take his annual vacation tour while serving as ambassador.

In his pamphlet "The Way to Wealth," Franklin once admonished, "Methinks I hear some of you say, must a man afford himself no leisure? I will tell thee, my friend, what Poor Richard says, employ thy time well if thou meanest to gain leisure." Amen!

CHAPTER 52

ON THE CHINESE

*"The Chinese are the most ancient, and from
long experience, the wisest of nations."*
—Benjamin Franklin, in a letter to his daughter (1784)

In his last will and testament, Benjamin Franklin listed among his prized possessions a Chinese gong, which he bequeathed to his grandson, William Temple Franklin.

We don't know how he acquired the Chinese gong, but it is an appropriate symbol, for traditionally gongs were used not only as percussion instruments but also to make a sound to clear the way for important officials and processions.

Among his many talents, Franklin was a musician and was fond of singing, dancing, and enjoying a lively social life in America and Europe. He invented the glass armonica, which he often played in conjunction with other musical instruments. At Franklin's home in Philadelphia, a list included "a Welch harp, bell harp, a set of tuned bells in a box, Viol de Gambo, all the spare Armonica Glasses and one or two of the spare cases."

Perhaps he added the Chinese gong to his musical list while ambassador to France. An inventory of Franklin's instruments in his estate includes a viola da gamba, bells, harpsichord, glass armonica, spinet, and a Chinese gong. At the home of Madame Helvévtius, Abbé Morellet would sing one of Franklin's favorite

THE GREATEST AMERICAN

Scottish ballads while Madame Brillon would play the pianoforte and Franklin the armonica. The abbé toasted him: "*Le verre en main / Chantons nôtre Benjamin*" ("With glass in hand / Sing to our Franklin").

Franklin's favorite Chinese philosopher was Confucius (551–479 BC), the most influential teacher of ancient China. Franklin first introduced Confucius to the American colonies when, in 1737, he ran a series of articles with excerpts from *The Morals of Confucius* in his weekly magazine *The Pennsylvania Gazette*. Franklin called the Chinese master's philosophy "the gate through which it is necessary to pass to arrive at the sublimest wisdom."

David Wang (St. John's University) claims that Franklin probably acquired a copy of *The Morals of Confucius* on his first trip to London 1824–25. Professor Wang makes the bold claim that Confucius was his moral exemplar and that eleven out of his thirteen virtues from his *Autobiography* were inspired by *The Morals of Confucius*. According to Wang, Franklin "consistently and systematically promoted the main principles of the Confucian moral philosophy" in his adult life.

Is this wishful thinking or a breakthrough about the source of Franklin's personal philosophy?

There are some of Franklin's virtues that are closely linked with Confucian philosophy. Here's what Confucius said regarding:

— Silence (virtue #2): "Silence is absolutely necessary to the wise man."

— Frugality (virtue #5): "He that seeks pride in his habits and loves not frugality is not disposed for the study of wisdom."

— Justice (virtue #8): "The first regards the justice that ought to be practiced between a king and his subjects."

— Moderation (virtue #9): "If we abandon ourselves to immoderate joy, or to an excessive sorrow..."

ON INTERNATIONAL RELATIONS AND TRAVEL

— Chastity (virtue #12): "The third recommends conjugal fidelity to husbands and wives."

Franklin is clearly attracted to the Stoic philosophy of meditation, calm, reason, silence, and avoidance of the extremes of anger, fear, and the emotions of mobs. But was this taken from Confucius, or from the Jewish King Solomon or the Roman stoic Marcus Aurelius?

In his *Autobiography*, Franklin wrote that he started his road to "moral perfection" and wrote down the list of thirteen virtues in the early 1730s, long before he published extracts from *The Morals of Confucius*. He cites the Roman Cato, Solomon's proverbs, and St. Paul and James of the New Testament, but nothing from Confucius. For his thirteenth virtue, humility, he cites only two mentors: "Imitate Jesus and Socrates."

According to Confucius, rulers and ministers had a special obligation to live a strict moral code and to teach it to their followers. Franklin approved of this approach. In a 1749 letter, he commended Rev. George Whitefield for preaching to high-ranking officials in government. "If you can gain them to a good and exemplary life, wonderful changes will follow in the manners of the lower ranks." He then cited Confucius on this principle. "When he saw his country sunk in vice, and wickedness of all kinds triumphant, he applied himself first to the grandees; and having by his doctrine won them to the cause of virtue, the commons followed in multitudes."

Finally, in 1784, he referred to a Chinese tradition in his opposition to the Society of the Cincinnati. If you read chapter 59 on George Washington, you will see that Franklin disagreed with the policy of honoring descendants of officers and veteran soldiers. Instead, he recommended that the Society of the Cincinnati adopt the Chinese tradition and "direct the badges of their order to be worn by their parents instead of handing them down to their children." He praised the Chinese for respecting their elders, while

THE GREATEST AMERICAN

criticizing the Europeans for promoting noblesse oblige among their heirs, causing an "odious mixture of pride and idleness." He would no doubt find this statement in *The Importance of Living* by the great Chinese philosopher Lin Yutang most agreeable:

> In China, the first question a person asks the other on an official call, after asking about his name and surname is, "What is your glorious age?"... Enthusiasm grows in proportion as the gentleman is able to report a higher and higher age, and if the person is anywhere over fifty, the inquirer immediately drops his voice in humility and respect.... People in middle age actually look forward to the time when they can celebrate their fifty-first birthday.... The fifty-first birthday, or the half-century mark, is an occasion of rejoicing for people of all classes. The sixty-first is a happier and grander occasion than the fifty-first and the seventy-first is still happier and grander, while a man able to celebrate his eighty-first birthday is actually looked upon as one specially favored by heaven.[40]

Franklin lived to the glorious age of eighty-four!

---

40 Lin Yutang, *The Importance of Living* (New York: John Day Company, in association with Reynal and Hitchcock, 1937), pp. 192–201.

PART VII

ON PERSONALITIES

CHAPTER 53

ON FAME AND VANITY

*"Pride breakfasted with plenty, dined with poverty,
and supped with infamy. And after all, of what use is this
pride of appearance, for which so much is risked, so much
is suffered? It cannot promote health; or ease pain; it
makes no increase of merit in the person, it creates
envy, it hastens misfortune."*
—*"The Way to Wealth," Poor Richard's Almanac (1758)*

*"Celebrity may for a while flatter one's vanity,
but its effects are troublesome."*
—*Ben Franklin*

Ben Franklin's *Autobiography*, the most famous memoir ever written since St. Augustine's *Confessions*, is known for the founder's list of thirteen virtues. What's interesting is that most of the platitudes are self-centered: silence, resolution, frugality, industry, sincerity, moderation, temperance, order, cleanliness, chastity, and tranquility.

What did he leave off the list? Franklin ignores some of the more essential Christian virtues dealing with others like forgiveness, gratitude, and charity.

Always the diplomat, when he wrote his memoirs he knew that his "plan of life" would be made public. In fact, his reputation

THE GREATEST AMERICAN

did not fit the list. He was famous for his silence, industry, and thrift, but not for orderliness, temperance, or chastity. His critics made their own list of Franklin peccadilloes: cunning, secretive, opportunist, hedonist, and above all, vain.

What about pride? In the beginning of his *Autobiography*, he took note of it, admitting that writing his own story "shall a good deal gratify my own vanity." He goes on to confirm, "I give it fair quarter whenever I meet with it, being persuaded that it is often productive of good to the possessor, and to others that are within his sphere of action; and therefore, in many cases, it would not be altogether absurd if a man were to thank God for his vanity among the other comforts of life" (*A*, p. 2).

When he showed this list of virtues around to friends, it did not yet contain the final ethic of "humility." A Quaker friend kindly informed him that he was generally thought to be proud, overbearing, and insolent in conversation. Franklin responded, "I determined endeavoring to cure myself, if I could, of this vice or folly among the rest, and I added humility to my list." He added number thirteen to the list: "Humility: Imitate Jesus and Socrates" (*A*, p. 109).

To work on his humility, he made an effort to be less dogmatic and willing to accommodate the views of others. "I even forbid myself, agreeably to the old laws of our Junto, the use of every word or expression in the language that imported a fixed opinion, such as certainly, undoubtedly, etc., and I adopted, instead of them, I conceive, I apprehend, or I imagine a thing to be so or so; or it so appears to me at present." In disagreeing with others, "I denied myself the pleasure of contradicting him abruptly, and of showing immediately some absurdity in his proposition" (*A*, p. 110).

As a result, his conversations "went on more pleasantly," and his opinions enjoyed a "readier reception and less contradiction." He claimed that for the last fifty years of his life "no one has

ON PERSONALITIES

ever heard a dogmatical expression escape me." Franklin became famous as the great compromiser in Congress, and consequently "I generally carried my points" (*A*, p. 110).

Yet, ultimately, he admitted too that he "cannot boast of much success in acquiring the reality of this virtue [humility]." He went add to write in the *Autobiography*, "In reality, there is, perhaps, no one of our natural passions so hard to subdue as *pride*. Disguise it, struggle with it, beat it down, stifle it, mortify it as much as one pleases, it is still alive, and will every now and then peep out and show itself; you will see it, perhaps, often in this history; for, even if I could conceive that I had completely overcome it, I should probably be proud of my humility" (*A*, pp. 110–111).

Indeed, fellow founder John Adams thought that Franklin suffered from an overweening ego and would take too much credit for establishing a new nation. After Franklin died in 1790, Adams wrote Benjamin Rush a letter in which he described his worst nightmare: "The history of our revolution will be one continued lie from one end to the other. The essence of the whole will be that Dr. Franklin's electric rod smote the earth and out sprang General Washington. Then Franklin electrified him, and thence forward those two conducted the policy, negotiations, legislations, and war."

John Adams's nightmare may have come true. In 2005, a survey was taken of the one hundred most popular Americans, and George Washington and Ben Franklin were ranked the two most influential founders (in the top five). John Adams didn't even make the list. Of course, it helps that Franklin's image is on the one hundred dollar bill, which recently surpassed the one dollar bill as the most commonly printed currency. No doubt it would please his vanity to know he is worth one hundred times more than a George Washington!

Before the American Revolution, Benjamin Franklin was the most famous American. Not for his *Autobiography*, which was not

THE GREATEST AMERICAN

published until years after his death, but for his scientific discoveries. His experiments in electricity, which he published in the 1750s, made him the first scientific American—and a household name among European elite.

"Famous, fascinating Benjamin Franklin—he would be neither without his accomplishments in science," states Harvard historian Joyce Chaplin. "Franklin's achievements as a natural philosopher played a central role in his meteoric rise in politics."[41]

For his scientific accomplishments, he was the first American to be awarded the coveted gold Copley Medal in 1753 and become a member of the distinguished Royal Society in 1756. He received several honorary degrees from Harvard College, Yale College, and the College of William & Mary. After receiving a doctorate degree from St. Andrews, he insisted on being called Dr. Franklin.

He acquired a certain degree of pride in developing his social connections with business colleagues (via his Junto and post office appointment), politicians (by running for office or being appointed to a political position), and the general public (by publishing his newspaper, *The Pennsylvania Gazette*, and various pamphlets). Critics labeled him an opportunist. In any case, his self-promotion paid off, so that by the age of fifty, he was the most well-known figure in Pennsylvania. By 1757, he was made colonial agent to London and embarked on a career as an international diplomat.

By time he reached Paris to be America's first ambassador, he commented that he might have too much of a good thing: "Medallions, pictures, busts, and prints made my face as well known as that of the moon in France," he wrote to a friend. "I had sat so much and so often for painters and statuaries that I grew perfectly sick of it. Celebrity may for a while flatter one's vanity, but its effects are troublesome. Besides being harassed with too much business, I was exposed to numberless visits, some of kindness and civility, but many of mere idle curiosity, from strangers of America

---

41   Joyce Chaplin, *The First Scientific American* (New York, Basic Books, 2007), preface.

ON PERSONALITIES

and of different parts of Europe, as well as the inhabitants of the provinces who came to Paris. These devoured my hours, and broke my attention, and at night I often found myself fatigued without having done anything" (*CA*, pp. 159–160).

The issue of vanity came up again in a famous letter to Franklin by his longtime femme fatale Madame Brillon in Paris. In a letter dated March 7, 1778, she graded her wise diplomatic friend on the seven deadly sins. Regarding pride, she wrote, "When a sage has always done good, solely for the love of goodness and the happiness of his fellowmen, and then if there happens to be glory at the outcome of this conduct, it is not its motivation; hence you are not proud" (*CA*, p. 165).

When Franklin returned to America after the revolution, he hurt his pride not a little when Congress failed to "make some liberal provision for ministers when they return home from foreign services"—to grant him a payment or even a track of land—as they did for Arthur Lee or John Jay. "But how different was what happened to me!" (*CA*, p. 372). Franklin was never reimbursed for his services or his opportunities lost in private affairs while ambassador.

CHAPTER 54

HAVE YOU READ FRANKLIN'S MASTERPIECE?

"Benjamin Franklin, tactless in his youth, became so diplomatic, so adroit at handling people, that he was made American Ambassador to France. The secret of his success? 'I will speak ill of no man,' he said, '...and speak all the good I know of everybody.'"
—*Dale Carnegie*

In 2006, in celebration of Benjamin Franklin's three hundredth birthday, the US Postal Service issued four commemorative stamps representing his four major accomplishments in life: printer, scientist, diplomat, and revolutionary. But the fact remains that if it weren't for the publication of his *Autobiography*, Franklin would not be considered America's most influential founding father.

Ever since his memoirs were published in the English in the early nineteenth century, Franklin's reputation as the founding father of American capitalism has gradually increased.

For over a hundred years, Franklin's *Autobiography* was required reading in school. Today, when I ask people if they have

ON PERSONALITIES

read it, only about 10 percent respond "yes." But for anyone who went to school in the 1920s or earlier, every hand would go up.

What is the book all about, and why has it engendered so much influence?

It's essentially the life of a self-made businessman and entrepreneur, the original rags-to-riches Horatio Alger story. The youthful Ben arrives in Philadelphia penniless and through "industry, thrift and prudence" achieves financial independence. By the age of forty-two, he is able to retire from his printing business and devote the remainder of his life to benefiting mankind with his inventions and civil affairs. He highlights thirteen virtues that anyone can adopt in their profession, so that no matter what their background, they can achieve success in life. Franklin embodies the belief that anyone can make it in America, the land of the free.

In his classic work, *The Protestant Ethic and the Spirit of Capitalism*, the great sociologist Max Weber uses Franklin as the supreme example of an individual who adopted the Calvinist virtues of honest work, punctuality, and frugality to achieve financial success.

These virtues were ideally suited to young entrepreneurs seeking their fortune in America. Steel magnate Andrew Carnegie and Pittsburgh banker Andrew Mellon credited the *Autobiography* with their achievements in business and charitable work. Franklin encouraged successful business leaders to devote their money and time to good public causes. Today's leaders in commerce, such as Bill Gates and Warren Buffett, are big fans of Franklin.

The book also had its impact in foreign countries, where it has been translated into over a dozen languages. The *Autobiography* was originally published in French in the late eighteenth century, and one of his first readers was Jean-Baptiste Say, the well-known French economist. Under Franklin's influence, Say popularized the word "entrepreneur" to describe the risk-taking, enterprising capitalist and developed Say's law, "Supply creates its own demand,"

THE GREATEST AMERICAN

suggesting that entrepreneurs and capitalists were the catalysts for economic growth.

The *Autobiography* has also been popular in China, where the Confucian principles of work and thrift have been well established.

If you haven't read it, or haven't read it since childhood, I encourage you to buy a copy of the *Autobiography* and read it (or listen to it on audiobook). There are over a dozen editions currently available online or in bookstores. In 2006, Regnery published my own version with a new introduction.

There is also a new translation into modern English by Blaine McCormick, a professor of business at Baylor University, entitled *Ben Franklin: America's Original Entrepreneur* (Entrepreneur Press, 2008). I recommend this version, especially if you or your children have trouble with Franklin's sometime archaic language.

Finally, I should note that Franklin's *Autobiography* was never finished. It covers the first fifty-one years of his long eighty-four-year history. He wrote it at various times as an elderly man when he was a London agent and ambassador to France, but his history only covers up to the year 1757, just when he was launching his career as a colonial agent in London. The *Autobiography* is silent on what Franklin did or thought about the American Revolution, his nine-year role as America's first ambassador, and the creation of a new nation.

Before he died, he asked his grandson Temple to complete his memoirs, but Temple never did.

Some two hundred years later, I am happy to announce that his *Autobiography* has been completed. In 2005, my wife and I started researching and compiling his autobiographical writings culled from *The Papers of Benjamin Franklin* published by Yale University Press, and in 2006, Regnery published *The Compleated Autobiography by Benjamin Franklin*.

It covers 1757–1790, the final thirty-three years of Franklin's life, all in his own words. In it, you'll discover what Frank-

ON PERSONALITIES

lin thought about the American Revolution, his fascinating life as America's first ambassador to France, his attitude toward John Adams, Thomas Jefferson, George Washington and the other founders, and his critical role at the Constitutional Convention. In compiling and editing his final thirty-three years, I discovered a number of great new quotes from Franklin, such as: "A virtuous and industrious people may be cheaply governed," and "The system of America is universal commerce with every nation; war with none." Words to live by!

CHAPTER 55

SEVEN DISCOVERIES IN COMPLETING FRANKLIN'S AUTOBIOGRAPHY

As many of you know, I am a direct descendant of Dr. Franklin, and always wondered if it were possible to complete Franklin's final thirty-three years that were missing from his *Autobiography*. Drawing upon numerous letters, journal entries, and essays collected and published in *The Papers of Benjamin Franklin* by Yale University Press, my wife and I were able to recreate Franklin's account of his life in *his own words*. *The Completed Autobiography by Benjamin Franklin* was published by Regnery in 2006, in honor of the three hundredth anniversary of Franklin's birth. Ol' Grandpa Ben's wish has been fulfilled.

The *Compleated Autobiography* reveals a very private Franklin, with colorful new insights into the man as diplomat, scientist, inventor, financier, philosopher, economist, and family man.

Here are seven new things I learned about Franklin in completing his story:

1. **The indispensable Franklin:** Washington won the American war at home, but Franklin won it abroad.

ON PERSONALITIES

Without Franklin's brilliant diplomacy, the French would never have provided the military and financial aid—over one billion dollars in today's money!—essential to achieving American independence from the British. Most historians agree that without French assistance, Washington's army could not have succeeded. (Over half the troops and ships were French at the crucial battle of Yorktown in 1781.) Franklin was the only one of five commissioners that the French adored. John Adams, for example, detested the French, and the French returned the favor. He was also instrumental in establishing America's early laws, from the Articles of Confederation to the US Constitution, both of which he helped write. Franklin deserves to be "co-father" of our nation.

Franklin's fundraising was so successful that France went bankrupt a few years later, leading to the French Revolution. He saw only the first year of the French Revolution, which caused him much pain. His economic plan to pay for the war was to create a "sinking fund" through taxation to pay off the war debts. Alexander Hamilton followed Franklin's plan and America prospered. France did not and the French Revolution self-destructed.

In sum, Franklin was responsible for two revolutions, the American Revolution of 1776 and the French Revolution of 1789.

2. **He had a gift for prophecy:** He was the first founder to recognize the inevitability of American independence. In 1771, five years before the Declaration of Independence, Franklin declared that "the seeds are sown of total disunion" from Britain (*CA*, p. 65). During the American Revolution, Franklin never doubted that the Americans would win. And after the war, he prophesized that "America will, with God's blessing, become a great and happy country" (*CA*, p. 301).

THE GREATEST AMERICAN

3. **The first financial guru:** Franklin suffered numerous personal and financial setbacks. Most people know of his rags-to-riches story in the *Autobiography*. But in the *Compleated Autobiography*, we learn that Franklin was seriously threatened on many occasions by (a) life threatening illnesses, (b) death or imprisonment by British officers, privateers, and spies, and (c), major financial setbacks. In 1774, the British fired Franklin as postmaster and colonial agent, cutting off his entire earning power (£1,800 a year). Fortunately, he had practiced what he preached, and he had over the years garnered considerable assets through frugality and economy—in stocks, bonds, bank accounts, and rental properties. Thus, his fortune was never in jeopardy, because of the financial techniques he mastered as a printer and retiree. "No revenue is sufficient without economy" (*CA*, p. 336). He died in 1790 at the age of eighty-four, a very rich man.

4. **Franklin became disenchanted with war, even after winning:** He repeatedly told his friends, "There is so little good gained, and so much mischief done generally by war.... There never was a good war, or a bad peace" (*CA*, p. 302). Why? First, it forever destroyed his close relationship with his son, William, and his friendship with British and American colleagues (including John Adams). Second, it cut short his dreams of technological and scientific revolution. The war essentially ended Franklin's pursuit of practical inventions, for which he was famous (Franklin stove, lightning rod, bifocals, and more.).

5. **Franklin became a devotee of Adam Smith's model of limited government:** After his bad experiences in pursuing favors from the British and American governments for his son and grandsons, he concluded that any private profession was preferable to public service. He explicitly

ON PERSONALITIES

endorsed Adam Smith's model of free trade ("no nation was ever ruined by trade"), open immigration (which "does not diminish but multiplies a nation"), and limited government ("not to govern too strictly"). In general, he said, "A virtuous and industrious people may be cheaply governed" (*CA*, p. 189). He favored economy in private and public affairs, and loathed excessive debt. But, like Adam Smith, he was no anarchist. Franklin supported an elastic currency ("as commerce requires"), free education for youth, and universal and fair tax policy to pay the "dues" for the "general welfare" (public goods).

6. **Franklin and women:** *The Compleated Autobiography* proves that Franklin was romantically active into his seventies and sought female companionship, including the temptation of a married woman and a proposal of marriage to another. Women found Franklin mesmerizing. Franklin confessed, "One must do mad things when one loves madly" (*CA*, p. 162).

7. **Franklin's personality change:** In many ways, Franklin underwent a personality change in the final years of his life. He went from a slaveholder to an abolitionist. As ambassador to Paris, he gave up on the "early to bed, early to rise" routine and became a late-night bon vivant, and upon returning to Philadelphia, he abandoned his famous "time management" and "spent the time idly" playing cards with his friends and family. In religion, he went from a religious freethinker to an active believer that "God governs in the affairs of men" as a result of the American Revolution, which he considered a "miracle in human affairs." But his religion was always a practical one: "good works" rather than "sermon-hearing." He wanted his final epitaph to read, "He lived usefully," rather than "He died rich" (*CA*, p. 392).

CHAPTER 56

ON MAKING ENEMIES

"Love your enemies, for they tell you your faults."
—*Poor Richard's Almanac*

If you read Franklin's famous *Autobiography*, you might come away with the feeling that Franklin never had an enemy to his name. He wanted you to think he was an early student of Dale Carnegie knowing "how to win friends and influence people." He worked hard to develop friendships and turn enemies into friends. After all, was he not America's first diplomat, beloved by the French people? He loved to fraternize. He organized his own association of tradesmen, the Junto, and joined many clubs when he was a colonial agent in London. If he had had a Rolodex, it would have contained thousands of names. "I find I love company, chat, a laugh, a glass, and even a song," he said, "and relish...the grave observations and wise sentences of old men's conversations" (*CA*, p. 18). And women's too!

Yet Franklin as a political animal had his share of hostile relationships, despite his diplomatic skills. His political adversaries included both Americans (the Penns, John Adams, and Arthur Lee) and British lords.

He even suffered a bitter fallout with his son, William, who sided with the British when the American Revolution began in 1776, and they never fully reconciled.

ON PERSONALITIES

When he traveled to London as colonial agent, he felt that Pennsylvanians like himself were "deceived, cheated and betrayed" by the Penns, the proprietors who insisted they were exempt from taxation. Franklin encountered more foes over the Stamp Act, both in America, when a mob threatened to destroy his home in Philadelphia when he initially went along with the act, and in England, when he finally opposed it. After the Thomas Hutchinson letters affair in 1773, Franklin was vilified in the "Cockpit" by the British Parliament and was fired as postmaster and colonial agent. He returned to America as a fully committed patriot and revolutionary in early 1775.

It was at this time that he wrote, "Enemies do man more good than harm. They point out to us our faults; they put us upon our guard; and help us to live more correctly. The best men have always had their share of envy and malice of the foolish and wicked, and a man has therefore some reason to be ashamed of himself when he meets with none of it. My good friend Rev. Whitefield once said, When I am on the road and see boys in a field pelting a tree, though I am too far off to know what tree it is, I conclude it has fruit on it" (*CA*, pp. 286–287).

In 1775, after the battle of Lexington and Concord, Franklin wrote (but did not send) the following famous letter to the British publisher William Strahan (*CA*, p. 109):

Philada. July 5, 1775
Mr. Strahan,

You are a member of Parliament, and one of that majority which has doomed my country to destruction. You have begun to burn our towns, and murder our people. Look upon your hands! They are stained with the blood of your relations!

THE GREATEST AMERICAN

You and I were long friends: You are now my enemy, and

I am,
Yours,
B. Franklin

Franklin and John Adams were friends when they signed the Declaration of Independence, but when Franklin became ambassador to France, they became adversaries. Adams (and Arthur Lee and the other commissioners) complained that Franklin was too old and disorganized and held a bias in favor of the French at the expense of American interests. Yet it turned out that Franklin was the only commissioner who loved the French people, and was able to raise monies, arms, and uniforms for the American cause.

One reason Franklin hated war so much was because it estranged his love of family as well as friendship with his fellow scientists. He and his son William became bitter opponents during the war, William remaining a loyalist as governor of New Jersey. "He saw everything with government eyes," his father commented. Their affection for each other never returned after the war, and the father disinherited the son. He wrote, "This is a disagreeable subject. I drop it" (*CA*, p. 125).

When Franklin died in early 1790 at the venerable age of eighty-four, twenty thousand people showed up at his funeral in his hometown of Philadelphia to honor the man who had almost single-handedly financed the revolution abroad and signed both the Declaration of Independence and the United States Constitution. And yet the Senate, in the hands of the Adamses and the Lees, refused to eulogize him for a year. It was only a generation later, after the publication of the *Autobiography*, that Franklin became a universal popular hero in America.

Historian Robert Middlekauff summarized it best: "This man of extraordinary talent of a range unsurpassed in the eighteenth

ON PERSONALITIES

century, made enemies, with few exceptions, only in politics.... The main contests of Franklin's life arose from political conflict— especially over questions of how free men should be governed and how they should conduct their public lives."[42]

---

42 Robert Middlekauff, *Benjamin Franklin and His Enemies* (University of California Press, 1998), pp. 209–210.

CHAPTER 57

ON JOHN ADAMS

"The life of Dr. Franklin was a scene of continual dissipation…. All the atheists, deists and libertines, as well as all the philosophers and ladies, are in his train."
—*John Adams (1779)*

"I am persuaded that Mr. Adams meant well for his country, was always an honest man, and often a wise one, but sometimes and in some things absolutely out of his senses."
—*Ben Franklin (1783)*

Benjamin Franklin worked hard at avoiding enemies, but the tumult of the times inevitably resulted in making them.

Franklin got along well with George Washington, Thomas Jefferson, and most of the other founders, but developed enmity with John Adams and the Lees of Virginia.

At first, Franklin and Adams were cordial allies in the Second Continental Congress and as members of the committee to draft the Declaration of Independence. Together, they served on a three-man committee that met with Lord Richard Howe in August 1776 on Staten Island to respond to the Olive Branch Petition. They only disagreed on Franklin's theory of colds while sleeping in the same room at an inn in New Brunswick. Adams, nursing a cold, wanted the windows closed, while Franklin insisted on keeping the windows open.

ON PERSONALITIES

But their breach became more serious in Paris when both served as commissioners to France during the American Revolution and their widening personality differences became apparent. Adams was dogmatic, outspoken, and cantankerous; Franklin was tolerant, quiet, and flirtatious. Adams hated the French; Franklin loved the French—and vice versa. "Adams felt comfortable confronting people, whereas Franklin preferred to seduce them, and the same was true of the way they dealt with nations," noted historian Walter Isaacson.

Adams complained about Franklin's diplomatic style, how he always arrived late to meetings, was disorganized, and accomplished little. He was convinced that Franklin and the French plotted against him and the new nation. Adams was especially annoyed at the old man's "*maladie d'amour*" ("lovesickness") with the French ladies. Abigail Adams expressed righteous indignation at the sight of Madame Helvétius, who invited Dr. Franklin and the Adamses to a dinner party and showed excessive physical affection for the old doctor. Abigail was distraught. "I was highly disgusted," she wrote a friend back home. As far as the Adamses were concerned, Franklin was an unrepented sinner.

Yet somehow Franklin amazed everyone, including the four other commissioners (John Adams, Ralph Izard, and Arthur and William Lee), in his ability to convince the French king and his court to send funds and supplies to the American cause. Adams and the other diplomats were entirely unsuccessful as fundraisers in France, while the indispensable Franklin raised millions in loans and supplies. It's worth repeating that Washington won the war at home, but Franklin won it abroad. Without Franklin's brilliant diplomacy, the French would never have provided the military and financial aid essential to achieving American Independence from the British.

After Benjamin Franklin died in 1790, John Adams and the Lee brothers controlled the Senate and refused to honor Franklin until a year later.

THE GREATEST AMERICAN

Years later, near the end of his life, Adams mellowed his criticism against his fellow founders. He began a lively discourse with Thomas Jefferson, and reassessed the virtues of his former antagonist Ben Franklin. "Had he been an ordinary man, I should never have taken the trouble to expose the turpitude of his intrigues," Adams wrote in 1810. "Franklin had a great genius—original, sagacious, and inventive, capable of discoveries in science, no less than of improvements in the fine arts and the mechanical arts. He had a vast imagination.... He had wit at will. He had a humor that, when he pleased, was delicate and delightful. He had a satire that was good-natured or caustic, Horace or Juvenal, Swift or Rabelais, at his pleasure. He had talents for irony, allegory and fable, that he could adapt with great skill, to the promotion of moral and political truth. He was a master of that infantile simplicity, which the French called naïveté, which never fails to charm."[43]

As Poor Richard once wrote, "An ill wound may be healed."

---

43 The Papers of John Adams: https://founders.archives.gov/documents/Adams/99-02-02-5574.

CHAPTER 58

ON THOMAS JEFFERSON

What did Franklin think about the author of the Declaration of Independence, Thomas Jefferson? Franklin had his share of disagreements with the other founding fathers, John Adams being the most prominent, but Jefferson was a "great and dear" friend throughout the American Revolution and after. Their admiration was mutual. Jefferson spoke highly of this seasoned veteran of international diplomacy, science, and letters.

They had much in common—a shared interest in science and technology; a liberal, enlightened view of religion; an appreciation of the fairer sex; and a confirmed optimism about the War of Independence and the future of America.

They differed on a few things. Jefferson preferred the idyllic life of the gentlemen farmer, far away from city life, but Ben Franklin loved the hustle and bustle of the big city—the bigger the better. He lived his entire life in cities, first Boston as a youth; second, Philadelphia as a budding businessman and civic volunteer; third, London as a colonial agent; and fourth, Paris as an ambassador. Franklin also defended commercial society and the monied interests of the big banks; Jefferson preferred rural and agricultural life, and hated paper money. (See chapters 8 and 9.)

THE GREATEST AMERICAN

They first met as delegates to the Second Continental Congress in 1775, Franklin representing Pennsylvania and Jefferson Virginia. They differed in age, Franklin being thirty-seven years his senior. Yet they both were taciturn philosophers, one in business and the other in law, who worked together on many committees.

Five delegates were assigned to draft the Declaration of Independence, including Franklin, Jefferson, and John Adams. After writing the draft, Jefferson asked Franklin to review it and make suggestions. He made only one, replacing the words "sacred and undeniable" with "self-evident," so that today it reads, "We hold these truths to be self-evident." (See chapter 49.)

Franklin sat next to Jefferson when the Declaration was revised by Congress. Noting Jefferson's discomfort as his document was mutilated, Franklin recounted the satirical story of a businessman who owned a hat shop. He first proposed a signboard that read "Hatter, makes and sells hats for ready money," but by time his friends had finished with their revisions, all that was left of the sign was the man's name and the figure of a hat. Jefferson was so impressed with the story that he recounted it in his diary.

On July 4, the day the Declaration of Independence was printed, Franklin, Jefferson, and Adams were again assigned to a committee in charge of designing the great seal of the United States. Both Franklin and Jefferson proposed the Latin phrase, "E pluribus unum" (Out of many, one).

They met again seven years later when Jefferson was sent to France to help negotiate commercial treaties and eventually a peace treaty with Britain. They spent nine months together before Franklin left for America, leaving Jefferson in charge as ambassador.

As a scientist and diplomat extraordinaire, Franklin was the most famous American in the world. Jefferson himself noted his scientific achievements in *Notes on the State of Virginia*, in which he rebuffed European charges that America, among other things, was devoid of genius. "In physics we have produced a Franklin, than

ON PERSONALITIES

whom no one of the present age has made more important discoveries, nor has enriched philosophy with more, or more ingenious solutions of the phenomena of nature," Jefferson wrote.

In fact, when Jefferson arrived in Paris, his appearance was little noticed. As one Parisian noted, "No one was more fashionable, more sought after in Paris than Doctor Franklin. The crowd chased after him in parks and public places; hats, canes, and snuffboxes were designed in the Franklin style, and people thought themselves very lucky if they were invited to the same dinner party as this famous man."

Jefferson and Franklin were the only American commissioners who seemed to appreciate the French people. While John Adams and the Lee brothers despised French culture, Jefferson was drawn into the night life of Franklin in the French salons and scientific circles. He sought introductions by Franklin to open the "door of admission for me to the circle of literati." It was at the salon of Madame Helvétius, a close friend of Franklin, where Jefferson met and established lasting relationships with members of the French literati such as the Comte de Volney, Comte Destutt de Tracy, and Pierre-Jean-Georges Cabanis.

Soon after Jefferson returned to the United States, he visited the "beloved and venerable Franklin" at his home in Philadelphia. They talked about the political upheaval in France, which deeply worried Franklin. Jefferson also encouraged Franklin to finish his *Autobiography*. Alas, he died a month later in 1790, leaving it to his descendants to complete his memoirs.

Jefferson maintained his devotion and administration for Franklin, and confessed the following story: "On being presented to any one as the Minister of America, the common-place question, used in such cases, was, 'C'est vous, Monsieur, qui remplace le Docteur Franklin?' 'It is you, Sir, who replace Doctor Franklin?' I generally answered, 'No one can replace him, Sir; I am only his successor.'"

CHAPTER 59

ON GEORGE WASHINGTON

Every year on the Monday before February 22, George Washington's birthday, we celebrate Presidents' Day. Ben Franklin would undoubtedly approve of a national holiday to honor the "Father of Our Country." He would have agreed with Henry "Light-Horse Harry" Lee, who said that George Washington was "first in war, first in peace, and first in the hearts of his countrymen."

Today critics aren't as charitable. They complain that Washington was vain to a fault, a lousy general who blundered repeatedly and extended the American Revolutionary War unnecessarily, and was a hypocrite on slavery because he supported emancipation but refused to free his slaves until his wife died.

Franklin would have none of that. Although he met Washington only a few times during the war, he was always supportive. On his ability as a general, Franklin wrote, "An American planter, who had never seen Europe, was chosen by us to command our troops and continued during the whole war. This man sent home to England, one after another, five of their best generals, baffled, their heads bare of laurels, disgraced even in the opinion of their employers." While ambassador to France, Franklin noted

ON PERSONALITIES

in a letter home that the French generals felt the same way, calling Washington "one of the greatest captains of the age" (*CA*, p. 212).

Franklin had only superlatives to describe Washington's victory at Yorktown on October 19, 1781. "No expedition was ever better planned or better executed. It made a great addition to the military reputation Gen. Washington had already acquired, and brightened the glory that surrounds his name and that must accompany it to our latest posterity" (*CA*, p. 248).

It should be pointed out that Franklin could also indirectly take credit for the victory at Yorktown, because without his Herculean diplomacy in raising the funds and armaments from the French, the victory could not have been achieved. Among the allies at Yorktown, most of the troops and all of the ships were French!

After the war, Franklin endorsed the retired Virginian as president of the Constitutional Convention in 1787. He was asked to nominate him but had to decline that day because of illness. Franklin was the oldest delegate to the Convention, but thought Washington represented the best of the younger generation to rule the nation.

Over eighty years of age, the "Sage of Philadelphia" had no interest in running for president. "I must soon quit the scene," he wrote, "but General Washington (and others) will live to see our country flourish, as it amazingly and rapidly did after the war was over."

The Philadelphian's compliments were reciprocated. In a letter to Franklin in 1789, Washington wrote, "If to be venerated for benevolence, if to be admired for talents, if to be esteemed for patriotism, if to be beloved for philanthropy can gratify the human mind, you must have the pleasing consolation to know that you have not lived in vain."

If Franklin disagreed with Washington on one issue, it was the Society of the Cincinnati, an association honoring officers who served in the American Revolution and their posterity. Washing-

THE GREATEST AMERICAN

ton was made the honorary president of the order. Franklin had no problem with paying tribute and honoring the soldiers themselves or their parents, but to honor descendants was, in his judgment, "groundless and absurd," and often "hurtful to that posterity." He praised the Chinese for their tradition of respecting their elders, while criticizing the Europeans for promoting noblesse oblige among their heirs, causing an "odious mixture of pride and idleness" (*CA*, pp. 311–312).

He suggested that the Cincinnati adopt the Chinese tradition and "direct the badges of their order to be worn by their parents instead of handing them down to their children."

It did little good—Washington stayed on as honorary president, and twenty-three signers of the Constitution joined. Even Franklin accepted honorary membership when he returned to America. The Society of the Cincinnati continues to this day.

In his final will and testament (a fascinating document), Franklin thought so much of his friend Washington that he willed his "fine crab-tree walking stick, with a gold head curiously wrought in the form of a cap of liberty" to him. Washington, he wrote, was "the friend of mankind" (*CA*, p. 405).

In 2005, AOL and the Discovery Channel did a nationwide poll to rank the top one hundred "greatest Americans." In the top five were two founding fathers: George Washington and Benjamin Franklin. The post office has issued more stamps with the images of Washington and Franklin than any other.

One stamp, issued in 1947 in honor of the centennial of stamp collecting, has portraits of both founders. And whose images grace the one dollar and the hundred dollar bill? Washington and Franklin.

PART VIII

ON CULTURE AND PERSONALITY

CHAPTER 60

ON A LIFELONG EDUCATION

"The used key is always bright."
—*Poor Richard's Almanac (1758)*

Benjamin Franklin is known as a famous inventor—of the Franklin stove, the lightning rod, and the bifocals, among other creations. But I just discovered a new invention by the first scientific American: According to Richard Beeman, history professor at the University of Pennsylvania, Franklin was the originator of a liberal arts education.

By liberal arts education is meant a study of a wide variety of subjects, not just one's profession.

"He was in the business of cultivating habits of mind. The Philadelphia Academy [now the University of Pennsylvania] was a broadly based platform for lifelong learning," Beeman states. "Of course Franklin is the perfect role model. He kept his mind open and his intellectual ambition fully fueled. As an educator he is my hero."

In 1732, he created the first public library by subscription. To encourage subscriptions, he wrote his pamphlet, *Proposals Relating to the Education of Youth in Pennsylvania*, which was distributed with his newspapers at no additional charge. "As in the scheme of the library, I had provided only for English books, so in this new scheme my ideas went no farther than to procure the means of a good English education," he wrote. (*A*, pp. 141–143)

Franklin was supportive of education for all youth, including the Negro School of Philadelphia. "The instruction of youth," he wrote, is one of the "most useful and honorable to the public."

THE UNIVERSITY OF PENNSYLVANIA

In 1749, Franklin proposed that the city build an institution of higher learning that would "teach everything that is useful and everything that is ornamental." Other major cities in the colonies had their schools of higher education, such as Harvard, Yale, and Princeton. Why not Philadelphia?

He urged students to have a broad-based education, to learn philosophy, history, logic, mathematics, religion, government, law, chemistry, biology, health, agriculture, physics, and foreign languages.

This academy later became the University of Pennsylvania, established in 1751. "I have been one of its trustees from the beginning, now nearly forty years," he wrote in his *Autobiography*, "and have had the very great pleasure of seeing a number of the youth who have received their educations in it, distinguished by their improved abilities, serviceable to public stations and ornaments to their country" (*A*, pp. 143–144).

THE REWARDS OF A GOOD EDUCATION

Thinking of going back to school? Should your children go to college?

Franklin himself had had only two years of formal school in Boston, followed by an apprenticeship, and he wanted more for his children and grandchildren. He wrote the following letter to his grandson Benny, who was at a private school when Franklin was ambassador to France. Here's what he said:

ON CULTURE AND PERSONALITY

> You see everywhere two sorts of people. One sort are those who are well dressed and live comfortably in good houses, whose conversation is sensible and instructive, and who are respected for their virtue. The other sort are poor, and dirty, and ragged and ignorant, and vicious, and live in miserable cabins or garrets on coarse provisions, which they must work hard to obtain, or which, if they are idle, they must go without or starve. The first had a good education given them by their friends, and they took pains when at school to improve their time and increase their knowledge. The others either had no friend to pay for their schooling, and so never were taught; or else when they were at school, they neglected their studies, were idle, and wicked, and disobedient to their masters, and would not be instructed; and now they suffer. (*CA*, p. 218)

Study after study demonstrates that the more educated you are the more money you are likely to earn. Getting a good education can put you ahead of the class. Natural intelligence is often not enough to become a professional doctor, lawyer, or accountant. In most cases, you need an advanced degree to be successful.

Franklin believed that students should be broadly educated in the liberal arts and not confine themselves to specialties. In 1766, he wrote letters of recommendation for two sons of business associates who planned on studying medicine at the University of Edinburgh. He cautioned them "to be very circumspect and regular in your behavior...that doing so you may bring a good character." Moreover, he counseled that they learn more than just the study of medicine, but "several branches of knowledge." By doing so, "You will from thence draw great aids in judging well both of diseases and remedies, and avoid many errors. I mention this, because I have observed that a number of physicians, here as well as in America, are miserably deficient in it" (*CA*, pp. 46–47).

But formal education isn't enough. As the publisher of the colonies' largest circulating newspaper, the *Pennsylvania Gazette*, he needed to stay up to date. He learned French, Italian, and Spanish, became a good chess player, and was a voracious reader. He commenced a subscription library in Philadelphia as an alternative to a bookstore, which was wanting in the colonies. As a result, "reading became fashionable," and in a few years, local citizens were observed to be "better instructed and more intelligent than people in other countries."

In reading the *Gazette*, I'm always amazed at the variety of interests Franklin enjoyed. He published both serious essays and satires on a wide range of topics, including health care, defense, business, drinking, religion, marriage, legal prose, and virtue. He wrote a long "History of North America" and in 1737, he reprinted *The Morals of Confucius*.

Not being especially religious, Franklin used Sundays as his "studying day" where he would read and improve his knowledge. It was during one of those Sundays that he developed his thirteen virtues and "project toward moral perfection" found in the *Autobiography*.

THE JUNTO: THE SOCIETY FOR USEFUL KNOWLEDGE

He established the Junto to get to know fellow tradesmen and learn of the latest technological advances. Each member would present papers each week on some subject of learning. The Junto helped Franklin immensely in expanding his business, and to keep informed about the latest business opportunities. Master your business, and keep up to date. As Poor Richard admonished, "The used key is always bright." (See chapter 6.)

Franklin was an avid reader from his childhood, and all great entrepreneurs keep informed by reading and attending conferences

ON CULTURE AND PERSONALITY

to become better people, better investors, and better entrepreneurs. He wrote in his *Autobiography*, "From a child I was fond of reading and all the little money that came into my hands was ever laid out in books." As a teenager, he read John Bunyan's *Pilgrim's Progress*, Plutarch's *Parallel Lives*, and Cotton Mather's *Essays to Do Good*, all of which influenced him greatly.

Throughout his adulthood, Franklin was a constant reader. In 1764, Franklin sailed to England for a second mission as colonial agent and commented that he had brought no books with him. But by late 1772, eight years later, he wrote, "I was amazed to see how many books had grown upon me since my return to England. I had brought none with me, yet had now a roomful, many collected in Germany, Holland and France, and consisting chiefly of such as contain knowledge that might hereafter be useful to America" (*CA*, pp. 75–76).

Poor Richard said it best: "Genius without education is like silver in the mine."

CHAPTER 61

ON FUNDRAISING

Ben Franklin was a fundraiser extraordinaire.

Did you know that he invented the "matching funds" technique in fundraising? I'm sure you have all been approached by charities where a wealthy contributor has agreed to match any donation you make. So if you agreed to donate $1,000 to a worthy cause, a donor would match it dollar for dollar, and the charity would get $2,000 for your effort. The matching funds technique is quite popular these days.

Franklin reveals his technique in the *Autobiography* (*A*, pp. 147–148). In 1751, he was approached by a medical doctor, Thomas Bond, to establish a private hospital for poor people in Philadelphia. Franklin was a firm believer in getting involved in local community activities, focusing primarily on private activities rather than the government. As Alexis de Tocqueville commented in *Democracy in America*, in England some great lord was behind a philanthropic project, and in France the government, but in America, every perceived problem seemed to produce a new benevolent association supported by volunteers.

Franklin financed all kinds of private initiatives, such as an academy for youth, which later become the University of Pennsylvania, the Negro School of Philadelphia, a subscription library,

ON CULTURE AND PERSONALITY

a voluntary militia, a fire department, and a scientific foundation (the American Philosophical Society). As historian Lorraine Smith Pangle notes, "Franklin was a tireless supporter of volunteer associations and philanthropic projects."

Dr. Bond approached Franklin for assistance after failing to get such support for his hospital for the poor. Franklin liked the project, so made a donation, wrote an editorial in the *Pennsylvania Gazette*, and solicited subscriptions from his friends. Still, the donations were insufficient to start building the hospital.

Frustrated, he decided to petition the Pennsylvania General Assembly for financial support. But they too were reluctant to use taxpayer's funds for a local project, even if it were for a good cause. "They considered [my proposal] as a most extravagant supposition, and utterly impossible," Franklin wrote.

In response, he came up with a clever idea. He suggested that the assembly pass a bill to give £2,000 to the hospital, but they would only have to donate the funds on the condition that private donations achieve an equal amount. It passed because nobody thought the hospital could raise £2,000 on its own.

Franklin went to work and urged citizens to donate, knowing that "every man's donation would be doubled" if they reached their goal. The additional motive worked, and the subscriptions by private citizens soon exceeded £2,000. The hospital claimed the public gift from the assembly and built the first hospital for the poor in Philadelphia.

Franklin was proud of his accomplishment. "I do not remember any of my political maneuvers, the success of which gave me at the time more pleasure for having made some use of cunning" (*A*, p. 149).

That's not to say that fundraising was easy. When he was ambassador to France, he was constantly under pressure to raise more funds for the American cause. After four years in Paris, he became depressed about the whole process. "I had long been humiliated

THE GREATEST AMERICAN

with the idea of our running about from court to court begging for money and friendship, which were the more withheld the more eagerly they were solicited." Yet, because the French people loved Franklin so much, he was able to raise millions, and in fact, he was the only one of the six commissioners to achieve success in France. John Adams finally collected some money from the Dutch, but only victory was achieved in the Battle at Yorktown in 1781.

Franklin was often on the other end of the fundraiser stick, and was frequently asked to donate to churches and other charitable causes. In exasperation, he wrote to a friend on the endless burdens of philanthropy: "Always supplications! Always demands for money! It is bad to have the reputation of being charitable. We expose ourselves to a thousand importunities and a good deal of expense as punishment for our pride, nay our vanity, which lets our small benefactions be known."

He added, "Charitable institutions, however originally well intended, and well executed at first for many years, are subject to be in a course of time corrupted, mismanag'd, their funds misapplied or perverted to private purposes. Would it not be well to guard against those by prudent regulations respecting the choice of managers, and establishing the power of inspecting their conduct, in some permanent body, as the monthly or quarterly meeting?" (*CA*, p. 343).

THE GEORGE WHITEFIELD STORY

His favorite story in this regard was when he was asked by Reverend George Whitefield to donate money for the creation of an orphanage in Georgia. Whitefield was a famous orator who had such a powerful and clear voice that he could be heard by an outdoor audience of twenty-five thousand. He invited Franklin to attend a sermon on the subject of the orphanage. Franklin reluctantly agreed, but made it clear that he disagreed with Reverend Whitefield; he wanted the orphanage to be built in Philadelphia.

ON CULTURE AND PERSONALITY

He arrived at the church determined not to give to the cause. He noted that he had in his pocket "a handful of copper money, three or four silver dollars, and five pistoles of gold." But, he thought, "I silently resolved he should get nothing from me."

But as the minister began speaking, Franklin softened a little and resolved to give the copper pennies. And then, "another stroke of his oratory made me ashamed of that, and determined me to give the silver; and he finished so admirably, that I emptied my pocket wholly into the collector's dish, gold and all" (*A*, pp. 127–129).

FRANKLIN AS A FUNDRAISER EXTRAORDINAIRE IN FRANCE

He found even a better example in later life. By early 1781, the American ambassador, age seventy-five, was suffering from the gout and other ailments. The war with Britain was in its sixth year with no end in sight. Franklin had successfully committed France to offer massive amounts of supplies and funds to the colonial cause, with very little to show for it.

Now a desperate Congress asked their diplomat to "make a fresh and strong application for more money," another loan of 25 million livres. Franklin was reluctant to do so but finally wrote a letter in his best diplomatic language to the foreign minister, Comte de Vergennes, asking for the 25 million.

In making the request for another loan, he wrote the following in his best diplomatic language:

> Passy, Feb. 13, 1781
> To His Excellency the Ct. de Vergennes:
>
> I am grown old. I feel myself much enfeebled by my late long illness; and it is probable I shall not long have any more concern in these affairs. I therefore take this occasion to express my opinion to your Excellency, that the present conjuncture

THE GREATEST AMERICAN

is critical; that there is some danger lest the Congress should lose its influence over the people, if it is found unable to procure the aids that are wanted; and that the whole system of the new government in America may be shaken. If the English are suffered once to recover that country, such an opportunity of effectual separation as the present may not occur again in the course of ages; and the possession of those fertile and extensive regions and that vast sea coast will afford them so broad a basis for future greatness, by the rapid growth of their commerce, and breed of seamen and soldier, as will enable them to become the terror of Europe and to exercise with impunity that insolence which is natural to their nation, and which will increase enormously with the increase of their power.

I am with great respect, your excellency's most obedient and most humble servant,

B. Franklin

He sent the letter off and waited. For over a week there was no answer from Versailles. Another week passed, and finally Franklin demanded an answer. He was told to take the next carriage to Versailles to meet with Vergennes. He left immediately.

When he entered the foreign minister's chambers, Franklin could tell that he was in trouble. Vergennes did not smile. He told him bluntly that, first, he knew the Americans were broke and did not have the funds to repay their loans, let alone the interest on the loans. And second, he confessed that sadly France was also broke, and the depreciation of the French currency had hurt their credit.

In sum, the foreign minister told Franklin that "the King of France could not possibly favor a loan for us [the Americans] as it

ON CULTURE AND PERSONALITY

would interfere with and be a prejudice to those under a necessity of supporting the war" (*CA*, pp. 224–225).

Then he paused and said (I paraphrase), *"But because of the love the King and the French people have for you, Dr Franklin, and the love you have for the French people, the King has resolved to grant the Americans the sum of six million livres—not as a loan, but a free gift!"*

Franklin had done it again. He squeezed blood out of a turnip.

Now that's what I call fundraising!

CHAPTER 62

ON THE IMPORTANCE OF GOOD HUMOR AND LAUGHTER

"I'll be hanged if this is not one of your American jokes!"
—*Paul Whitehead, British author (1773)*

"Ben Franklin was the first American humorist. He invented American humor and the one-liner."
—*Paul Johnson, Humorists (2010)*

British historian Paul Johnson claims that not only was Ben Franklin the first scientific American, but the "founding father of American laughs," a polymath who "invented the national mood in which American humor has flourished: that the world is a good and cheerful place, and everyone has an equal right to be happy in it."

Having studied the life and works of Franklin, I heartily agree. The inveterate prankster and socialite loved to tell jokes, puns, and double entendres to his friends, write political satires of his enemies, and send salacious bagatelles to his French ladies. (I might add that, in my experience, Ben Franklin impersonators largely fail to capture this vital aspect of Franklin's personality. They are far too serious.)

ON CULTURE AND PERSONALITY

Poor Richard's Almanac, published from 1733 to 1758, is full of funny one-liners:

1. A countryman between two lawyers is like a fish between two cats.
2. Three can keep a secret—if two are dead.
3. There are three friends in life—a faithful wife, an old mistress, and ready money!
4. Creditors have better memories than debtors.
5. A man who boasts of his ancestors does but advertise his own insignificance.

Franklin is portrayed as quite witty in the musical *1776*. In one scene, John Adams and John Dickinson almost come to blows over a debate about independence from England. The debate wakes Franklin, played magnificently by Howard Da Silva, who is sleeping.

> **Franklin:** Please Mr. Dickinson, but must you start banging? How is a man to sleep?
>
> [*Laughter from Congress*]
>
> **Dickinson:** Forgive me, Dr. Franklin, but must YOU start speaking? How is a man to stay awake?
>
> [*More laughter*]
>
> **Dickinson:** We'll promise to be quiet—I'm sure everyone prefers that you remained asleep.
>
> **Franklin:** If I'm to hear myself called an Englishman, sir, I assure you I prefer I'd remained asleep.
>
> **Dickinson:** What's so terrible about being called an Englishman? The English don't seem to mind.
>
> **Franklin:** Nor would I, were I given the full rights of an Englishman. But to call me one without those rights is like calling an ox a bull.

THE GREATEST AMERICAN

He's thankful for the honor, but he'd much rather have restored what's rightfully his.

[*Laughter*]

Dickinson: When did you first notice they were missing, sir?

[*More laughter*]

The dialogue is, of course, invented but very Franklin-esque.

Like Jonathan Swift, Franklin frequently used satire to poke fun of the British. For instance, in 1773, he wrote an anonymous essay in a British newspaper called "An Edict of the King of Prussia," a hoax he invented about King Frederick II announcing that the Germans were going to impose a 4.5 percent duty on all English trade to pay for a war between Prussia and France—a play on the Stamp Act. The day the essay was published, Franklin watched a group of Londoners read the account with great indignation. One said, "Damn his imprudence! I dare say, we shall hear by next post that he is upon his march with one hundred thousand men to back this." Suddenly, another Brit realized who the author was. Looking at Franklin, he said, "I'll be hanged if this is not some of your American jokes upon us." Franklin had fooled them, and everyone laughed heartily. (See *CA*, pp. 77–78.)

Franklin loved to play chess, and on one occasion when he was ambassador to France, he was playing a late-night game with the Duchess of Bourbon. Early in the game, the duchess made a move that inadvertently exposed her king. Franklin promptly took the king. Checkmate! "Ah," responded the duchess, "we do not take kings so." Replied Franklin famously, "We do in America."

Franklin once played the game all night, and his opponent at one point announced that it was light outside. Franklin threw open the shutters. "You are right, it is daytime." The incident inspired him to write a bagatelle at his "discovery" that light appeared at 6 a.m. Playing on the habit of the French aristocracy not rising

ON CULTURE AND PERSONALITY

before noon, he announced this "discovery" to the French, and suggested that if they simply get up earlier and go to bed earlier (a Poor Richard's famous refrain), they could save a lot of money on candles—close to 97 million livres, "an immense sum that the city of Paris might save every year by the economy of using sunshine instead of candles." He suggested changing the time to encourage the French to being tricked into rising earlier—and thus inventing the idea of daylight savings time! He humorously said he wanted no royalty or reward for his invention. "I expect only to have the honor of it" (*CA*, pp. 314–317).

In September 1777, when Franklin was ambassador in France, he attended an event that included both the French foreign minister Comte de Vergennes and the British ambassador. They each proposed a toast. Vergennes went first: "To his majesty, Louis the Sixteenth, who, like the moon, fills the earth with a soft, benevolent glow." The British ambassador followed: "To George the Third, who, like the sun at noonday, spreads his light and illuminates the world."

Franklin responded, "I give you George Washington, general of the armies of the United States, who, like Joshua of old, commanded the sun and the moon to stand still, and both obeyed!"[44]

As ambassador to France, he enjoyed flirting with young French ladies as a diversion from work. He (a widower) and Madame Brillon, a talented but married woman, exchanged a series of teasing letters about the temptations of the flesh, in which he writes, "I will mention the opinion of a certain father of the church...that the most effectual way to get rid of a certain temptation is to comply with and satisfy it. Pray instruct me how far I may venture to practice upon this principle?" (*CA*, p. 167)

Later he pursued another French beauty, Madame Helvétius. As a beautiful widow and thirteen years his junior, she was fascinated by Doctor Franklin. He proposed to her, but she rejected

---

44 See the Lehman Institute, "Benjamin Franklin, Thinking Outside the Box," https://lehrmaninstitute.org/history/essays5.html

THE GREATEST AMERICAN

him. Heartbroken, he composed a charming little piece titled "The Elysian Fields," imagining a scenario where, after death, he ascended to heaven and discovered that her late husband and his own late wife, Debbie, were now married. In the piece, he praised Madame Helvétius's beauty, claiming it surpassed that of his deceased wife, and suggested they "avenge ourselves."

Franklin once wrote to his sister Jane about an ancient poem:

> A man of words and not of deeds,
> Is like a garden full of weeds.

Franklin reversed the saying, so that it read:

> A man of deeds and not of words
> Is like a garden full of——

He did not say the word, but added, "tis something the very reverse of a perfume" (*CA*, p. 16).

Franklin is famous for his scientific spoofs and essays of mock science. For example, in a letter to Abbé Morellet, he celebrated the wonders of wine: "We hear of the conversion of water into wine at the marriage in Cana, as of a miracle. But this conversion is, through the goodness of God, made every day before our eyes. Behold the rain which descends from heaven upon our vineyards; there it enters the roots of the vines, to be changed into wine; a constant proof that God loves us, and loves to see us happy. The miracle in question was performed only to hasten the operation."

Promoters of beer have changed Franklin's quote from wine to beer, so as to read, "Beer is proof that God loves us and wants to see us happy." The joke is now on Franklin, who loved wine, not beer.

One of his most notorious satires is "A Letter to a Royal Academy," published in 1780, in which Franklin proposed that "learned physicians, chemists, etc. of this enlightened age" undertake research about "a great quantity of wind" that is "created or produced in the bowels of human creatures" and that is "usually

ON CULTURE AND PERSONALITY

offensive to the Company, from the fetid Smell that accompanies it." Franklin suggested that the Royal Academy seek to develop a drug, "wholesome and not disagreeable," which can be mixed with "common Food or Sauces" with the effect of rendering flatulence "not only inoffensive, but agreeable as Perfumes." The essay ends with a pun on the British coin of the realm, saying that compared to the practical applications of this discussion, other sciences are "scarcely worth a FART-HING" (*CA*, p. 306).

CHAPTER 63

ON CHESS, SPORTS, AND OTHER GAMES

"Life is a kind of chess. It is not merely an idle amusement, but can be useful in the course of human life."
—Ben Franklin

Sports and games of leisure were not as advanced as they are today. In Ben Franklin's day, there was no basketball, football (soccer), or baseball. Cricket and golf were invented in the United Kingdom, but there is no evidence that he played either game.

Swimming was one of Franklin's favorite physical activities in an era where only a small number of people knew how to swim (Captain James Cook, for example, never learned how to swim). When living in London from 1724 to 1726, the youthful Franklin displayed his "many feats of activity, both upon and under water, that surprised and pleased those to whom they were novelties" (*A*, p. 57).

Board and card games were much more popular. Franklin's favorite pastime was the game of chess. Chess was invented in India around AD 600 and has enjoyed universal appeal. It became especially popular in the US since Bobby Fischer, the youngest American grandmaster ever, caught the imagination of the American public in the early 1970s, when he beat the Russian Boris Spassky

ON CULTURE AND PERSONALITY

for the world championship. Over thirty million Americans now play the game.

Ben Franklin helped popularize the game in America, and in fact, was the first American to write about it in his 1786 essay, "The Morals of Chess." He probably picked up the game during his first trip to London in 1724–26, where he "delighted in" playing various board games.

He was fascinated with games of skill, such as magic squares and magic circles, which he could do in his head. Over time, he gained a preference for the "noble game of chess" above card playing and other forms of entertainment, because of its complexity, skill, and lessons of life.

We don't have any record of his games, but he was undoubtedly an above-average player. He had a reputation as a "good" chess player in London and played at the Café de La Régence, where the best players gathered in Paris. An observer noted that Franklin had a "passion for late-night games."

One of the most notorious stories about Franklin and the French ladies involved chess. On one occasion, the famous ambassador to France played chess with Madame Brillon while she was "in the bath." Franklin wrote a friend, "She has among other elegant accomplishments that of an excellent musician, and with her daughters who sing prettily, and some friends who play, she kindly entertains me and my grandson with little concerts, a dish of tea and a game of *chess*. I call this my Opera; for I rarely go to the Opera at Paris."

After one late evening, she wrote him, "Madame Brillon is a little miffed about the six games of chess Mr. Franklin won so inhumanly and she warns him that she will spare nothing to get her revenge!"

In response, Franklin apologized, "I fear that because we were so overly engrossed in the game of chess as to forget everything else, we caused great inconvenience to you, by detaining you so

THE GREATEST AMERICAN

long in the bath.... Never again will I consent to start a game in your bathing room" (*CA*, pp. 163–164).

Franklin found chess a useful tool of diplomacy. In late 1774, he was brought into the peace negotiations with the British when he was invited to play chess by Lord Howe's sister, "fancying she could beat me." In fact, her invitation was a ruse to engage Franklin in discussions with Lord Howe prior to the American Revolution. Unfortunately, his negotiations turned into a stalemate, and he was forced to return to America in 1775, preparing his country for all-out war (*CA*, pp. 90–92).

During the war with England, Franklin compared war to the game of chess. "Knowing that war is full of changes and uncertainty, in bad fortune I hope for good, and in good I fear bad. I play this game [of war] with almost the same equanimity as when I play chess. I never give up a game before it is finished, always hoping to win, or at least get a stalemate; and when I have a good game, I guard against presumption, which is often very damaging and always very dangerous; and when I am presumptuous, I try to conceal it to spare myself shame if my luck changes."

In his "The Morals of Chess," he opined, "The Game of Chess is not merely an idle amusement; several very valuable qualities of the mind, useful in the course of human life, are to be acquired and strengthened by it, so as to become habits ready on all occasions; for life is a kind of Chess, in which we have often points to gain, and competitors or adversaries to contend with, and in which there is a vast variety of good and ill events, that are, in some degree, the effect of prudence, or the want of it. By playing at Chess then, we may learn: 1st, *Foresight*, which looks a little into futurity, and considers the consequences that may attend an action...2nd, *Circumspection*, which surveys the whole Chess-board, or scene of action:—the relation of the several Pieces, and their situations;...3rd, *Caution*, not to make our moves too hastily."

According to Madame Brillion, Franklin played chess so much that it gave the old man a severe case of the gout (arthritis). She

ON CULTURE AND PERSONALITY

encouraged Franklin to write a satire called "Dialogue Between the Gout and M. Franklin," reprinted in part below:

> FRANKLIN: Eh! Oh! Eh! What have I done to merit these cruel sufferings [the gout]?
>
> GOUT: Many things; you have ate and drank too freely, and too much indulged those legs of yours in their indolence.... Your amusements, your recreation, at least, should be active.... But what is your practice after dinner? Walking in the beautiful gardens...would be the choice of men of sense; yours is to be fixed down to chess, where you are found engaged for two or three hours! This is your perpetual recreation.... Wrapt in the speculations of this wretched game, you destroy your constitution....
>
> FRANKLIN: Oh! Oh!—for heaven's sake leave me! And I promise faithfully never more to play at chess, but to take exercise daily, and live temperately (*CA*, pp. 219–222).

Of course, Franklin never did give up his sedentary lifestyle, and he continued to suffer from the gout, gallstones, and other old-age maladies. But he remained optimistic. "There are many sorrows in this life, but we must not blame Providence inconsiderately, for there are many more pleasures. This is why I love life" (CA, p. 347).

Chess was one of those pleasures, even if he lost. He once said, "I prefer to lose a really good game than to win a bad one."

CHAPTER 64

ON WINNING FRIENDS AND INFLUENCING PEOPLE

Dale Carnegie's most famous book, published in 1936, is entitled *How to Win Friends and Influence People*. One of Carnegie's mentors was none other than Ben Franklin, who knew and practiced the secrets of social interaction and successful diplomacy.

In fact, Carnegie drew many lessons from Franklin. He wrote, "Benjamin Franklin, tactless in his youth, became so diplomatic, so adroit at handling people, that he was made American Ambassador to France."

Franklin was considered the most affable of the founders. John Adams was known to be cantankerous and argumentative, while Thomas Jefferson and George Washington were aloof. When the public was polled, "Which founder would you like to have a beer with?" Franklin won handily. Though considered a genius, the Philadelphia diplomat could spend his evenings equally at ease with a top scientist or a lowly cobbler. And he was famous for his way with the ladies too.

The French was so endeared by Franklin's diplomatic ways that he practically bankrupted the king's treasury to finance the Amer-

ON CULTURE AND PERSONALITY

ican Revolution. While George Washington won the war at home with his military prowess, Franklin won the war abroad with his savoir faire.

But it's important to note that Franklin's social skills did not come naturally. He learned in the school of hard knocks how to win friends and influence people. Earlier in his career, he would get into arguments with his friends, always trying to prove how much smarter he was. He lost friends and alienated people.

When it came to arguing, Franklin quickly learned this lesson: "If you argue and rankle and contradict, you may achieve a victory sometimes; but it will be an empty victory because you will never get your opponent's good will."

So, he decided to take a different tack. "I will speak ill of no man, and speak all the good I know of everybody."

He gave an example in his *Autobiography* on how he befriended an enemy, a gentleman of fortune and education who opposed Franklin in the Pennsylvania legislature. He wrote, "I did not, however, aim at gaining his favor by paying any servile respect to him, but, after some time, took this other method. Having heard that he had in his library a certain very scarce and curious book, I wrote a note to him, expressing my desire of perusing that book, and requesting he would do me the favor of lending it to me for a few days. He sent it immediately, and I returned it in about a week with another note, expressing strongly my sense of the favor" (*A*, p. 124).

When they next met in the House, Franklin reported that the man approached him and for the first time expressed "great civility." "He ever after manifested a readiness to serve me on all occasions, so that we became great friends, and our friendship continued to his death. This is another instance of the truth of an old maxim I had learned, which says, 'He that has once done you a kindness will be more ready to do you another, than he whom you yourself have obliged.' And it shows how much more profitable it

THE GREATEST AMERICAN

is prudently to remove, than to resent, return, and continue inimical proceedings" (*A*, p. 124).

In another part of the *Autobiography*, Franklin explained his new social philosophy: "I made it a rule to forbear all direct contradiction to the sentiments of others, and all positive assertion of my own. I even forbid myself, agreeably to the old laws of our Junto, the use of every word or expression in the language that imported a fixed opinion, such as certainly, undoubtedly, etc., and I adopted, instead of them, I conceive, I apprehend, or I imagine a thing to be so or so; or it so appears to me at present. When another asserted something that I thought an error, I denied myself the pleasure of contradicting him abruptly, and of showing immediately some absurdity in his proposition; and in answering I began by observing that in certain cases or circumstances his opinion would be right, but in the present case there appeared or seemed to me some difference, etc. I soon found the advantage of this change in my manner; the conversations I engaged in went on more pleasantly. The modest way in which I proposed my opinions procured them a readier reception and less contradiction; I had less mortification when I was found to be in the wrong, and I more easily prevailed with others to give up their mistakes and join with me when I happened to be in the right" (*A*, pp. 109–110).

"And this mode, which I at first put on with some violence to natural inclination, became at length so easy, and so habitual to me, that perhaps for these fifty years past no one has ever heard a dogmatical expression escape me. And to this habit (after my character of integrity) I think it principally owing that I had early so much weight with my fellow-citizens when I proposed new institutions, or alterations in the old, and so much influence in public councils when I became a member; for I was but a bad speaker, never eloquent, subject to much hesitation in my choice of words, hardly correct in language, and yet I generally carried my points" (*A*, p. 110).

ON CULTURE AND PERSONALITY

Franklin didn't always live up to his social strategy. He still had his share of enemies, including the Pennsylvania proprietor Thomas Penn, fellow commissioner Arthur Lee, and even fellow founder John Adams. But when he died, over twenty thousand people showed up at his funeral.

CHAPTER 65

ON KNOWLEDGE, BOOKS, AND SUCCESS

Charlie Munger, Warren Buffett's partner in the Berkshire Hathaway investment company, was certainly right when he said, "In my whole life, I have known no wise people who didn't read all the time—none, zero." Successful people are constant readers on a variety of subjects. "To be a successful investor," admonished Munger, "You must draw from many disciplines."

In his *Autobiography*, Franklin confessed he was "fond of reading and all the little money that came into my hands was ever laid out in books." He read John Bunyan's *Pilgrim's Progress*, Plutarch's *Parallel Lives*, and Cotton Mather's *Essays to Do Good*, "which perhaps gave me a turn of thinking that had an influence on some of the principal future events of my life." It was his "bookish" nature that caused his father to encourage young Benjamin to apprentice in his older brother James's printing business. There he had access to better books. "Often I sat up in my room reading the greatest part of the night, when the book was borrowed in the evening and to be returned early in the morning" (*A*, pp. 1–14).

He met Matthew Adams, "an ingenious tradesman," who invited him to his library and lent him books. He "now took a fancy to poetry," and started writing for James's newspaper *The*

ON CULTURE AND PERSONALITY

New-England Courant. He improved his writing skills by imitating the writers of another publication, *The Spectator.*

After becoming a profitable printer in Philadelphia, his first public project was the creation of the first subscription library in North America in 1730. At that time, books still were quite expensive and out of the reach of the average worker. According to Franklin's *Autobiography*, there was not a good bookshop in any of the colonies south of Boston. In New York and Philadelphia, printers were stationers and sold only paper, almanacs, and a few common schoolbooks. "Those who loved reading were obliged to send for their books from England," which was expensive.

To make books more available to members of the Junto, the club that Franklin had organized, he proposed that members bring their books to their meeting room so that they would be a "common benefit, each of us being at liberty to borrow such as he wished to read at home." Later, he decided to extend the book-lending plan by commencing a public subscription library. Franklin drew up the proposal and charged ten shillings a year to be a member. But "so few were the readers at that time in Philadelphia, and the majority of us so poor, that I was not able, with great industry, to find more than fifty young persons, mostly young tradesmen, willing to pay down for this purpose."

Still, Franklin proceeded with the plan; it eventually became so successful that it was imitated throughout the colonies. Franklin was convinced the first subscription library had significant impact economically and politically. "These libraries have improved the general conversation of the Americans, made the common tradesmen and farmers as intelligent as most gentlemen from other countries, and perhaps have contributed in some degree to the stand so generally made throughout the colonies in defense of their privileges" (*A*, pp. 82–83). Franklin was a book lover and collector throughout his adult life as a businessman, colonial agent, and public servant.

THE GREATEST AMERICAN

In 1772, after arriving in England eight years earlier, Franklin wrote to a friend, "I settled into my new apartment on Craven Street [in London].... I was amazed to see how many books had grown upon me since my return to England." In 1778, the town of Exeter, Massachusetts, decided to change its name to Franklin in honor of Benjamin. After the war, the city wrote to Franklin requesting a donation of a bell, but he wrote back offering a more practical gift of 116 books for use by the town's residents. On November 20, 1790, those attending Franklin's town meeting voted to lend the books to all Franklin inhabitants free of charge. This vote established the Franklin collection as the first public library in the United States. The original Franklin collection is still housed in a bookcase in Franklin Public Library's Reading Gallery.

CHAPTER 66

FRANKLIN SAID WHAT?!

Which of the following quotes did Ben Franklin actually say or write?

A. "Beer is proof that God loves us and wants us to be happy."

B. "Tell me and I forget. Teach me and I remember. Involve me and I learn."

C. "Some people die at twenty-five and aren't buried until seventy-five."

D. "By failing to prepare, you are preparing to fail."

Answer: None of the above.

In today's internet world, famous people are constantly being misquoted and getting away with it, especially in politics and finance. Frequently I hear that Mark Twain said, "No man's life, liberty or property is safe while the legislature is in session." A truer statement was never made, but Mark Twain didn't say it. It originated with Gideon J. Tucker, a New York judge, in 1866.

Ben Franklin is probably misquoted more than any other founding father. In the early 1990s, Rollins College in Winter Park, Florida, placed a statue of Franklin sitting on a bench read-

THE GREATEST AMERICAN

ing the Declaration of Independence. The president of the college asked me to appear in costume as Ben Franklin and say a few words at the dedication. (As a direct descendant, I occasionally dress up as the old man.) I agreed to do so, but then I noticed the quote they had for Franklin and saw that it appeared to be a made-up quotation about education. "Tell me and I forget. Teach me and I remember. Involve me and I learn." It sounded too modern to be a legitimate quote.

To check on its veracity, I contacted Ellen Cohn, the longtime editor of *The Papers of Benjamin Franklin* at Yale University, and she immediately debunked the quote. Upon my recommendation, the college changed the saying to a real one: "Genius without education is like silver in the mine."

What about the alleged statement on T-shirts that are sold in taverns, on Bourbon Street, and even at the National Constitution Center in Philadelphia: "Beer is proof that God loves us and wants us to be happy"?

He never wrote it. He did tour Germany once or twice, but there's no evidence that he was a fan of beer. Actually, his favorite beverage was wine, especially the heavy Portuguese Madeira port. Here's what he actually wrote: In a letter dated July 5, 1779, to the Abbé Andre Morellet, ambassador Franklin wrote (this is a translation of the original French): "We hear of the conversion of water into wine at the marriage in Cana, as of a miracle. But this conversion is, through the goodness of God, made every day before our eyes. Behold the rain which descends from heaven upon our vineyards, and which incorporates itself with the grapes to be changed into wine; a constant proof that God loves us, and loves to see us happy!"

Somehow the beer lobby made the switch and made Franklin a beer lover. I complained to the National Constitution Center that the T-shirt was a misquote, but to no avail. Commerce supersedes truth. It reminds me of a great quote from *Poor Richard's*

ON CULTURE AND PERSONALITY

Almanac, "When the beer enters, out goes the truth." Actually, he said, "When the wine enters, out goes the truth" (honest).

What about Poor Richard's famous line, "A penny saved is a penny earned"? Truly advice worth living. But the original maxim was not as memorable:

> "A penny spar'd is twice got." (George Herbert's *Outlandish Proverbs,* circa 1633)

> "This I did to prevent expences, for.... A penny sav'd, is a penny got." (Edward Ravenscroft's *Canterbury Guests,* 1695)

Franklin used something similar in *Poor Richard's Almanac*: "A penny saved is two pence dear. A pin a day is a groat a year." It rhymes but is hardly memorable. A better line is this one: "An investment in knowledge pays the best interest."

In politics, Franklin is often alleged to have said, "Who gives up liberty for security, deserves neither." He actually wrote the following in a letter to the governor of Pennsylvania on November 11, 1755, before the American Revolution, "Those who would give up essential liberty, to purchase a little temporary safety, deserve neither liberty nor safety." Same theme, different words. This example reminds me of Winston Churchill's famous line, "blood, sweat, and tears." Actually, he said "blood, toil, tears, and sweat" in his speech before the House of Commons on May 13, 1940. The rock 'n roll band wisely choose a more memorable line.

Should we really complain if Franklin is misquoted? Accuracy is important in a world of social media. Today, historians are questioning the old views about the founders, whether Thomas Jefferson sired black children, or Ben Franklin really flew a kite. Regarding long-established maxims, the fact is that Franklin himself often stole old aphorisms and proverbs without giving any attribution to the original authors. Ultimately, it's the thought that counts, unless it does not represent the spirit of the author.

PART IX

ON RELIGION AND PHILOSOPHY

CHAPTER 67

THE BENEFITS OF A USEFUL RELIGION

"Don't judge a man by his Sunday appearance."
—*Poor Richard's Almanac*

There is much misinformation about Benjamin Franklin's religious views. His friends accused him of being a "free thinker," a Deist and heretic, and even an atheist because he was not a regular churchgoer. He was critical of the Puritans and other Calvinists who preached that salvation came through God's graces only and not by good deeds.

While traveling in Europe in the summer of 1761, he visited the town of Flanders in Holland and noted the difference between Sunday activity there compared to the "excessive strict" observation of Sunday in Connecticut. In Connecticut, Franklin wrote, "a man could hardly travel on that day without hazard of punishment; while where I was in Flanders, every one traveled, and in the afternoon both high and low went to the play or the opera, where there was plenty of singing, fiddling and dancing. I looked round for God's judgments but saw no signs of them. The cities were well built and full of inhabitants, the markets filled with plenty, the people well favored and well clothed; the fields well tilled; the

THE GREATEST AMERICAN

cattle fat and strong; the fences, houses and windows all in repair" (*CA*, pp. 19–20).

When he proposed marriage for his grandson Temple, who was a Protestant, to the daughter of Catholic friends in France, Madame Brillon raised the issue of religion. Franklin tried to play down her concerns, saying, "In every religion, besides the essential things, there are others which are only forms and fashions, as a loaf of sugar may be wrapped in brown or white or blue paper, and tied with a string of flax or wool, red or yellow; but the sugar is always the essential thing" (*CA*, p. 229).

At the end of his life, he asked Reverend Ezra Stiles, president of Yale College, not to publish his views for fear of being "exposed to criticism and censure."

Yet Franklin was a deeply spiritual man, albeit unorthodox, and as we shall see, more religious toward the end of his life. He begins his famous *Autobiography* thanking God for a happy and productive life. Although he was not a regular churchgoer, and used his Sundays for study, he created his own private liturgy.

In fact, he had a close friendship with numerous religious leaders of varying faiths throughout his life and gave anonymously to almost all the churches in Philadelphia, including the Friends Meeting House (Quakers) and the Jewish synagogues.

He urged his business friends to donate to good causes, including churches, and he practiced what he preached. For Franklin, good works were more valuable than attending church.

Franklin's emphasis on "useful" religion is apparent in his list of thirteen virtues of moral principles in the *Autobiography*. He begins his discussion by complaining about a Presbyterian minister who engaged in "polemic arguments" rather than how to make us "good citizens" by adopting the virtues of temperance, frugality, industry, moderation, chastity, and humility. In virtue number thirteen, he admonished: "Imitate Jesus and Socrates."

ON RELIGION AND PHILOSOPHY

Franklin firmly believed that anyone could achieve personal and financial success in this life, starting from scratch, if they lived by his three fundamental virtues: industry, thrift, and prudence.

After the American Revolution, Franklin gradually became more religious. The Revolutionary War had convinced him that America's independence was a "miracle in human affairs," and brought about by the "blessing of God." He told the Constitutional Convention in 1781: "I have lived a long time; and the longer I live, the more convincing proofs I see of this truth, that God governs in the affairs of men! If it had not been for the justice of our cause, and the consequent interposition of Providence in which we had faith, we must have been ruined. If I had ever before been an atheist, I should now have been convinced of the being and government of a Deity. It is He who abases the proud and favors the humble! May we never forget his goodness to us, and may our future conduct manifest our gratitude" (*CA*, p. 365).

A month before he died, he told Reverend Stiles that while he doubted the divinity of Jesus Christ, he "believ[ed] in one God, creator of the universe. That he govern[ed] it by his providence. That he ought to be worshiped. That the most acceptable service we can render to him is doing good to his other children. That the soul of man is immortal, and will be treated with justice in another life" (*CA*, p. 385).

CHAPTER 68

FRANKLIN, THE PRACTICAL PHILOSOPHER

*"I would rather it have said, He lived
usefully, than, He died rich."*
—*Ben Franklin (1750)*

I recently picked up a book called *101 Great Philosophers: Makers of Modern Thought*, by Madsen Pirie. He identified Benjamin Franklin as one of his favorite American philosophers along with Thomas Jefferson, William James, John Dewey, John Rawls, and Robert Nozick.

Franklin is known as an inventor, writer, businessman, and statesman, but was he also a philosopher? How would one characterize Franklin's philosophy?

To understand his way of life, consider the story of the time he arrived in England as a colonial agent in 1757. His ship almost wrecked off the coastline of Cornwall, and the religiously inclined passengers were so happy to be alive that they vowed to build a shrine to a saint. But Franklin took a more practical approach: "If I were to vow at all, it should have been to build a lighthouse" (*CA*, p. 5).

ON RELIGION AND PHILOSOPHY

Later in life, after he returned to an independent America, an admirer sent him a letter indicating that the town of Franklin, Massachusetts, planned to build a bell tower for their church and asked if he would like to make a contribution. He sent them instead some books.

In a word, Franklin's philosophy was pragmatism, putting theory into practice, whether it be in his contributions to science, religion, or creating a new government. He was the earliest pragmatist, in the tradition of Ralph Waldo Emerson, Henry James, and John Dewey.

One of his favorite ancient philosophers was the Roman politician Cicero (106–43 BC). In fact, Franklin reprinted Cicero's long essay, *On a Life Well Spent*, in the *Gazette* in 1744. "The best armor of old age," Cicero wrote, "is a well spent life preceding it; a life employed in the pursuit of useful knowledge, in honorable actions and the practice of virtue."

Franklin practiced what Cicero preached. We have many examples of this practical "what works" approach to life. In his scientific pursuits, he wrote with simplicity and clarity, with little obfuscation. His experiments in electricity were not exercises in curiosity or high theory, but were meant ultimately to be useful to the common man. His inventions were practical devices, such as the lightning rod, the Franklin stove, bifocals, and charting the Gulf Stream across the Atlantic Ocean.

His religion was on the practical side. Several of Poor Richard's refrains point in this direction:

1. "A good example is the best sermon."
2. "A plowman on his legs is higher than a gentleman on his knees."
3. "Don't judge men's wealth or piety by their Sunday appearance."
4. "Many have quarreled about religion that never practiced it."

THE GREATEST AMERICAN

5. "A long life may not be good enough, but a good life is long enough."

In the *Autobiography*, Franklin described an occasion when he attended a sermon by a preacher who focused entirely on "polemic arguments" and "peculiar doctrines of our sect," which he found "very dry, uninteresting, and unedifying, since not a single moral principle was inculcated or enforced, their aim seeming to be rather to make us Presbyterians than good citizens" (*A*, p. 98).

Later, he wrote his sister Jane that "good works among some sorts of people are so little valued, and good words admired in their stead; I mean seemingly pious discourses instead of humane benevolent actions." He quoted a poem:

> A man of words and not of deeds,
> is like a garden full of weeds.

Later in life, he wrote, "Doubtlessly, faith has its use in the world; I do not desire to see it diminished, nor would I endeavor to lessen it in any man. But I wish it were more productive of good works than I have generally seen it: I mean real good works, works of kindness, charity, mercy, and public spirit; not holiday-keeping, sermon-reading or hearing, performing church ceremonies, or making long prayers, filled with flatteries and compliments, despised even by wise men, and much less capable of pleasing the Deity" (*CA*, p. 387).

In politics, he was seldom dogmatic, utopian, or intransigent. He learned from business to be a dealmaker, which led to the Great Compromise in the Constitutional Convention in 1787. On the final day of the convention, he urged his fellow delegates to "doubt a little of their own infallibility," and sign the document.

Franklin was also pragmatic when it came to war, which he regarded as wasteful and unnecessary. He wrote, "What vast additions to the conveniences and comforts of living might mankind have acquired if the money spent in wars had been employed in

ON RELIGION AND PHILOSOPHY

works of public utility! What an extension of agriculture…what rivers rendered navigable…what bridges, aqueducts, new roads, and other public works, edifices and improvements rendering England a complete paradise. But millions were spent in the great war doing mischief…and destroying the lives of so many thousands of working people who might have performed useful labor!" (*CA*, p. 302).

CHAPTER 69

ON GIVING AND CHARITY

"Great alms-giving lessens no man's living."
—*Poor Richard's Almanac*

"Gain all you can, save all you can, give all you."
—*John Wesley's Sermon #50 (1744)*

No doubt Benjamin Franklin was influenced by John Wesley's famous Sermon #50 on "The Use of Money" that he gave in the 1740s to his Methodist congregations.

Franklin was a profound believer in Wesley's three virtues—industry, thrift, and charity. There's a reason why John C. Bogle, founder of the Vanguard Group of mutual funds, calls Franklin not only America's first entrepreneur but "may well be our finest one." Bogle was impressed with Franklin's work ethic and his thriftiness. In fact, Bogle's mutual funds are famous for being the no-load funds with the lowest cost. Franklin would like that.

But there's another reason. Before and after retirement, Franklin set the standard for what a successful businessman should be like in his community. In his belief that "man is a social animal," he engaged in numerous civic activities to improve the city of Philadelphia.

ON RELIGION AND PHILOSOPHY

He didn't just manage his fortune and play golf every day. He devoted his time and funds to make a difference in the public arena for the common good. As a result of his example and leadership, Franklin helped establish Philadelphia as the leading political, cultural, and social center of colonial America. It was no accident that the Continental Congress met in Philadelphia to declare independence and write a new constitution.

Franklin was a tireless supporter of volunteer associations and philanthropic projects. Rather than depend on government and the great lords, as they did in Europe, Americans offered a better way: volunteer collective action and self-help individualism. He was especially influenced by the writings of Daniel Defoe's *An Essay Upon Projects* and Cotton Mather's *An Essay Upon the Good.* Here's a list of his civic accomplishments:

— He established the Junto in 1727, a club of mutual improvement consisting of merchants and local businesspeople, which served to increase "our influence in public affairs, and our power of doing good."

— He published the *Pennsylvania Gazette* in 1729, not just for profit, but to influence the general public and to inform and shape public opinion. He firmly believed in the vigorous exchange of ideas through a free press.

— He created the Library Company in 1731, the first private subscription circulating library in the nation.

— He organized the first volunteer fire company in 1736. His subsequent invention of the lightning rod helped local citizens to prevent fires in their communities.

— He created the American Philosophical Society in 1743 to encourage experiments and share discoveries in science and technology—electricity, agriculture, medicine, geology, mathematics, chemistry, man-

THE GREATEST AMERICAN

ufactures, and geography—whatever would benefit "mankind in general."

— He organized the Pennsylvania militia in 1748, a voluntary private military to defend colonial interests against the growing threat of French and Spanish privateers. He started a lottery to pay for a battery weapon and talked a neighboring governor into lending cannon.

— He proposed a formal education with the establishment of "the Academy" in 1751 that grew into the University of Pennsylvania. "Nothing is of more importance for the public weal, than to form and train up youth in wisdom and virtue," he wrote. It was the first secular non-religious education institution in the country.

— He established in 1751 the first hospital in Philadelphia, particularly "for the reception and cure of poor sick persons," especially those "whose poverty is made more miserable by the additional weight of a grievous disease." He raised the funds through his ingenious invention of the matching grant. He persuaded the legislature to promise £2,000 if the friends of the hospital could raise the same amount privately, and they did.

— He organized in 1751 the first insurance company in the colonies; fire was the number one adversary. The full name was the "Philadelphia Contributionship for the Insurance of Houses from Loss by Fire." It was called a mutual insurance plan, "whereby every man might help another, without any disservice to himself."

ON RELIGION AND PHILOSOPHY

— He helped organize the City Watch in 1752. He worked tirelessly to improve street lighting, by fitting it with four panes of glass and piercing the top and bottom to allow for ventilation, and paving the city's roads. "By talking and writing on the subject," Franklin wrote in his *Autobiography*, "I was at length instrumental in getting the street paved with stone between the market and the bricked foot-pavement that was on each side next the houses."

Franklin summed up the ideal businessman: "When I disengaged myself...from private business, I flattered myself that, by the sufficient though moderate fortune I had acquired, I had secured leisure during the rest of my life for philosophical studies [his scientific experiments] and amusements...and enlarge my power of doing good."

CHAPTER 70

FRANKLIN'S VERSION OF THE FIRST THANKSGIVING

"Instead of a fast they proclaimed a thanksgiving."
—*Benjamin Franklin (1785)*

Since 1941, Americans have celebrated the Thanksgiving holiday every fourth Thursday in November. It's not quite a unique American celebration, but close. Only Canada has a similar official holiday, the second Monday of October. Historically, the Greeks and Romans celebrated "harvest" days and Jews held the "Feast of Tabernacles."

What is the origin of Thanksgiving? According to tradition, a year after the Pilgrims landed in Plymouth Rock, they gathered together with the local Indians for a traditional English harvest festival that lasted three days. The winter of 1620–21 was especially harsh for the Puritans, who lost 46 of the original 102 who sailed on the *Mayflower*. Fortunately, the fall harvest in 1621 was a bountiful one, and fifty-three Pilgrims invited to the festival ninety Indians who had helped them survive the first winter.

There wasn't another Thanksgiving festival until fifty-five years later. Finally, in June 1676, the governing council of Charlestown,

ON RELIGION AND PHILOSOPHY

Massachusetts, held a meeting to decide the best way to express thanks to God for their good fortune.

Ben Franklin probably had this meeting in mind when he wrote his version of the first Thanksgiving. He writes:

> There is a tradition that in the planting of New England, the first settlers met with many difficulties and hardships, as is generally the case when a civilized people attempt to establish themselves in a wilderness country. Being so piously disposed, they sought relief from heaven by laying their wants and distresses before the Lord in frequent set days of fasting and prayer. Constant meditation and discourse on these subjects kept their minds gloomy and discontented, and like the children of Israel there were many disposed to return to the Egypt which persecution had induced them to abandon.
>
> At length, when it was proposed in the Assembly to proclaim another fast, a farmer of plain sense rose and remarked that the inconveniences they suffered, and concerning which they had so often wearied heaven with their complaints, were not so great as they might have expected, and were diminishing every day as the colony strengthened; that the earth began to reward their labor and furnish liberally for their subsistence; that their seas and rivers were full of fish, the air sweet, the climate healthy, and above all, they were in the full enjoyment of liberty, civil and religious.
>
> He therefore thought that reflecting and conversing on these subjects would be more

THE GREATEST AMERICAN

> comfortable and lead more to make them contented with their situation; and that it would be more becoming the gratitude they owed to the divine being, *if instead of a fast they should proclaim a thanksgiving.* His advice was taken, and from that day to this, they have in every year observed circumstances of public felicity sufficient to furnish employment for a *Thanksgiving Day*, which is therefore constantly ordered and religiously observed (*CA*, pp. 331–332).

Franklin loved this account because it fit better into his positive approach to community life and religious affairs. He preferred singing, dancing, good food and drink, fun games, social conversation, and good works of charity to the piety of fasting, long prayers, sermonizing, church ceremonies, and the excessively strict observation of the Sabbath.

Franklin would be especially pleased to see that the turkey is the bird of choice in the main Thanksgiving meal. The turkey ("wild fowl" included ducks, geese, and turkeys) was part of the first Thanksgiving. In a letter to his daughter Sarah in 1784, he said he preferred the turkey over the eagle as the symbol of America. "In truth," he wrote, "the turkey is in comparison a much more respectable bird, and a true original native of America.... He is besides, tho' a little vain and silly, a bird of courage, and would not hesitate to attack a grenadier of the British guards who should presume to invade his farm yard with a red coat on" (*CA*, p. 313).

The council of Charlestown, Massachusetts, declared June 29 as a day of thanksgiving. In 1789, George Washington tried to proclaim the first Thursday in November a national day of thanksgiving, and John Adams followed suit, but Thomas Jefferson discontinued the holiday. Magazine editor Sarah Josepha Hale kept the idea alive in her editorials in Boston's *Ladies' Magazine*, and

ON RELIGION AND PHILOSOPHY

finally, in 1863, President Abraham Lincoln proclaimed the last Thursday in November as the national day of Thanksgiving.

Thanksgiving was proclaimed by every president after Lincoln. The date was changed a couple of times, most recently by Franklin Roosevelt, who set it up one week to the next-to-last Thursday in order to create a longer Christmas shopping season. Public uproar against this decision caused the president to move Thanksgiving back to its original date two years later. And in 1941, Thanksgiving was finally sanctioned by Congress as a legal holiday, as the *fourth* Thursday in November.

CHAPTER 71

ON DYING AND THE AFTERLIFE

If life's compared to a feast,
Near fourscore years I've been a guest:
I've been regaled with the best,
And feel quite satisfied.

'Tis time that I retire to rest;
Landlord, I thank ye! Friends, good night.
A man is not completely born until he be dead:
Why then should we grieve?
—"B. F.'s Adieu!" (1784, age seventy-eight)

In chapter 22, I wrote about Franklin writing his last will and testament. But what about dying and the afterlife? Was the grand old man cheerful as he went to the grave, or did he follow the likes of poet Dylan Thomas, who urged his modern-day friends to fight to the bitter end: "Do not go gentle into that good night. Rage, rage against the dying of the light."

In completing Franklin's *Autobiography* in 2006, I discovered that the famous octogenarian took a well-deserved rest from his labors and turned to family, friends, and spiritual matters. Although his wife Deborah had passed away and he continued to suffer from the gout, kidney stones, and other ailments, he drew

ON RELIGION AND PHILOSOPHY

comfort from his loved ones and neighbors. "I feel myself a free man…I amuse myself in reading or writing, or in conversation with friends, joking, laughing, and telling merry stories, as if I were a young man about fifty. My children and grandchildren, the Baches, are all well, living in my house," he wrote (*CA*, p. 381).

He tried his hand at playing cards in the evenings, but sometimes felt a bit guilty not being engaged in some worthwhile pursuit. "I have indeed now and then a little compunction in reflecting that I spend time so idly: but another reflection comes to relieve me, whispering, 'You know the soul is immortal; why then should you be such a niggard of a little time when you have a whole eternity before you?' So being easily convinced, I shuffle the cards again, and begin another game" (*CA*, pp. 351–352).

He outlived almost all of his friends and enemies, and frequently attended funerals and sent letters of condolences. He often sent copies of a favorite letter he wrote when he was fifty years old that reflected his positive attitude toward death. He wrote his stepniece Elizabeth:

> I condole with you, we have lost a most dear and valuable relation, but it is the will of God and nature that these mortal bodies be laid aside, when the soul is to enter into real life; 'tis rather an embryo state, a preparation for living; a man is not completely born until he be dead: Why then should we grieve that a new child is born among the immortals? A new member added to their happy society? We are spirits. That bodies should be lent us, while they can afford us pleasure, assist us in acquiring knowledge, or doing good to our fellow creatures, is a kind and benevolent act of God. When they become unfit for these purposes and afford us pain instead of pleasure—instead of an aid, become an encumbrance and answer none

> of the intentions for which they were given—it is
> equally kind and benevolent that a way is pro-
> vided by which we may get rid of them. Death is
> that way (*CA*, p. 391).

Franklin wasn't regular churchgoer or true believer, but he harbored no doubts about the existence of God or an afterlife. His creed was simple: "I believe in one God, creator of the universe. That he governs it by his providence. That he ought to be worshipped. That the most acceptable service we can render to him is doing good to his other children. That the soul of man is immortal, and will be treated with justice in another life respecting its conduct in this" (*CA*, p. 385).

What about the evils of mankind and the injustices Franklin saw? "The more I see the impossibility, from the number and extent of his crimes, of giving equivalent punishment to a wicked man in this life, the more I am convinced of a future state in which all that here appears to be wrong shall be set right, all that is crooked made straight. In this faith let us comfort ourselves" (*CA*, p. 275).

Regarding Jesus of Nazareth, he wrote Rev. Ezra Stiles, president of Yale College, that he considered his "system of morals and his religion the best the world ever saw," but still had "some doubts as to his divinity." He then added, "it is a question I do not dogmatize upon, having never studied it, and think it needless to busy myself with it now, when I expect soon an opportunity of knowing the truth with less trouble" (*CA*, p. 385).

A few years before passing away, he expressed curiosity about the next life from a scientific viewpoint, wondering what space travel would be like in the spirit world. He wrote a friend, "having seen during a long life a good deal of this world, I feel a growing curiosity to be acquainted with some other, and can cheerfully with filial confidence resign my spirit to the conduct of that great and good parent of mankind, who created it, and who has so gra-

ON RELIGION AND PHILOSOPHY

ciously protected and prospered me from my birth to the present hour" (*CA*, p. 392).

When he was only twenty-three years of age, he wrote the following epitaph, and gave it to many of his friends over the years—a fitting expression of his firm belief in a better life after death:

The Body of
B. Franklin,
Printer;
Like the cover of an old book,
Its contents torn out,
And stript of its lettering and gilding,
Lies here, food for worms,
But the work shall not be wholly lost:
For it will, as he believ'd, appear once more,
In a new & more perfect edition,
Corrected and amended
By the author.

CHAPTER 72

CLAIMED BY THE MASONS AND THE MORMONS

In chapter 6, Franklin's exclusive, by-invitation-only club, the Junto, was described. Initially it was a secret organization limited to twelve individuals, like the Apostles at the University of Cambridge.

Franklin found secret organizations appealing. Freemasonry was one such organization because it was exclusive, sociable, and non-denominational. Today the brotherhood of Freemasons are usually good citizens who do charitable work, but during the eighteenth century, they were much more controversial. The Masonic Lodges were allegedly based on the rites of Solomon's Temple, the Knights Templar, and the Egyptian pyramids. The Freemasons were infamous for their solemn oaths, handshakes, and secret signs, enforced by severe penalties.

It was rumored that judges, sitting in court, may be easier on a masonic prisoner who made a secret sign to the judge.

Four years after creating the Junto, in 1731, Franklin became an active and enthusiastic Freemason, members of which had great influence in Pennsylvania, the colonies, and Europe. A minority of

ON RELIGION AND PHILOSOPHY

the founding fathers were members, but they were highly influential, including George Washington, James Madison, Paul Revere, John Paul Jones, John Hancock, and James Monroe. Benedict Arnold was also a member. Eight of Washington's aides were Freemasons. When Washington attended the laying of the foundation stone of the Capitol in 1793, he wore his masonic apron.

In Britain, members included Edmund Burke, and in France, Marquis de Lafayette.

Franklin drafted the first bylaws of the St. John's Lodge #1 (which is still standing), and in 1734, printed *The Constitutions of the Free-Masons*, the first formally sponsored Masonic book in America. It wasn't long before he became the grand master of all of Pennsylvania's Freemasons.

When a public controversary arose about the goings on in the St. John's Lodge, he wrote his parents, "As to the Freemasons...I must entreat her [Franklin's mother] to suspend her judgment till she is better informed, unless she will believe me when I assure her that they are in general a very harmless sort of people, and have no principles or practices that are inconsistent with religion and good manners."[45]

When he became ambassador to France in 1778, he joined the Masonic Lodge of the Nine Sisters, which consisted, to some extent, of free thinkers. Most members were sympathetic to the American cause, and Franklin joined to benefit his diplomatic mission.

After joining the lodge, he met the controversial Voltaire and invited him to become a member. John Adams wrote cynically of the occasion, "The two aged actors upon the greater theater of philosophy and frivolity then embraced each other by hugging one another in their arms and kissing each other's cheeks, and then the tumult subsided.... How charming it was! Oh, it was enchanting to see Solon and Sophocles embracing!"[46]

---

45 Ben Franklin's letter to Josiah and Abiah Franklin, April 13, 1738.
46 John Adams Journal, April 29, 1778.

THE GREATEST AMERICAN

Franklin's membership in the Masonic Lodge led to accusations of spying for the British.

For more information, see *The Freemasons: A History of the World's Most Powerful Secret Society* by Jasper Ridley (Arcade Press, 2001).

FRANKLIN IN THE AFTERLIFE SEEKS OUT THE MORMON PROPHET

The Mormons also have a fascinating connection with Benjamin Franklin after his death.

Ben Franklin did not fear death; in fact, he looked forward to entering the world of spirits and eventually the resurrected soul. He wrote a friend, "Having seen during a long life a good deal of this world, I feel a growing curiosity to be acquainted with some other, and can cheerfully with filial confidence resign my spirit to the conduct of that great and good parent of mankind, who created it, and who has so graciously protected and prospered me from my birth to the present hour" (*CA*, p. 392).

In Mormon lore, after the Latter-day Saints moved to Utah, the spirit of Franklin, along with other prominent Americans, appeared in 1887 before Wilford Woodruff, the president of the St. George Utah Temple (he would later become president of the church).

The St. George Temple in southern Utah was the first Mormon temple built by the Mormons after they were driven out of the East by anti-Mormons forty years earlier.

Mormon temples are unique sacred buildings, where faithful members engage in various ceremonies, including marriages and baptisms by proxy for people who have not been baptized during their lifetimes. Some comparisons have been made between the Mormon temples and the Mason temples—Mormons also make secret covenants, handshakes, and oaths, and wear an apron. Perhaps that may be one reason the spirit of Franklin found the Mormon ceremonies attractive.

ON RELIGION AND PHILOSOPHY

President Woodruff spoke about it to church members: "Before I left St. George, the spirits of the dead gathered around me, wanting to know why we did not redeem them. Said they, 'You have had the use of the Endowment House [the temple] for a number of years, and yet nothing has been done for us. We laid the foundation for the government you now enjoy, and we never apostatized from it, but we remained true to it and were faithful to God.'"[47]

President Woodruff indicated that the founding fathers waited on him for two days and two nights as he and his assistant, Brother John D. T. McAllister, were baptized for the signers of these historic documents of freedom, along with fifty other prominent men (such as Columbus and presidents of the United States). Among them were George Washington and Benjamin Franklin.

One of the reasons why the spirits of Franklin, Washington, and the other founders might find the Mormon faith appealing is the church's defense of the Constitution. In Latter-day Saint scripture the Lord says: "And for this purpose have I established the Constitution of this land, by the hands of wise men whom I raised up unto this very purpose, and redeemed the land by the shedding of blood" (Doctrine and Covenants 101:80).

But the story does not end there for Franklin. Several years later, on the night of March 19, 1894, President Woodruff recorded a dream following his meditations about the future and the work he had for the dead. In his dream Ben Franklin appeared to him, who sought additional temple blessings. "I spent some time with him and we talked over our temple ordinances which had been administered for Franklin and others. He wanted more work done for him than had already been done. I promised him it should be done. I awoke and then made up my mind to receive further blessings for Benjamin Franklin and George Washing-

---

47 Wilford Woodruff, *Discourses of Wilford Woodruff* (Salt Lake City: Bookcraft, 1946), pp. 160–161.

THE GREATEST AMERICAN

ton."[48] The temple records indicate that Franklin and Washington were ordained high priests that would make them leaders in the world of spirits.

---

48 Mattias F. Cowley, *Wilford Woodruff: History of His Life and Labors* (Salt Lake City: Deseret News, 1909), p. 586.

PART X

PERSONAL

CHAPTER 73

FRANKLIN'S 13 VIRTUES

"I wished to live without committing any fault at any time. [So] I conceived the bold and arduous project of arriving at moral perfection."
—*Ben Franklin*

In some ways, Franklin saw himself, like Adam Smith, as a moral philosopher. Probably the biggest reason why Franklin's *Autobiography* became the world's most famous life story is his list of thirteen virtues. Schools assigned it "must" reading for students after the Civil War and into the 1920s.

In his memoirs, he reported that sometime around 1730, after he married Deborah, he decided to create his own plan on "moral perfection." He was a skeptic of formal religion and hated doctrinal debates. He wanted to focus on proper conduct.

So he came up with twelve virtues, followed by some pithy comments:

1. Temperance: Eat not to Dullness, drink not to elevation.
2. Silence: Speak not but what may benefit others or yourself. Avoid trifling Conversation.
3. Order: Let all your Things have their Places. Let each Part of your Business have its Time.

THE GREATEST AMERICAN

4. Resolution: Resolve to perform what you ought. Perform without fail what you resolve.
5. Frugality: Make no Expense but to do good to others or yourself: i.e. Waste Nothing.
6. Industry: Lose no Time. Be always employ'd in something useful. Cut off all unnecessary Actions
7. Sincerity: Use no hurtful Deceit. Think innocently and justly; and, if you speak; speak accordingly.
8. Justice: Wrong none, by doing Injuries or omitting the Benefits that are your Duty.
9. Moderation: Avoid Extremes. Forbear resenting Injuries so much as you think they deserve.
10. Cleanliness: Tolerate no Uncleanness in Body, Clothes, or Habitation
11. Tranquility: Be not disturbed at Trifles, or at Accidents common or unavoidable.
12. Chastity: Rarely use Venery but for Health or Offspring; Never to Dullness, Weakness, or the Injury of your own or another's Peace or Reputation.

After making the list, he worked up a chart to measure his success in meeting these twelve virtues. He was surprised to discover how hard it was to break old habits, especially keeping everything in "order." Franklin's contemporaries always commented on how messy Franklin was, even as a diplomat.

What's interesting are the virtues that he left off the list. The Scout Law also has twelve virtues, but Franklin's ignores some of the more essential ones like courtesy, bravery, and reverence. Most of his virtues are self-centered. For example, he fails to mention forgiveness, repentance, gratitude, and charity, four of the most famous Christian principles.

Yet he wrote to a friend, "Doubtlessly, faith has its use in the world; I do not desire to see it diminished, nor would I endeavor to lessen it in any man. But I wish it were more productive of good

PERSONAL

works than I have generally seen it: I mean real good works, works of kindness, charity, mercy, and public spirit; not holiday-keeping, sermon-reading or hearing, performing church ceremonies, or making long prayers, filled with flatteries and compliments, despised even by wise men, and much less capable of pleasing the Deity" (*CA*, p. 387).

He also left off an important one in business and finance: prudence. He considered it third of his financial trinity in his booklet, "The Way to Wealth," after industry and thrift. By prudence, he meant to beware of taking on too much risk or debt. I suppose "moderation" might be similar.

Franklin wrote about his "plan of life" when he was ambassador in France in 1784, and knew that his memoirs would be made public. The list of virtues was, in many ways, a ruse and an act of conceit. For his reputation did not fit many of the virtues he listed. As noted earlier, he was famous for his silence, industry, and thrift, but not for orderliness, temperance, or chastity. His critics made their own list of Franklin peccadilloes: cunning, secretive, opportunist, hedonist, and vain.

In fact, after he showed this list around, a Quaker friend kindly informed him that he was generally thought to be proud, overbearing, and insolent in conversation. Franklin responded, "I determined endeavoring to cure myself, if I could, of this vice or folly among the rest, and I added humility to my list." He added: "Humility: Imitate Jesus and Socrates" (*A*, p. 109).

CHAPTER 74

MAN OF LETTERS: ON THE IMPORTANCE OF LETTER WRITING

"If you would not be forgotten,
As soon as you are dead and rotten,
Either write things worth reading,
Or do things worth the writing."
—*Poor Richard's Almanac*

Franklin recognized early on the importance of the pen. In his lifetime, he wrote numerous columns, essays, pamphlets, and letters to the editor (usually anonymously) on a variety of topics. Personal correspondence was Franklin's primary way of talking to his friends and relatives.

The *Papers of Benjamin Franklin* being edited at Yale University contain over thirty thousand items. Half of them are personal letters that he wrote in his eighty-four-year lifetime—to his wife Deborah and other family members, his fellow business colleagues, scientists, politicians, and diplomats. Some days he wrote as many as thirty letters of correspondence.

He maintained a sixty-year correspondence with his youngest sister, Jane, which was covered in a book called *Book of Ages: The*

PERSONAL

Life and Opinions of Jane Franklin, by Harvard historian Jill Lapore. Their relationship was so close that they called each other Benny and Jenny. They exchanged loving, gossipy, bantering, and vexing letters over more than sixty years. Her letters have disappeared but most of his were preserved. Jane had a tough life, having twelve children but only one survived, and he suffered one tragedy after another.

In completing Franklin's *Autobiography* (1757–1790), I read many of his letters. Some of my favorites are found in the chapter on 1775–76, the start of the American Revolution.

His involvement in political affairs was so intense that he wrote few letters during this time (1775–76). Fortunately, Arthur Lee, one of the American commissioners to France, wrote a lengthy letter summarizing Franklin's perspective during this critical time in US history. Without that letter, I don't think I could have compiled a "compleated" picture of 1776, that critical year, in Franklin's own words.

Franklin did send a letter to his estranged son William (Billy) after the war was over, but relations between them had soured, since William fought on the British side during the war. (The letter below is quoted in part.)

> Passy, France, August 16, 1784
> Dear Son,
>
> Nothing has ever hurt me so much and affected me with such keen sensations, as to find myself deserted in my old age by my only son; and not only deserted, but to find him taking up Arms against me, in a Cause wherein my good fame, fortune and life were all at stake. You conceived, you say, that your duty to your King and regard for your country required this. I ought not to blame you for differing

in sentiment with me in public affairs. We are men, all subject to errors. Our opinions are not in our power; they are formed and governed much by circumstances that are often as inexplicable as they are irresistible. Your situation was such that few would have censured your remaining neutral, though there are natural duties which precede political ones, and cannot be extinguished by them. This is a disagreeable subject. I drop it. And we will endeavor as you propose mutually to forget what has happened relating to it, as well as we can.

Your affectionate father,
B. Franklin

On a lighter note, he did have some wonderful correspondence with his favorite lady friend, Madame Brillon, while ambassador to France in the late 1770s. "Madame Brillon wished to divert me for a moment from my affairs with a little amusement." They exchanged letters about books, philosophy, religion, and even sex. He spent an evening twice a week at her home with her husband and children, where "she kindly entertained me and my grandson with little concerts, a dish of tea, and a game of chess. I call this my opera." He wrote to a friend, "The French ladies had a thousand ways of rendering themselves agreeable by their various attentions and civilities, & their sensible conversation. 'Tis a delightful people to live with."

Although he was a strong advocate of technological advances, I suspect Franklin would have misgivings about replacing personal letter writing with emails and texting as today's modern methods of correspondence. Sadly, writing handwritten letters has become a lost art.

PERSONAL

When I get a personal handwritten letter from a friend or acquaintance, I cherish it. Several years ago, I received just such a letter from the historian David McCullough in response to my sending him an inscribed copy of *The Compleated Autobiography by Benjamin Franklin*. He wrote in his own hand, "Your idea of completed Franklin's Autobiography is ingenious and inspired!"

I encourage you to follow in Franklin's footsteps by sending friends and colleagues a handwritten letter or note.

CHAPTER 75

ON ENJOYING THE HOLIDAYS

"Be always at war with your vices, at peace with your neighbors, and let each new year find you a better man."
—*Poor Richard's Almanac*

You would never think of Ben Franklin as an advocate of carefree leisure, long vacations, or relaxing with friends and relatives during the holidays. He had to be up and doing!

He was famous for lines like these from *Poor Richard's Almanac*:

1. "Laziness travels so slowly that poverty should overtakes him."
2. "The honest man takes pains, and then enjoys pleasures; the knave takes pleasures, and then suffers pain."

And this one:

"Life with Fools consists in Drinking; With the wise Man, Living's Thinking."

For Franklin, "time is money," and he warned, "Doth thou love life? Then do not squander time, for that's the stuff life is made of."

PERSONAL

Christmas time and other holidays should be taken seriously, not for idle pleasure and amusement. "How many observe Christ's Birth-day! How few, his Precepts! O! 'tis easier to keep Holidays than Commandments," said Poor Richard. "'Tis not a Holiday that's not kept holy."

In reading his *Papers*, I found that Franklin often spent the holidays writing letters about business matters and scientific pursuits. He was always in a hurry.

Yet, as the father of American thrift and hard work became older, he mellowed. At the age of seventy, as ambassador to France, he learned a lot from the French, who were famous for frivolity, late-night dinners, and sleeping in. He adopted their lifestyle, much to the consternation of Puritan workaholic John Adams. No more "early to bed, early to rise, makes a man healthy, wealthy and wise" for Ben Franklin. He stayed out late and sometimes slept until noon. He later wrote a friend, "I find I love company, chat, a laugh, a glass, and even a song...and at the same time relish...the grave observations and wise sentences of old men's conversations" (*CA*, p. 18).

And he did not forget the ladies. Among the French belles, he soon forgot his ditty: "Women & Wine, Game & Deceit, Make the Wealth small and the Wants great." His new refrain was "If you would be loved, love and be lovable" and "With bounteous Cheer, Conclude the Year."

Christmas time was a time to relax and share the rich bounties of life. Said Franklin, "In *Christmas* feasting pray take care; Let not your table be a Snare; But with the Poor God's Bounty share. Adieu my Friends! till the next Year."

In Paris, Franklin attended dinners and parties galore. He regularly visited the home of Madame Brillion de Jouy, who played music for him. On Christmas Day 1781, he wrote Madame Brillon, who was away in Nice, addressing her "*ma chere amie*," and expressing how much he missed her "charming noels" of Christmas past.

THE GREATEST AMERICAN

Upon returning to Philadelphia after the war, he talked of spending his time "so idly" during the long winter of 1785–86 with family and friends, "in conversation, books, my garden, and cribbage." During the holidays, it was time for playing cards and chess (his favorite game). "I passed a winter agreeably in that manner in Passy a few years ago when Polly Stevenson visited us from London," he wrote.

Did he feel guilty about so much play time? "I have indeed now and then a little compunction in reflecting that I spent time so idly; but another reflection comes to relieve me, whispering, 'You know the soul is immortal; why then should you be so stingy of a little time when you have a whole eternity before you?' So being easily convinced, I shuffled the cards again, and began another game" (*CA*, pp. 351–352).

As for holiday gifts, Franklin often sent presents to friends and family. But the best gift was gathering together for a party. "A true friend is the best possession."

On New Year's Day, he wrote his last surviving sister, Jane Mecum, "Our good God has brought us…to the beginning of a New Year. The measure of health and strength we enjoy…is a great blessing. Let us be cheerful and thankful."

Perhaps this poem would best befit Franklin at this time of year:

"Reader, farewell, all Happiness attend thee;
May each *New Year*, better and richer find thee."

CHAPTER 76

ON FAMOUS ANCESTORS AND THE FAMILY TREE

"A man who makes boast of his ancestors does but advertise his own insignificance."
—*Ben Franklin*

Doing genealogy and the family tree are big business these days, especially since the introduction of the internet. Familysearch.org and Ancestory.com are popular sites that attract millions of interested citizens. In 1999, *Time* magazine named genealogy as one of the four most popular topics on the internet, behind sex, finance, and sports.

Ben Franklin himself was a genealogist, being "curious in collecting family anecdotes," and wrote extensively in the beginning part of his *Autobiography* about his ancestors in England. He proudly noted that "Franklin" meant "free man," and noted that he was uniquely the "youngest son of the youngest son for five generations."

He learned this fact when he and his son William traveled to his ancestral home of Ecton, England, in 1758, when he was a colonial agent. He wrote, "Billy and I travelled over a great part of

THE GREATEST AMERICAN

England; and among other places visited the town my father was born in and found some relations in that part of the country still living (Thomas Franklin in Leicestershire, and his daughter Sally Franklin, who later lived with me in London). We went to Ecton, being the village where my father was born, and where his father, grandfather, and great-grandfather had lived. We went first to see the old house and grounds; the land is now added to another farm, and a school kept in the house: it is a decayed old stone building, but still known by the name of Franklin House."

He and his son visited the church where the births, marriages, and burials of his ancestors were recorded for two hundred years. The rector's wife remembered a great deal about the Franklin line. "She entertained and diverted us highly with stories of Thomas Franklin, who was a conveyancer, something of a lawyer, clerk of the county court, and clerk to the archdeacon, in his visitations; a very leading man in all county affairs, and much employed in public business. He set on foot a subscription for erecting chimes in their steeple, and completed it, and we heard them play. He found out an easy method of saving their village meadows from being drowned, as they used to be sometimes by the river, which method is still in being; but when first proposed, nobody could conceive how it could be; but however, they said, if Franklin says he knows how to do it, it will be done. His advice and opinion was sought for on all occasions, by all sorts of people, and he was looked upon, she said, by some as something of a conjurer. He died just four months before I was born, on the same day of the same month" (*CA*, pp. 13–14).

Franklin explained that he was named after an uncle who was a silk dyer in London. Franklin's father, Josiah, married young and moved to New England around 1682. He had seven children from his first wife, and after she died, he married another and had ten more children. Ben was the youngest son of the second wife, Abiah Folger.

PERSONAL

However, Franklin thought every man and woman should stand on their own, and not depend on famous ancestors to get ahead in life. He criticized the "blue blood" tradition in Europe that "families may be perpetuated with estates."

When Europeans came to Franklin for advice about moving to America, he said, "There were many in Europe who hoped for offices and public employments, who valued themselves and expected to be valued by us for their birth or quality." He warned them, "Those bear no price in our markets. In America, people do not inquire concerning a stranger, *What is he?* But *What can he do?*" (*CA*, p. 292).

It should be noted that Franklin was famous for nepotism in his career, arranging for his son William to be the royal governor of New Jersey, his son-in-law Richard Bache to be the postmaster in Philadelphia, and his grandson Temple to be his secretary in France—most of which he later regretted.

HOW I'M RELATED TO "GRAMPA BEN"

I've had a lifelong interest in the "grandfather" of our nation, going back to a long-standing tradition in my mother's line of being related to Franklin through his daughter, Sally. My mother, Helen Louise McCarty (1925–2007) even looks like Franklin's profile. For years no one knew exactly how we were related other than the fact that it was rumored to be through an illegitimate line long ago. In the late 1970s, my wife and I decided to do some genealogical work in Philadelphia. We could trace back our ancestors to the Franklin family, but there was a missing generation. Then we discovered a will proving that my siblings and I were direct descendants through Benjamin Franklin's grandson Louis Bache, who according to his will, had two "natural sons" from an unmarried servant, one of whom was also named Louis. It turned out that the missing generation was due to the fact that there were two Louis Baches! Louis Jr. was raised by his father (shades of Ben and his illegitimate son William) and is my direct ancestor. This relationship was hidden by the Baches because of the embarrassment of Louis Bache Sr. having two illegitimate sons. But it all came out in Louis Sr.'s will.

It turns out that Ben Franklin is my eighth-generation grandfather through the Louis Bach line. So, I have 1/512th of Franklin's blood.

I often joke that the only thing I inherited from Grampa Ben was that we are both left-handed. However, my career has sometimes followed Franklin's footsteps as a publisher, author, financial advisor, public servant, world traveler, and innovator.

HAVE FRANKLIN DESCENDANTS MADE ANY CONTRIBUTIONS?

Franklin honored his ancestors for doing good, but he offered no guarantees in honoring his descendants, especially after enduring his beloved son William's betrayal during the American Revolution. He had more faith in his other children and grandchildren, such as Temple and Benny. As *Poor Richard's Almanac* states, "Let our fathers and grandfathers be valued for *their* goodness, ourselves for our own," adding, "A man who makes boast of his ancestors does but advertise his own insignificance."

Benjamin ("Benny") Franklin Bache (1769–1798) went on to some notoriety as the editor of the *Philadelphia Aurora* newspaper and was jailed for his personal attacks on George Washington and John Adams. After his release, he suddenly died of yellow fever. Several biographies have been written about Bache.

Another Benjamin Franklin Bache (1839–1900), the great grandson of Benjamin Franklin and the son of Louis Bache Jr., was famous for two inventions: the fireman's pole and the keychain! The apple doesn't fall far from the tree. He was a captain in the Civil War and lived in Louisville, Kentucky.

CHAPTER 77

ON LOVE, SEX, AND MARRIAGE: FRANKLIN'S HARD-TO-GOVERN PASSIONS

*"There are three friends in life—a faithful wife,
an old mistress, and ready money!"*
—*Poor Richard's Almanac*

*"Keep your eyes wide open before marriage,
and half shut after marriage."*
—*Poor Richard's Almanac*

Eventually, I knew a chapter on Franklin's infamous reputation as a lady's man had to be written. We know the public Franklin as a printer, diplomat, and founding father. But privately, there was another side to Franklin: a freethinker, a nudist, a hoaxer, a clubber, and bon vivant extraordinaire whom women couldn't resist. The giant of Philadelphia wasn't a distant, stoic figure like the reserved George Washington or the uptight John Adams. He was a charismatic, lively American playboy who defied the prudish norms of a sexually repressed Puritan society. With an irresistible charm, Benjamin Franklin captivated women with his humor, storytelling, fame, and worldly sophistication. A thoroughly modern founding father, Franklin was free of the usual inhibitions that plagued many of his peers.

From fancy-free youth to octogenarian sage, ol' Ben was a man who fueled the flames of passion throughout his life. We are constantly reminded of his humanness and his playboy image. In his *Autobiography*, he readily admitted that "the hard-to-be-governed passion of youth had hurried me frequently into intrigues with low women that fell in my way" (*A*, p. 81, always censored in early editions). Luckily, he escaped catching a venereal disease, although his sexual exploits proved expensive and the cause of one unfortunate consequence, the birth of a "natural" son William by a mother Franklin whose name was never revealed. In 1730, at the age of twenty-four, he moved in with his common-law wife, Deborah. The marriage was informal because Debbie was previously married and her irresponsible husband left for the Caribbean without a divorce, and it was uncertain whether he would return (rumor had it that he died in a brawl). She raised William in their home, and thus Franklin said he "corrected that great erratum as well as I could" (*A*, p. 82).

The relationship between Billy and Franklin's wife was tempestuous. Debbie made it known to friends that he was not her own. She was frequently hostile to him. According to a clerk who worked for the family, Deborah referred to Billy as "the greatest villain upon earth" and heaped upon him "invectives in the foulest terms I ever heard from a gentlewoman."[49]

In his memoirs, written for public consumption, he would have us believe that he daily plotted a life of thirteen virtues, among them temperance, moderation, and chastity. He urged his young readers to "rarely use venery but for health or offspring." And did not Poor Richard warn, "Women & wine, game & deceit, makes the wealth small and wants great"? Yet his own story suggests that he surely practiced all the more a "healthy" sex life. "He went

---

49 Isaacson, *Benjamin Franklin*, p. 77.

PERSONAL

to women hungrily, secretly, and briefly," states Carl Van Doren (p. 91).

"ADVICE TO A YOUNG MAN ON THE CHOICE OF A MISTRESS"

The Philadelphia publisher fueled the promiscuous rumors with his own writings. Many of those convinced of Franklin's philandering point to excerpts from a provocative little letter published anonymously in 1745, entitled "Advice to a Young Man on the Choice of a Mistress."

The anonymous writer counsels a young man on the pros and cons of taking on a mistress. It was banned from publication in America until the early twentieth century, when Franklin was revealed as the true author.

Titillated by Franklin's "advice" on choosing a mistress, most readers ignore his sound advice in the first part of the letter, where he extols the virtues of marriage. "Marriage is the proper remedy" to the sex drive, he wrote. "It is the most natural state of man, and therefore the state in which you are mostly likely to find solid happiness.... It is the man and woman united that makes the complete human being.... If you get a prudent, healthy wife, your industry in your profession, with her good economy, will be a fortune sufficient."

However, if the reader refused to take his counsel to marry, Franklin suggested that he should take on an older woman as a mistress. The advantages? Older women are better conversationalists, more tender and amiable, more prudent and discreet, and better experienced in the art of love. Do not worry about their physical appearance, he advised, for "in the dark all cats are grey." And lastly, older women are preferred because "they are so grateful!!"

"THE SPEECH OF MISS POLLY BAKER"

Two years later, in 1747, an article appeared in the *Gentlemen's Magazine* in London under the title "The Speech of Miss Polly Baker." It was again published anonymously.

The author ostensively defended a single mother in England who was prosecuted for the fifth time for having an illegitimate child. She proclaimed before the court, "Can it be a crime to add to the king's subjects, in a new country that really needs people? I own it, I should think it a praiseworthy, rather than a punishable action. I have debauched no other woman's husband, nor enticed any other youth…. But how can it be believed that heaven is angry at my having children, when to the little done by me toward it, God has been pleased to add His divine skill & admirable workmanship in the formation of their bodies, and crowned the whole by furnishing them with rational and immortal souls?"

In this op-ed, Franklin protests the inequality of the prevailing justice system, which punished women for out-of-wedlock sexual relations by imposing fines and whippings while the father of the child went without punishment.

MARRIAGE AND SEPARATION

Despite these missives, Franklin, while living in Philadelphia until 1757, appears to be a faithful husband to his wife Deborah, with whom he had two children, a boy Francis (or Franky), who died tragically at age four from smallpox, and a daughter Sarah, who later married, had children, and cared for Franklin in his final years.

Husband and wife worked closely together to make the printing business a financial success. "She proved a good and faithful helpmate, assisted me much by attending the shop; we throve together, and have ever mutually endeavored to make each other happy" (*A*, p. 82).

PERSONAL

However, we do know of one encounter with a young beauty that tested his fidelity. In one of his many trips as deputy postmaster, in 1754, he met a flirtatious twenty-three-year-old brunette named Catharine Ray, described by historian Thomas Fleming as a young lady who would torment men "with her dancing eyes and low-cut gowns." The forty-nine-year-old traveling businessman was smitten, and they spent many evenings together in Boston in a dance of desire and tête-à-tête. At one point, Franklin talked about sex and suggested he could be her lover, but she recoiled and reminded him that he was a married man. He retreated. "His rational head had prevailed over his wayward heart."

On his way back home to Philadelphia, Franklin dreamed of a romantic encounter with Ray, but as he drew closer to home, he began driving his horse faster and faster until "a very few days brought me to my own house and to the arms of my good old wife and children."[50]

Deborah was made aware of their correspondence, but their marriage was severely tested after Franklin sailed to England in 1757 as colonial agent. As husband and wife, they lived separately for the remaining seventeen years of their marriage (he returned briefly for a couple of years, 1762–64).

Ben begged Debbie to join him abroad, but she had an "invincible aversion to crossing the seas" and refused to accompany him to London in 1757, despite numerous pleas. Once in England, his publisher friend William Strahan (who would later published Edward Gibbon's *The History of the Decline and Fall of the Roman Empire* and Adam Smith's *Wealth of Nations* in the fateful year of 1776) wrote a letter to Debbie encouraging her to sail to England by telling her "There are many ladies here that would make no objection to sailing twice as far after him" (*CA*, p. 8).

In any case, they grew distant, and Franklin was still in London when Debbie died in December 1774.

---

50 Thomas Fleming, *The Intimate Lives of the Founding Fathers* (New York: Harper, 2010), 82–83.

FRANKLIN'S RELATIONSHIP WITH MARGARET STEVENSON

For years, Franklin stayed at a boarding house at 36 Craven Street (now a museum), run by widow Margaret Stevenson. He was amiable to her and maintained a lifelong friendship with her daughter, Polly. Ben and Margaret lived in the same house for fifteen years, which included a long period during which the time and setting were right for sexual relations. Franklin scholar Claude-Anne Lopez concludes, "He lived abroad for fifteen years of the last seventeen years of his marriage. It strains credulity to imagine that so vigorous a man was never unfaithful in all that time. But whatever he may have done to another's peace, he did no injury to anyone's reputation."

Historian Thomas Fleming is convinced that they had informal, though never legal, marriage.

THE HELLFIRE CLUB

Meanwhile, in London, Franklin enjoyed the clubs and the social life. "I find I love company, chat, a laugh, a glass, and even a song… and wise sentences of old men's conversation."

Though not a member, he was known to occasionally frequent the "Order of the Friars of St. Francis of Wycombe," better known as the infamous Hellfire Club, which catered to the hard-drinking and womanizing habits of wealthy patrons. Created by the British politician Francis Dashwood, the Hellfire Club served as the meeting place outside of London for "persons of quality" who wished to partake in mock rituals, worship the devil and false gods, and engage in obscene parodies of religious rites, which allegedly included prostitutes dressed up as nuns. It was mostly a parody of Elizabethan mores.

FRANKLIN AND THE FRENCH LADIES

Following the signing of the Declaration of Independence from England in 1776, Franklin was appointed US ambassador to

PERSONAL

France. The French lionized America's first ambassador. "This is the civilest nation upon Earth," he wrote in a letter. "Tis a delightful people to live with." "All my pleasant dreams are laid in that city," he said. His nine years in Paris were remembered as "the sweet society of a people whose conversation is instructive, whose manners are highly pleasing, and who...[have] the art of making themselves beloved by strangers."[51]

Franklin was a cause célèbre. While procuring financial and military assistance and a treaty with France, he received gifts, awards, and honors. Portraits, medallions, and engravings of the old man became popular. He dined with the Duc de La Rochefoucauld, met with Anne-Robert Turgot and Voltaire, and later presented himself before the youthful King Louis XVI and Queen Marie Antoinette at Versailles. Marie Antoinette called Franklin *l'ambassadeur electrique*. Jean-Antoine Houdon made his famous bust of Franklin. A widely circulated epigram, attributed to Turgot, declares, *Eripuit coelo fulmen sceptrumque tyrannis* ("He seized the lightning from Heaven and the scepter from tyrants").

The celebrated diplomat was there for nine long years as the war dragged in what one could describe as *une affaire de coeur* ("a matter of the heart"). It was in Paris that his reputation grew as a charmer of French ladies. Franklin, now a widower in his seventies, was capable of the most courteous gallantry, compliments, witticisms and bagatelles, and entertained the French women as a distraction from his many duties and controversies. "Women, especially, flocked to see him, to speak to him for hours on end," commented his friend Jean-Baptiste Le Roy. Franklin was a defender of women's rights and treated them as his equals. He wrote his step-niece in 1779, "Somebody gave it out that I loved ladies; and then everybody presented me their ladies (or the ladies presented themselves) to be embraced, that is to have their necks kissed. For as to kissing of lips or cheeks it is not the mode here, the first is

---

51 Paul Leicester Ford, *The Many-Sided Franklin* (New York: The Century Co., 1899), p. 505.

reckoned rude, and the other may rub off the paint. The French ladies have however a thousand other ways of rendering themselves agreeable" (*CA*, p. 161).

"*Mon cher Papa*" responded passionately to the French tradition of flirting and developed a considerable relationship with several beautiful French women, including the glamorous Madame Anne-Louise Brillon; Anne-Catherine de Ligniville, known as Notre Dame d'Auteuil or Madame Helvétius; and La Comtesse d'Houdetot. "*Ame du héros, et du sage!*" the countess greeted him at his visit to her home in Sanois.

Members of the American diplomatic party (Arthur Lee, Ralph Izard, and John Adams) did not respond so favorably to French coquetry. Madame Brillon wrote Franklin, "Do you know, my dear Papa, that people have the audacity to criticize my pleasant habit of sitting upon your knees…" (*CA*, pp. 169–170).

Madame Brillon invited Franklin to visit her regularly for tea, to play chess, and listen to music. She was an artist and a musician in her early thirties, married to a man twenty-four years her senior. She quickly developed a loving friendship with the old philosopher and diplomat. He, in turn, sent her copies of his famous bagatelles, such as "Dialogue Between the Gout and M. Franklin," and an essay called "To the Royal Academy of Brussels" (which ends with the famous refrain, "And I cannot but conclude, that…the philosophers…are, all together, scarcely worth a FART-HING.")

Madame Brillon beckoned her friend, "Come tomorrow to take tea, come every Wednesday and Saturday, come as often as you wish, my heart calls you, expects you, is attached to you for life.… You pass a Wednesday then without me actually? And you will say after that, I love you furiously in excess; and I, my good papa, who do not love you furiously—but very tenderly, not in excess; I love you enough to be sorry not to see you every time it is possible to me or to you; which loves the more, and the better of us twain?"[52] Ben responded, *"Je vous aime."* Historians "have

---

52 Ford, *The Many-Sided Franklin,* 302.

PERSONAL

marveled at the spell she held over the old statesman, wondering how far that spell carried, whether he was really in love, whether there really could be an affair."[53]

At one point, Franklin did write a friend, "I was always happy when I was with her, enjoying her sweet society, seeing her and hearing her speak. It is true that I sometimes suspected my heart of wanting to go further, but I tried to conceal it from myself" (*CA*, p. 162).

In 1778, Madame Brillon comments on Franklin's ability to withstand the seven deadly sins: pride, envy, avarice, gluttony, anger, sloth, and lust. He passed all counts except the last. She wrote: "The seventh—I shall not name it. All great men are tainted with it: it is called their weakness. I dare say this weakness removed the roughness, the austerity that unalloyed philosophy might have left with them. You have loved, my dear brother; you have been kind and lovable; you have been loved in return! What is so damnable about that? Go on doing great things and loving pretty women; provided that, pretty and loveable though they may be, you never lose sight of my principle: always love God, America, and me above all" (*CA*, p. 165).

The prudish John and Abigail Adams were not amused, and considered Franklin an unregenerate sinner. Mrs. Adams, who was in Paris with her husband, was appalled by the behavior of the French ladies. She noted how Madame Helvétius, widow of a French scientist, "then gave him [Franklin] a double kiss, one upon each check, and another upon the forehead. When we went into the room to dine, she was placed between the Doctor and Mr. Adams. She carried on the chief of the conversation at dinner, frequently locking her hands into the Doctor's, and sometimes spreading her arms upon the backs of both the gentlemen's chairs, then throwing her arm carelessly upon the Doctor's neck." Abigail Adams was distraught. "I was highly disgusted," she said.

---

53 Claude-Anne Lopez, *Mon Cher Papa* (New Haven: Yale University Press, 1966), 33.

THE GREATEST AMERICAN

Madame Anne-Catherine Helvétius was Madame Brillon's chief rival for Franklin's friendship. As a beautiful widow and thirteen years Franklin's junior, she was fascinated by Doctor Franklin. He was not just "*mon cher Papa*," but "*mon cher ami*." Eventually she was courted by the old man, and at one point he proposed to her, though she ultimately rejected his advance.

THE SUM OF HIS PASSIONS

Given Franklin's past social life and his *tête-à-tête* in France, it is easy to conclude that he had numerous *affaires de coeur*. Given his age, perhaps the French saw more the amicable old papa rather than the womanizer his enemies made him out to be. Claude-Anne Lopez and other historians at Yale, where his official papers are being published, have disputed Franklin's alleged philandering and the widespread view, promoted by his political opponents and humorless contemporaries, that he was the most lecherous of the founding fathers. "It so happens that, apart from the existence of William (who was treated as a legitimate son), there is hardly any explicit evidence to convict Franklin of either promiscuity or its opponent."

Lopez and other historians point out that Franklin delighted in irreverent hoaxes, risqué remarks, and suggestive allusions, all of which encouraged the rumor mill that he had multiple illegitimate children. He had, in fact, only one.

All of which is not to say that Franklin was a saint. "Franklin traveled a great deal once he reached his forties; he lived abroad for fifteen of the last seventeen years of his marriage. It strains credulity to imagine that so vigorous a man was never unfaithful in all that time. But whatever he may have done to another's peace, he did no injury to anyone's reputation."

Another scholar summarizes his views regarding Franklin: "Most of the gossip about Franklin's sexual exploits in Paris can be safely discounted. He was seventy years of age when he arrived in

PERSONAL

France in 1776. During his long stay there he often suffered from gout and sometimes hardly walk. He had other ailments during this period. But his mind remained active in his afflicted body, and perhaps it led him to expectations and even hopes impossible of fulfillment. Indeed, reading his correspondence of this period and remembering what we know of his physical condition, we might conclude that Franklin's sex life was very much like Jane Austen's novels—all talk and no action."[54]

"THE OLD MAN'S WISH"

Franklin loved to sing, and one of his favorites was "The Old Man's Wish."

> May I govern my passions with absolute sway
> Grow wiser and better as my strength wears away,
> Without gout or stones by gentle decay.

One of his detractors presented his old age in a more critical light:

> Franklin, though plagued with fumbling age,
> Needs nothing to excite him,
> But is too ready to engage,
> When younger arms invite him.

---

54 Robert Middlekauff, *Benjamin Franklin and His Enemies* (Oakland: University of California Press, 1998), 115–116.

CHAPTER 78

ON MARRIAGE AND FAMILY LIFE

"The married state is, after all our jokes, the happiest,
being comfortable to our natures."
—*Ben Franklin (1783)*

Chapter 77 was about Franklin's controversial views on love and sex. What about marriage and family life? He was all for it. Previously, I noted that the young Franklin suffered from his "hard-to-be-governed passions" and fathered an illegitimate child, William. But he finally settled down and moved in with his common-law wife, Deborah, who bore him two children (a son who died tragically of smallpox at age four, and a dutiful daughter Sally). Debbie was no raving beauty and had a fierce temper. She was not clever or inventive like her famous husband, but she worked hard in helping him get ahead in his business.

In print, Franklin defended marriage. "Keep your eyes wide open before marriage, and half shut after marriage," he counseled in *Poor Richard's Almanac*. In his banned essay, "Advice to a Young Man on the Choice of a Mistress," readers often forget that the sage encouraged the skirt chaser to consider a wife rather than a mistress in order to subdue those "violent natural inclinations." He wrote, "Marriage is the proper remedy. It is the most natural state

PERSONAL

of man, and therefore the state in which you are most likely to find solid happiness." Franklin argued that the youth's arguments against marriage were "not well-founded." Marriage, according to the practical philosopher, makes "the complete human being." He added, "Separate, she wants his force of body and strength of reason; he, her softness, sensibility, and acute discernment. Together they are more likely to succeed in the world. A single man has not nearly the value he would have in that state of union. He is an incomplete animal. He resembles the odd half of a pair of scissors." He concluded, "if you get a prudent, healthy wife, your Industry in your Profession, with her good economy, will be a fortune sufficient."

Indeed, Franklin himself wrote in his *Autobiography* that his wife "proved a good and faithful helpmate, assisted me much by attending the [printing] shop." He was financially successful because of their partnership.

Debbie was a homebody who never strayed from her native Philadelphia. Unfortunately, her "invincible aversion to crossing the seas" caused a rift that gradually harmed their marriage. When Ben Franklin was appointed colonial agent to represent Pennsylvania in London, he left her behind, despite regular pleas to change her mind. He was away for six straight years, and then following a two-year stint at home, another nine years. They grew apart. For years, Franklin stayed at a boarding house at 36 Craven Street (now a museum), run by Margaret Stevenson, and rumors exist even today that Franklin was a bigamist. Ben and Margaret lived in the same house for fifteen years, which included a long period during which the time and setting were right for sexual relations, but no one knows for sure if they developed. He was amiable to her and maintained a lifelong friendship with her daughter, Polly. Claude-Anne Lopez concludes, "He lived abroad for fifteen years of the last seventeen years of his marriage. It strains credulity to imagine that so vigorous a man was never unfaithful in all that time. But whatever he may have done to another's peace, he did no injury to anyone's reputation."

323

THE GREATEST AMERICAN

Franklin returned to America in 1775, following the death of his wife. After signing of the Declaration of Independence, Franklin returned to Europe to become ambassador to France to raise funds and arms for the revolution.

A widower in his seventies, Franklin became so entranced by the French ladies that he entertained remarrying and living the rest of his days there.

His favorite *"maladie d'amour"* ("lovesickness") was the talented and beautiful Madame Brillion, but she was married. "I despair of ever finding another woman I could love with equal tenderness," he wrote a friend.

He pursued another French beauty, Madame Helvétius. As a beautiful widow and thirteen years his junior, she was fascinated by Doctor Franklin.

He proposed marriage, but the French finance minister Anne-Robert-Jacques Turgot convinced her to turn him down. He was devastated and wrote a delightful bagatelle, "The Elysian Fields," in which he dreamed about going to heaven and finding that her late husband and his late wife, Debbie, were now married. Praising Madame Helvétius's beauty over that of his departed wife, he urged them "to revenge ourselves" (*CA*, p. 175). Apparently, they never did.

His luck running out with the French, Franklin grew homesick and, with his two grandsons, returned home to America in 1785, where he was greeted as a hero. Though old and in pain, he loved being surrounded by friends and loved ones, especially his grandchildren. "I was now in the bosom of my family, and found four new little prattlers, who clung about my knees of their grand papa, and afforded me great pleasure."

When Franklin died in 1790 at the ripe age of eighty-four, he instructed his heirs to bury his body next to his faithful wife Deborah in Philadelphia.

CHAPTER 79

ARE WE IN MORAL PROGRESS OR DECLINE?

"Benjamin Franklin and other founding fathers are considered to be both products of the Enlightenment and promoters of its philosophy of science and reason as the bases of a moral social order in the New World."
—Michael Shermer, The Moral Arc

Michael Shermer, publisher of *Skeptic* magazine and a former columnist for *Scientific American*, has written a provocative book called *The Moral Arc*, in which he made two claims:

First, that science and reason have lead humanity toward "truth, justice, and freedom."

Second, that mankind is making steady progress in moral improvement.

Ben Franklin would be pleased with both hypotheses, as he was a strong defender of the scientific method and the Enlightenment, and sought to make moral progress in his own life and in others.

Franklin himself was a Deist who was skeptical about the value of organized religion. The best example of this rational rather than

THE GREATEST AMERICAN

religious approach can be found in a story surrounding the editing of the Declaration of Independence. After Thomas Jefferson had written the first draft, he passed it along to Franklin for his perusal. The aging philosopher made only one significant change. Jefferson had written "We hold these truths to be sacred and undeniable." In heavy backlashes with his left hand, Franklin crossed out the last three words "sacred and undeniable" and replaced them with the simple word "self-evident," so as to read: "We hold these truths to be self-evident, that all men are created equal, that they are endowed by their Creator with certain inalienable Rights, that among them are Life, Liberty and the pursuit of Happiness."

Walter Isaacson comments, "The idea of 'self-evident' truths was one that drew less on John Locke, who was Jefferson's favorite philosopher, than on the scientific determinism espoused by Isaac Newton and on the analytic empiricism of Franklin's close friend David Hume."[55]

Franklin was, after being a printer by profession, a scientist who used the scientific method to test theories by gathering data. Shermer applied this approach to politics: "Their understanding of the provisional nature of findings led them to develop a social system in which doubt and dispute were the centerpieces of a functional polity." Franklin himself said the same thing, "By the collision of different sentiments, sparks of truth strike out, and political light is obtained" (*CA*, p. 335).

The founding fathers thought of democracy as they would have science—as a method, not an ideology. Franklin was never much of an ideologue, but rather a pragmatic problem solver. The legislature would engage in a scientific experiment: Try this, try that, compromise, see what works. That's how Franklin operated his printing business. As Thomas Jefferson wrote, "No experiment can be more interesting than that we are now trying, and which we trust will end in establishing the fact that man may be governed by reason and truth." Franklin said something similar. When the

---

55   Walter Isaacson, *Benjamin Franklin: An America Life,* p. 312.

PERSONAL

founders met in Philadelphia to create a new constitution, he said, "We are experimenting in politics" (*CA*, p. 370).

What about moral progress? Franklin's list of thirteen virtues in the *Autobiography* is a case study in secular humanism. Rather than focusing on guilt, forgiveness, and the Christian spiritual values of faith, hope, and charity, Franklin adopted a more universal list, including silence, sincerity, tranquility, and moderation. He tried his hand at living all thirteen virtues but found it an "arduous project of arriving at moral perfection." His overarching theme was "be always at war with your vices, at peace with your neighbors, and let each new year find you a better man" (*A*, p. 99).

Teresa Jordan, an author living in southern Utah, decided to live all thirteen virtues of Franklin's *Autobiography* one at a time for a year, and wrote a book on the subject called *The Year of Living Virtuously (Weekends Off): A Meditation on the Search for Meaning in an Ordinary Life.*

Like Franklin, she found herself "so much fuller of faults than I had imagined."

Yet, today, Shermer argues that moral progress is gaining ground, as evidenced by the declining number of wars and crime, and increased standard of living. "The experimental methods and analytical reasoning of science helped create the modern world of liberal democracies, civil rights and civil liberties, equal justice under the law, open political and economic borders, free minds and free markets. More people in more places have greater rights, freedoms, liberties, literacy, education, and prosperity—the likes of which no human society in history has ever enjoyed."

Franklin would be pleased at the progress of mankind.

CHAPTER 80

FRANKLIN AND HIS CRITICS

*"Let all men know thee, but no man
know thee thoroughly."*
—*Poor Richard's Almanac*

Was Benjamin Franklin an indispensable public servant or cunning chameleon? A hard-headed entrepreneur or an opportunistic privateer? A devoted family man or a notorious womanizer? A scientist and inventor or a hoaxer and self-promoter? A believer or a heretic? The first civilized American or the most dangerous man in America?

HONORING THE FOUNDER ON HIS 300TH BIRTHDAY

Probably all of the above. But no matter how you come down on this debate, one thing is clear: Franklin's stature has increased dramatically since his death in 1790.

I was privileged to be a part of this celebration in April 2006, when I was invited to speak at the first-day-of-issue ceremony in Philadelphia for the four Franklin commemorative stamps honoring Franklin as a printer, scientist, postmaster, and statesman. I've always been an admirer of this versatile genius since reading his famous *Autobiography*, which is regarded as the first "how-to"

PERSONAL

self-improvement book in America, championing the virtues of industry, thrift, and prudence.

Over the years, I've collected dozens of books on Franklin, including the voluminous *Papers of Benjamin Franklin*, being compiled and edited by Yale University Press. It was while reading through these *Papers*, now approaching fifty volumes, that I came up with the idea of finishing Franklin's *Autobiography*. Franklin's memoirs end abruptly in 1757, just as he was about to embark on his career as an international political figure. He lived another thirty-three years as a colonial agent, revolutionary, signer of the Declaration of Independence, America's first ambassador, and delegate to the Constitutional Convention. In going over his *Papers*, I realized that it might be possible to gather his autobiographical writings from his letters, journals, and essays to complete his story, all in his own words. My wife, Jo Ann, and I worked together to create *The Compleated Autobiography by Benjamin Franklin*, published in 2006 by Regnery.

THE DARK SIDE OF FRANKLIN

But perhaps my admiration of Franklin is misplaced. While studying Franklin, I discovered a great deal of animosity among historians and pundits toward wise ol' Dr. Franklin. For example, I came across an article called "Benjamin Franklin Was All Wet on Economics," written by a college student for the Mises Institute website. The author focused on Franklin's "labor theory of value" and his support for paper money. No doubt, the philosopher was misguided on some issues. But by taking a broader view of his economics, a case can be made that he was a sound thinker.

Actively involved in the creation of the three major documents of American government (the Declaration of Independence, the Articles of Confederation, and the US Constitution), Franklin was an advocate of a limited central government. He was no free-thinking anarchist. In economics, he did favor paper money and a "real

THE GREATEST AMERICAN

bills" doctrine of expanding the money supply beyond specie, though "no more than commerce requires." Easy money would facilitate trade, he wrote, when gold and silver are scarce. During the American Revolution, he justified the runaway inflation of the Continentals as an indirect way for all Americans to pay for the war, although he begged Congress to improve the creditworthiness of the United States by paying interest in hard currency. He was a strong supporter of Hamiltonian-style central banking and an investor in the Bank of North America. (His likeness on the one hundred dollar bill—the highest denomination—of an irredeemable American paper currency would greatly please his vanity.)

He argued that the state should be actively engaged in the free education of youth and other public services, and in dispelling the ignorance of public fads and superstitions. From several sources, it appears that Franklin was in league with Jefferson in emphasizing the theme of "life, liberty, and the pursuit of happiness" as the goal of government, downplaying Locke's inalienable right to property. Property, he wrote, is purely a "creature of society" and can be legitimately taxed to pay for civil society. He was quite critical of Americans unwilling to pay their fair share of society's "dues" (*CA*, pp. 298–99).

MURRAY ROTHBARD AS DISSENTER

Among libertarian writers, the leading detractor is Murray Rothbard, who describes Franklin in his now five-volume history *Conceived in Liberty* as "perhaps the most overinflated [leader] of the entire colonial period in America."[56] At every turn in the history of the American Revolution, Rothbard deprecates Franklin's achievements and accentuates his peccadilloes: The sly ol' Dr. Franklin is "a sinister, subversive devil...an opportunist par excellence...cunning...fawning...meddling...opportunistic hedonist...."

---

56 Murray N. Rothbard, *Conceived in Liberty*, vol. 2 (New York: Arlington House, 1975), p. 64.

PERSONAL

Franklin, according to Rothbard, was a warmonger, a Tory imperialist, and a speculator with his "cronies" who engaged in a "pattern of plunder of the American taxpayer" during the war.[57] His Albany Plan in 1754 was far more than an innocent way to unify the nation, but rather was a deliberate attempt to establish a "central supergovernment."[58]

Rothbard demeans Franklin's significant role in the Paxton Boys crisis, where Scottish Irish frontiersmen massacred twenty innocent Indians and then marched on Philadelphia to present their grievances in 1763 after the French and Indian War. Of the event, Rothbard writes, "Franklin was treating the Paxton Boys rather as citizens to be forgiven, with grievances to be pondered, than as murderers"[59]

In Franklin's own account of the incident, he refers to the Paxton Boys as "murderers...cruel, wicked men...who committed an atrocious act." It's totally different than Rothbard's description. Franklin did meet with the Paxton Boys and convinced them to disperse on the promise that Franklin would "consider" their grievances, but that's a far cry from condoning their wickedness.

In his long history, Franklin comes off almost as badly as the "deep-dyed conservative" George Washington, who is characterized as a fumbling, inept general who sought to "crush liberty and individualism" among his soldiers and impose a "statist" army, losing one campaign after another.

Rothbard would have preferred "the forgotten hero," the "brilliant, gifted" Charles Lee as the American general, "champion of liberty and guerrilla war."[60] And instead of Franklin as envoy

---

57 Rothbard, *Conceived*, vol. 4, p. 359.
58 Rothbard, *Conceived*, vol. 2, p. 233.
59 Rothbard, *Conceived*, vol. 2, p. 74.
60 Rothbard, *Conceived*, vol. 4, pp. 34, 35. In all my readings of contemporary historians, I couldn't find a single one who considered Major General Charles Lee a better commander than Washington. To give one example, here is what respected historian Thomas Fleming wrote: "Lee fancied himself a military genius, a great politician,

THE GREATEST AMERICAN

to France, Rothbard would have favored the "estimable liberal and Wilkite" Dr. Arthur Lee.[61] Never mind that other historians uniformly describe Lee as a "bilious" and "cantankerous" patriot who hated the French and accomplished little. Rothbard also likes Thomas Paine, author of the libertarian pamphlet, *Common Sense*, and promoter extraordinaire of the American cause. Interestingly, Rothbard ignores the fact that Paine's mentor was none other than Benjamin Franklin, and that Franklin was a lifelong supporter of Paine's call for independence. What did Paine see that Rothbard couldn't?

SUDDENLY FRANKLIN BECOMES A RADICAL

Rothbard never explains the fact that somehow by July 1776, the "Tory imperialist" had suddenly become a "radical revolutionary," along with John Adams and Thomas Jefferson. Franklin was indeed one of the first founders to call for independence. As early as 1771, he predicted that the "seeds are sown of total disunion" between England and her colonies, and in 1775, drafted a resolution to Congress to dissolve "all ties of allegiance" with a country that fails to "protect the lives and property of their subjects," adding: "It has always been my opinion that it is the natural right of men to quit, when they please, the society or state, and the country in which they were born, and either join with another or form a new one as they may think proper" (*CA*, pp. 65, 120). Furthermore, Franklin, like Rothbard, appears to be an advocate of natural rights: "I am a mortal enemy to arbitrary government and unlimited power. I am naturally very zealous for the rights and liberties of my country, and the least encroachment of those invaluable privileges is apt to make my blood boil" (*CA*, p. 80). No libertarian couldn't have said it better.

---

and a philosopher all in one explosive package. Unfortunately, he neither looked nor acted the part." *1776: Year of Illusions* (New York: W. W. Norton, 1975), p. 137.

61   Rothbard, *Conceived*, vol. 3, p. 218.

PERSONAL

Franklin is given no credit for the "radical" and "libertarian" Pennsylvania Constitution written in 1776 and endorsed by Franklin throughout his lifetime. And what about Franklin's critical role in raising military and financial aid in France? He's given little credit other than the following sentences from Rothbard's poison pen: "The wily old tactician Franklin proved to be a master at the intricacies of lying, bamboozling, and intriguing that form the warp and woof of diplomacy. Moreover, the old rogue was a huge hit with the French, who saw him as the embodiment of reason, the natural man, and *bonhomie*."[62] Not surprisingly, Rothbard is deadly silent about Franklin's thrill of victory and Arthur Lee's agony of defeat when it came to fundraising for the American cause. Franklin single-handedly raised all the loans and munitions for the Americans, despite the counterefforts of Francophobes Arthur Lee, Ralph Izard, and John Adams. (Adams was able to raise a loan of five million guilders from the Dutch but only after the Americans defeated the British at Yorktown.)

FRANKLIN'S CHANGING VIEWS ON WAR AND THE MILITARY

Rothbard also ignores Franklin's libertarian views regarding military service. Franklin favored a private militia over a publicly financed army. According to Lorraine Smith Pangle, "Although he willingly did his part as a common soldier, he had no taste for a good fight, no love of danger, no attraction to the glories of heroic self-overcoming. So much did he hate tyranny and love liberty, reason, and gentle persuasion that he could not see the need for military discipline."[63] He opposed military conscription and was against fines or corporal penalties in the military. He wouldn't have gotten far in George Washington's army.

---

62 Rothbard, *Conceived*, vol. 4, pp. 232–33.
63 Lorraine Smith Pangle, *The Political Philosophy of Benjamin Franklin* (Baltimore: Johns Hopkins University Press, 2007), p. 116.

THE GREATEST AMERICAN

Finally, Rothbard fails to quote Franklin's negative views on war in general, which is surprising given Rothbard's anti-war sentiments. After the Revolutionary War ended, Franklin wrote, "When will men be convinced that even successful wars do at length become misfortunes to those who unjustly commenced them, and who triumphed blindly in their success, not seeing all its consequences. There is so little good gained, and so much mischief done generally by wars that I wish the imprudence of undertaking them was more evident to princes. For in my opinion there never was a good war, or a bad peace. What vast additions to the conveniences and comforts of living might mankind have acquired if the money spent in wars had been employed in works of public utility! What an extension of agriculture...what rivers rendered navigable...what bridges, aqueducts, new roads, and other public works, edifices and improvements rendering England a complete paradise...millions were spent in the great war were spent doing mischief...and destroying the lives of so many thousands of working people who might have performed useful labor!" (*CA*, p. 302)

To show how severe Rothbard's attack is, consider that the only biography he recommends is Cecil B. Currey's *Code Number 72, Ben Franklin: Patriot or Spy?*, which accuses Franklin of being a double agent for the British. (Carl Van Doren's *Benjamin Franklin*, published in 1938, is considered the most comprehensive biography.) Currey is a tough-minded researcher but, like Rothbard, ignores evidence that doesn't fit his agenda. "I have not...pretended to write a 'balanced' picture of Franklin (for I have focused on his shadows)."[64] Currey put together a sizable amount of circumstantial evidence that Franklin played both sides of the conflict while ambassador to France. "The story involved treason, breaches of security, lackadaisical administration, privateering, misplaced truth, war profiteering, clandestine operations, spy apparatus, intrigue, double-dealing." Today we know that Franklin and Adams were

---

64 Cecil B. Currey, "The Franklin Legend," *Journal of Christian Reconstruction* 3, no. 1 (Summer 1976), p. 143.

PERSONAL

surrounded by spies, including one of their secretaries Edward Bancroft. "A cell of British Intelligence was located at Franklin's headquarters in France, and Benjamin Franklin—covertly perhaps, tacitly at least, and possibly deliberately—cooperated with and protected this spy cell operating out of his home in France from shortly after his arrival in that country until the end of the war."[65]

It is true that Franklin loved England before he loved France. He lived in London for nearly twenty years and considered it home more than Philadelphia. His son, William, was so enamored with the British Empire that he remained a loyalist throughout the war, thus giving rise to the rumor that Franklin was a double agent. In France, Franklin met with British agents and listened to their offers of honors, emoluments, and bribes. He did little to hide his activities and papers from alleged spies, whether French or British. And, yes, he was identified clandestinely as "Number 72."

But it is also clear that Franklin broke with his son, William, and was so bitter about being deserted "in a cause wherein my good fame, fortune and life were all at stake" that they never reconciled. Currey is correct that the British had a codename for Franklin, but so did the French ("Prométhée," the Greek God that brought fire from the heavens). The British also had code numbers for almost everyone, including George Washington ("Number 206"). And British and French spies were so common that Franklin simply ignored them.

While the circumstantial evidence against Franklin is sometimes damning, it's important to look at the big picture. If indeed Franklin was playing both sides of the war, would he have worked so enthusiastically to obtain essential aid from France? If you buy Currey's argument, you could just as easily make the argument that Arthur Lee and even John Adams were traitors because both seemed to make every effort to insult the French and sabotage

---

65 Cecil B. Currey, *Code Number 72: Ben Franklin, Patriot or Spy?* (Hoboken, NJ: Prentice Hall, 1972), pp. 12, 266.

Franklin and his fundraising efforts. Practically every historian today agrees that without Franklin, the French would not have given the financial and military support necessary to win the battle at Yorktown.

Today, Currey's scurrilous book is out of print, and for good reason. If you look at all the evidence and read Franklin's own *Papers* (as contained in the *Compleated Autobiography*), Currey's extreme thesis doesn't add up. Franklin clearly switched sides from loving the British Isles to hating the Crown and his ministers. Franklin considered the War of Independence "the greatest revolution the world has ever seen" and a "miracle in human affairs" (*CA*, pp. 130–32).

OTHER EXPOSÉS ON FRANKLIN'S ELECTRICAL EXPERIMENTS AND THE SLAVE TRADE

Like Rothbard and Currey, other historians have written with an agenda when it comes to Franklin. Tom Tucker wrote an entire book called *Bolt of Fate* (2003), contending that Franklin's famous kite experiment was faked, that it was one of Franklin's hoaxes. His evidence? Franklin never wrote about the kite story for years, and the only detailed account was written by his friend Joseph Priestley some fifteen years after the event. Yet, according to Priestley, Franklin dreaded the ridicule of performing an unsuccessful experiment in public, so he used as his only witness his son William, who never denied the kite test, even after they were estranged.

In *Runaway America* (2004), David Waldstreicher argues that Franklin masked his true feelings about slavery, and that he was a slave trader and slave owner in an age of supposed freedom and equality. Here, again, the author appears prejudiced, and deliberately ignores or downplays contrary evidence, such as: In 1763, Franklin visited the Negro School of Philadelphia, which he helped establish, examined the students, and discovered "a higher opinion of the natural capacities of the black race.... Their apprehension

PERSONAL

seems as quick, their memory as strong, and their docility in every respect equal to that of white children" (*CA*, p. 26). (Waldstreicher ignores this quote.) Franklin was never much of a slaveholder compared to Washington or Jefferson. The two slaves who acted as his servants escaped in London before he returned to America in 1775, and he didn't bother to track them down. Two years before he died, he became the first president of the Philadelphia Society for the Abolition of Slavery and helped introduce legislation in Congress to abolish slavery once and for all.

FRANKLIN'S LOVE AFFAIR WITH WOMEN

Franklin has been blamed for abandoning his devoted wife, Deborah, and becoming an old lecher in London and France. Again, there is plenty of evidence to support Franklin the philanderer. He wrote several risqué bagatelles, such as "Advice to a Young Man on the Choice of a Mistress" and "The Speech of Miss Polly Baker," which defended a single mother who was prosecuted for the fifth time for having an illegitimate child. Franklin himself had a "natural" son, William. In his *Autobiography*, he confessed that, as a young man, his "hard-to-be-governed passion of youth" led him into "intrigues with low women" (*A*, p. 81). (This paragraph was censored in grade schools until the early twentieth century.) Carl Van Doren comments, "He went to women hungrily, secretly, and briefly."[66]

In 1730, Franklin entered into a common-law marriage with Deborah Read, who had previously been married to a man who abandoned her without a divorce. Together, they raised William and had two children of their own: Franky (who died of smallpox at age four) and Sally, who cared for Franklin in his final years. There is no hard evidence that Franklin sired any other illegitimate children, despite all the rumors. (It didn't help that his son William

---

66 Carl Van Doren, *Benjamin Franklin* (New York: Viking Press, 1938), p. 91.

THE GREATEST AMERICAN

had an illegitimate son, William Temple, who, in turn, had an illegitimate son in Paris; that makes three generations.) He settled down into a faithful relationship with his wife in Philadelphia and focused on his printing business.

However, their relationship changed in the last eighteen years of their marriage, when they lived separate lives. But he did not abandon her by any means. When he made colonial agent in 1757, he begged her to come with him to London, but she had a mortal fear of crossing the ocean and refused repeatedly to join him. "I have a thousand times wished [my wife] with me, and my little Sally," he wrote from London. Gradually, they drifted apart, writing largely about mundane household matters and local gossip. Claude-Anne Lopez, a Franklin expert, says during this time, "It strains credulity to imagine that so vigorous a man was never unfaithful in all that time."[67] In fact, historian Thomas Fleming makes the case that he had an informal intimacy with his landlady Margaret Stevenson while living at his Craven Street residence in London.[68] His wife Deborah died in late 1774, when Franklin was still in London.

Two years later, as a widower, he was back in Europe. It was there that he developed a considerable friendship and correspondence with several beautiful French women, including Madame Brillon, who was an artist, musician, and wife of a diplomat. Their relationship supposedly never went beyond friendship, although Franklin admitted to a friend that "I sometimes suspected my heart of wanting to go further" (*CA*, p. 162). Their letters were intimate and flirtatious, and fun to read. (See chapter 6 of *The Compleated Autobiography*.) Franklin considered it his "amusement" from a grueling schedule. Gossip spread about the two: Her husband once

---

67 Claude-Anne Lopez and Eugenia W. Herbert, *The Private Franklin: The Man and His Family* (New York: W. W. Norton, 1975), pp. 26–27.

68 Thomas Fleming, *The Intimate Lives of the Founding Fathers* (New York: Harper, 2010), pp. 73–124.

PERSONAL

found them kissing. They played a game of chess in her bathroom. She sat on his lap at a dinner party, attended by puritans John and Abigail Adams, who were "disgusted" by Franklin's behavior. One of his critics wrote this ditty:

> Franklin, though plagued with fumbling age,
> Needs nothing to excite him,
> But is too ready to engage,
> When younger arms invite him.

It should be pointed out that the old doctor was seventy years of age when he arrived in France in 1776. During his long stay, he suffered severely from the gout and painful kidney stones, and sometimes could hardly walk. It is doubtful that he fulfilled his sexual fantasies in any meaningful way. Historian Robert Middlekauff concludes, "Reading his correspondence of this period and remembering what we know of his physical condition, we might conclude that Franklin's sex life was very much like Jane Austen's novels—all talk and no action."[69]

HIS HERETICAL RELIGIOUS VIEWS

Franklin was often criticized by contemporary Christians for his heretical religious views. He was not a churchgoer and had doubts about the divinity of Jesus. But he believed in God and thought that the American Revolution was a "miracle in human affairs." A Deist for most of his life, he supported a pragmatic religion that favored good works and charity more than simple faith and hope. "I mean real good works, works of kindness, charity, mercy, and public spirit; not holiday-keeping, sermon-reading or hearing, performing church ceremonies, or making long prayers, filled with flatteries and compliments, despised even by wise men, and much less capable of pleasing the Deity." Franklin was famous for en-

---

69   Robert Middlekauff, *Benjamin Franklin and His Enemies* (Oakland: University of California Press, 1998), pp. 115–16.

THE GREATEST AMERICAN

gaging in innumerable civic and charitable causes throughout his adult life—and into the afterlife, with his perpetual fund for young tradesmen in Boston (as established in his will).

FATHER OF AMERICAN CAPITALISM

In many ways, Franklin was America's first champion of free enterprise and commercial society. Austrian economists would be pleased with his emphasis on entrepreneurship, industry, and thrift. Eugen von Böhm-Bawerk and Max Weber recognized his genius, and so did American capitalists Andrew Carnegie and Thomas Mellon, who were deeply influenced by his *Autobiography*. (It was required reading in grade schools until the 1920s.) Franklin anticipated the incredible material and technological progress since our founding. An incurable optimist, Franklin was always bullish on America, and life in general. At the end of the War for Independence, he predicted, "America will, with God's blessing, become a great and happy country." The United States, he said, is "an immense territory, favored by nature with all advantages of climate, soil, great navigable rivers and lakes...[and] destined to become a great country, populous and mighty." He told potential European immigrants, that the country "affords to strangers... good laws, just and *cheap* government, with all the liberties, civil and religious, that reasonable men can wish for." (He underlined the word "cheap.")

Franklin was sympathetic to the laissez-faire economics (known back then as "political economy") of the day advocated by Adam Smith in his *Wealth of Nations* (published in 1776) and the French school known as the Physiocrats. They supported free trade and an unregulated market. Franklin wrote a friend in support of "*Laissez nous faire*: Let us alone.... *Pas trop gouverner*: Not to govern too strictly."

He was a devoted free trader, writing famously, "No nation was ever ruined by trade." He added, "To lay duties on a commod-

PERSONAL

ity exported which our friends want is a knavish attempt to get something for nothing. The statesman who first invented it had the genius of a pickpocket. Most of the statutes, acts, edicts, and placards of parliaments, princes and states, for regulating, directing, and restraining of trade have either political blunders or jobs obtained by artful men for private advantage under the pretence of public good. In general the more free and unrestrained commerce is, the more it flourishes."

Historian Lorraine Smith Pangle concludes that Franklin's "good businessman...contributes to the common good of society, generates employment, multiplying pleasures, and drawing energies away from deadly religious quarrels and military adventurism into more constructive channels...he [Franklin] early developed a robust faith in what Adam Smith would later call the 'invisible hand' to provide us with all the materials and innate capacities we need, and through free markets, to distribute labor, resources, and products in a way that is most beneficial to all."[70]

Surely Murray Rothbard would approve!

NO SOCIAL LIBERTARIAN!

What were Franklin's politics? He was no social libertarian, despite his image as a libertine and religious freethinker. While he is famous for reading books in the nude, frequenting the salacious Hellfire Club in London, and flirting with French ladies in Paris, he wrote stern letters to his daughter Sally, chastising her for wanting to wear the latest fashions while a war was going on, and refused to buy his grandson Benny a gold watch while in France. He dressed plainly and constantly preached economy. He promoted at all times frugality and industry in both public and private life. Readers might be surprised by Franklin's attack on the growth

---

70 Lorraine Smith Pangle, *The Political Philosophy of Benjamin Franklin* (Baltimore: Johns Hopkins University Press, 2007), pp. 18–19, 29. I highly recommend Pangle's fascinating book. It's the best work I've read on Franklin's political and economic philosophy.

of taverns in Philadelphia upon his return from England in 1762. He hated mobs of any kind, and though a defender of free speech, railed against scurrilous newspaper reports.[71] He favored the entrepreneurial can-do spirit of Americans in his *Autobiography* and, in later writings, lambasted public offices of privilege and aristocracies by birth. In an open letter to European immigrants, he wrote, "I told them those bear no prices in our markets. In America, people do not inquire concerning a stranger, *What is he?* but *What can he do?*"

LIMITED GOVERNMENT

Franklin was opposed to a strong centralized executive branch. In his original draft of the Articles of Confederation, which left the states free and sovereign and the central authority weak— something Rothbard himself was sympathetic to—he proposed twelve members of the executive branch instead of one president to disperse political power. He was opposed to public "offices of profit." As Bernard Faÿ concludes, "They [Congress] were directly opposed to Franklin's philosophical tendency, which might be summed up in this formula: the least government possible is the greatest possible good."[72]

SUPPORTING VOLUNTEER ORGANIZATIONS RATHER THAN GOVERNMENT

Finally, Franklin was ahead of his time in financing good causes with his business profits. He was civil minded early in his career,

---

71 Some libertarians are critical of Franklin for opposing the notorious "outlaw" John Wilkes, a defender of free speech who was imprisoned for libeling the king of England in 1768 and the "drunken mad mobs" supporting "Wilkes and Liberty." This is another case of Franklin's social conservativism before the American Revolution. Interestingly, after the war, Wilkes's sister and mother came over to America and stayed at the Franklin home in Philadelphia. See *The Compleated Autobiography*, pp. 59–62, 349.

72 Bernard *Faÿ, Franklin: Apostle of Modern Times (Boston: Little, Brown, and Company, 1929), p. 504.*

PERSONAL

helping to finance the first fire company, the nation's oldest property insurance company, and Philadelphia's own hospital, library and militia, all with mostly private funds. "America's first entrepreneur may well be our finest one," concludes John Bogle, founder of the Vanguard family of mutual funds.

As Pangle notes, "Franklin was a tireless supporter of volunteer associations and philanthropic projects." Rather than depend on government and the great lords, as they did in Europe, Americans offered a better way: volunteer collective action and self-help individualism.

He wasn't particularly fond of poor laws or public welfare programs, but he strongly believed in supporting private charities and noble causes. He was an unwavering advocate for civil organizations over government initiatives. He backed volunteer groups such as the Junto, the Library Company, local newspapers, the City Watch, the Union Fire Company, the Pennsylvania Academy, the Negro School of Philadelphia, the American Philosophical Society, and the Pennsylvania militia, which served as a private alternative to public defense.

CONCLUSION: "ENEMIES DO A MAN SOME GOOD"

Like all the founders, Benjamin Franklin had his share of foibles, but in many ways he was ahead of his time. How do you balance his mammoth achievements with his inscrutable flaws? Before you make up your mind, I suggest you spend a few days reading Franklin's own account of his life, starting with his *Autobiography* and finishing with *The Compleated Autobiography*, which is drawn from his own letters, journals, and essays. You might see a different Franklin from what his critics and I have written.

Libertarians are not used to winning. They prefer being in the minority. They figure that if they are victorious, they must be compromising their principles. That's probably what galled Murray Rothbard the most about Franklin—he was so damned successful as a scientist, businessman, and diplomat.

THE GREATEST AMERICAN

Of course, Franklin wasn't entirely successful in life. He had his share of enemies. This was his philosophy about his critics: "As to the abuses I have met with, I number them among my honors. One cannot behave…without drawing the envy and malice of the foolish and the wicked.… The best men have always had their share of this treatment…and a man has therefore some reason to be ashamed when he meets with none of it.… Enemies do a man some good by fortifying his character.… I call to mind what my friend good Rev. Whitefield said to me once: 'I read the libels writ against you, when I was in a remote province, where I could not be informed of the truth of the facts; but they rather gave me this good opinion of you, that you continued to be useful to the public: for when I am on the road, and see boys in a field at a distance, pelting a tree, though I am too far off to know what tree it is, I conclude it has fruit on it" (*CA*, pp. 44–45).

Now that's a quote from Franklin all libertarians can appreciate.

"One would think that a man laboring disinterestedly for the good of his fellow-creatures could not possibly…make himself enemies; but there are minds who cannot bear that another should distinguish himself even by greater usefulness; and though he demand no profit, nor anything in return but good will…they will endeavor to deprive him of that, first by disputing the truth of his experiments, then their utility, and being defeated there, they will finally dispute his right to them, and would give the credit of them to a man that lived 3000 years ago, or at 3000 leagues distance, rather than to a neighbor or friend" (*CA*, pp. 230–231).

WHAT WOULD BENJAMIN FRANKLIN SAY TODAY: A WARNING TO AMERICA

Originally published by Investment U (Vol. 2, Issue 3),
January 17, 2000.
By Mark Skousen
Editor, Forecasts & Strategies

Today is Ben Franklin's birthday.

What would this founding father extraordinaire, the first scientific American, and financial guru say about America today?

As a sixth-generation grandson of the famous man, I imagined contacting the grandfather of our nation through modern technology and asking him directly.

Here are my questions and his responses:

SKOUSEN: Hello, Dr. Franklin, are you there?

DR. FRANKLIN: Yes, I am here. I pray you may forgive my lateness, as I was engaged in some important business in another galaxy. Space travel is most agreeable in the world of spirits!

SKOUSEN: Dr. Franklin, happy birthday! We are delighted to have you as our guest to answer some questions.

THE GREATEST AMERICAN

FRANKLIN: I'm honored. Let's get started. Time is money! What is your first question?

SKOUSEN: Thanks, Dr. Franklin. Our first question is, how do you feel about being on the $100 bill?

DR. FRANKLIN: Oh! It does indeed please my vanity to be 100 times more valuable than the father of our nation, my good friend Gen. Washington!

SKOUSEN: Speaking of Gen. Washington, I see that recently you and Gen. Washington were voted among the top five greatest Americans of all time. How does it feel to be a celebrity?

DR. FRANKLIN: To be perfectly honest, I am perfectly sick of it! When I was minister to France, besides being harassed with too much business, I was exposed to numerous visits, some of kindness and civility, but many of mere idle curiosity. These devoured my hours, and broke my attention, and at night I often found myself fatigued without having done anything. I sometimes feel the same way here in the world of spirits, with a constant stream of visitors and relatives I never knew I had!

SKOUSEN: Are you concerned about inflation and the declining value of the $100 bill?

DR. FRANKLIN: In life nothing is certain but death and taxes, but now I see I must add inflation to the list. With your constant inflation, it seems I become more popular every day, and

PERSONAL

now my face is as well-known as the moon. My only fear is that your government will soon abandon banknotes entirely in favor a cashless society, leaving the greatest nation in the world with no daily reminder of its most famous philosopher!

SKOUSEN: Many experts blame our central bank, the Federal Reserve, for the constant depreciation of our currency. Should the Fed go back on a gold standard to return discipline to our government and to stop the inflation?

DR. FRANKLIN: I favor a hard currency with considerable flexibility according to commerce. Because of our lack of sufficient quantity of hard money in our country, I published a pamphlet in Philadelphia favoring paper money in moderate quantities, and found it to be highly beneficial to commerce. But during the Revolutionary War, the public demanded more than was necessary because they were not willing to pay their taxes. The Continental dollar depreciated rapidly and hurt our credit both here and abroad, and I often was unable to sleep at night because of the financial distress.

SKOUSEN: What do you think of the nation's huge deficits, the tax increases, big government, the wars in the Middle East, the Great Recession, the Patriot Act, CEO scandals, gun violence, and a declining dollar?

DR. FRANKLIN: Stop! Stop! I see nothing has changed since I left this sad world over 200 years ago. Upon my return from France, I saw in the

THE GREATEST AMERICAN

public papers frequent complaints of hard times, etc. There can be no country in which there are not some sort of troubles. And it is always in the power of a small number to make a great clamor. So my advice to you is to take a cool view of the general state of affairs, and perhaps the prospects will appear less gloomy than you have imagined.

SKOUSEN: So you are still an optimist about the future of the United States?

DR. FRANKLIN: Long ago I said that with God's blessing, America is destined to become a great and happy country. I still believe this. When I see the extravagant rejoicing every 4th of July, the day on which we signed the Declaration of Independence, thereby hazarding our lives and fortunes, I am convinced of the universal satisfaction of the people with the revolution and its grand principles. No nation has ever enjoyed a greater share of human felicity.

SKOUSEN: Aren't you worried about another crash or depression around the corner, with all these debts piling up?

DR. FRANKLIN: There are always croakers, as we called them, who are predicting ruin. When I lived in Philadelphia, one such elderly man who had a wise and grave manner came frequently by my door at the printing house to give me a detail of misfortunes and bankruptcies, and to predict that all was going to destruction, and that I should sell all my real estate and business, etc. etc. Fortunately, I ignored him, and at last I had

PERSONAL

the pleasure of seeing him pay five times as much for one piece of land as he might have bought when he first began his croaking.

SKOUSEN: But what if you are wrong, and we are hit with a great depression, or war? We live in uncertain times. How can we protect ourselves?

DR. FRANKLIN: Poor Richard always says, "An empty bag cannot stand." I always made it a policy to live simply and frugally, so that by my economy I was able to build up substantial savings and investments. This policy proved favorable to me during the American Revolution. In 1774, a great source of my income was cut off when I was dismissed by the Crown as postmaster general and colonial agent, and I lost £1,800 a year in income. But my family and I survived because I had bank accounts in three countries, some bonds and stocks, and income properties.

INDEX

4th of July. *See* Independence Day

18th century life...... 114, 130, 254
  average lifespan 107
  Caribbean islands 170
  crossing the Atlantic Ocean 87
  Europe's poor 130–131
  golf and cricket........................... 103
  mortgages................................... 124
  quacks....................................... 103
  travel 197

401(k) 56

1776 (musical)........................249

abolitionist 30, 221
  See also slaves/slavery

Abolition of Slavery................337
  See also slaves/slavery

Academy for Education of Youth. 26

Adams, Abigail ..30, 177, 227, 319, 339

Adams, John................1, 3, 7, 30,
    82, 104, 162, 177, 179, 211,
    217, 219, 220, 222, 224,
    226–228, 231, 244, 249,
    258, 261, 284, 291, 305,
    310–311, 318, 319, 332,
    333, 335, 339
  friend and adversary 224
  personality................................258

quotes
  Benjamin Franklin 7
  slavery 165

Adams, Matthew 262

Adam Smith Institute 27

affluence.................. 77. *See* wealth

affordable housing 124

agriculture 2

air bath..................................104

air quality 104

Albany Plan of Union..... 201, 331

Alexander the Great...............188

Alger, Horatio 34, 215

Algeria 167

ambassador..........xxi. *See* American
    Ambassador to France

America
  a warning to 345

American Ambassador to France .
    34, 70, 125, 161, 175, 214,
    224, 243, 250, 258, 316.
  See also France
  animal magnetism *(1784)* 103
  Paris *(1776-1785)* 25

American Dream 1, 121–126
  father of 7

THE GREATEST AMERICAN

American Economic Association . 137

American laughs. *See* humor
founding father of 248

American Philosophical Society
.........26, 162, 243, 279, 343

American Revolution *(1776)*.... 1,
80, 131, 139, 151, 152, 155,
162, 163, 171, 177, 211,
216, 219, 227, 229, 273,
310, 330, 339. *See also* War of
Independence *(1775-1783)*;
See also Declaration of Independence
Washington's troops arrive in
New York..........................177

American spirit......................... 39

ancestors........................... 307–310

Ancestory.com.........................307

anger 205

animal magnetism 87, 103, 107

Antigua 170

Antoinette, Queen Marie 317

AOL 234

Apple 38

Aristotle 27

Arkad 11, 45

Arnold, Benedict......................291

arthritis .... 105. *See* gout

Articles of Confederation135, 180,
219, 329, 342

Asia 199

assemblyman 125

astrology.................................108

atheist 271

Atlantic Ocean
lifetime transversment of............87

Aurelius, Marcus 205

Austen, Jane 321

austerity ....76–79, 138. *See
also* personal finances
Canadian fiscal crisis *(1994)*.......79

Australia..................................150

Austria 87

avarice 163, 181

Bache Jr., Louis 309–310

Bache, Richard 81, 309
postmaster in Philadelphia 169

Bache Sr., Louis.......................310

Bailyn, Bernard 58

bald eagle 175

Bancroft, Edward 335

bank accounts ..12, 53, 57, 66, 220

Bank of Douglas, Herod &
Company 75

Bank of England 140
£20 note..........................113–114

Bank of North America 3, 32,
53, 57, 140, 154, 330

Bank of the United States ... 3, 154

bankruptcy....................61, 63, 76

bank stocks............................... 12

battery 89

Battle of Concord....................223

Battle of Lexington.................223

Battle of Yorktown *(1781)*...... xxi,
219, 233, 244

Baumol, William J..................142

Baylor University.........13–14, 216

becoming rich .... 10–12.
See also wealth

Beeman, Richard.....................237

Beethoven 87

INDEX

Bell, Alexander Graham 26
bell har 203
Belloste, Dr. Augustin 105
Belloste's pills 105
Bellow, Adam 168
BEN. *See* Franklin Templeton
Ben Franklin five-and-dime.
    See also Walmart
Benjamin Franklin Institute of
    Technology (BFIT) 8
Berkshire Hathaway 14, 17,
    37–38, 262
Bible 31, 167
    Genesis 2
    New Testament 205
bifocal lenses 26, 36, 86, 93,
    108, 123, 220, 237, 275
bigamist 323
Bill of Rights 171
    Fourth Amendment 171–172
birth xxi
    three hundredth anniversary 14
blacks 3, 124, 166, 336
    achieving success 124
bladder 105
bleeding (medical practice) ....
    107–108
Blinder, Alan S. 142
boats
    managing 201
Bogle, John C. 278, 343
Böhm-Bawerk, Eugen von 340
bonds 220
Bond, Thomas 242
books 262–264
    See also publications
Boston. *See* Massachusetts: Boston

Bourbon, Duchess of 250
Bourbon Street 266
Bradford, Andrew 148
bravery 298
Bridgen, Edward 151
Brillion de Jouy, Madame
    Anne-Louise 109, 204,
    213, 251, 255–256, 272,
    302, 305, 318–319, 338
Britain/British .. xxi, 118, 134, 162,
    186, 219, 245, 250, 291
    agents 171
    Crown .. 52, 59, 134, 139, 147, 169
    Empire 183
    House of Commons 267
    Intelligence 335
    Parliament 134, 161, 201, 223
    Royal Academy 123, 252
    Royal Society 91, 212
        Copley Medal *(1753)* 86, 91, 212
        induction *(1756)* 91
    solders 171
Brockliss, Laurence 104
Browns & Collinson 74
budgeting. *See* personal finances
Buffett, Warren 14, 17, 31, 37,
    39, 215, 262
Bunyan, John 241, 262
Burke, Edmund 291
business/businessman 5–38,
    16, 102, 274, 281
    management 13–15
    success 16–19
    three virtues 55
Cabanis, Pierre-Jean-Georges .. 231
Caesar, Julius 188
Café de La Régence 255
Cage, Nicolas 16
California 9

353

THE GREATEST AMERICAN

University of 121

calm 205

Calvinist....................................271

    virtues 215

Cambridge University 290

    Apostles....................................20

Canada.................... 114, 150, 282

    Conservative Party 79

    financial crisis *(2008)* 79

    fiscal crisis *(1994)*........................79

    Liberal Party................................79

Cantillon, Richard.................... 24

capitalism 7

    American.......................2, 7, 38, 74

    father of 7–9, 13, 113, 134,
        138, 214, 340–341

    free-enterprise 1

Capitol

    foundation *(1793)*....................291

Caribbean 10

Carleton University................114

Carlyle, Dr. Alexander.............116

Carlyle, Thomas 35

Carnegie, Andrew..... 8, 13, 17, 31,
    34, 126, 215, 340

Carnegie, Dale 34, 123, 214,
    222, 258

census data 99

central banking........................140

Chaplin, Joyce.................. 85, 212

charismatic............................311

charity 2, 29, 209, 242,
    278–281, 339

    corruption................................244

charm 3

chastity......205, 209–210, 272, 298

    See thirteen virtues

chess 15, 240, 250, 254, 306,
    318, 339

childhood........................... 44, 240

    allowance 44

children........xxi, 45, 124, 238, 287

China 127, 183, 199, 203–206, 216

    yearly growth............................183

Chinese gong 203

Chrétien, Jean 79

Christensen, Clayton..............129

Christian/Christians 339

    European.................................167

    virtues 209

Christmas................................305

Churchill, Winston 267

Cicero 275

Citizens' Stamp Advisory
    Committee...................153

City Hospital. *See* Pennsylvania:
    Hospital

city life 32

City Watch.........29, 162, 281, 343

civic accomplishments.... 279–281

civic responsibility..................... 8

civil service.............................. 29

Civil War....................... 151, 297

Clark, Gregory 121

Clason, George..............11, 45, 47

cleanliness 209, 298

    See thirteen virtues

CMA CGM *Benjamin Franklin*...
    127–128

CNBC54

Coca-Cola 38

Cockpit 117, 223

Cohen, I. Bernard 90

Cohn, Ellen............................266

354

INDEX

coinage............ 139. *See also* Dollar;
   See also colonies/colonists:
   copper penny

Colbert, Jean-Baptiste 25, 119

colds, theory of........ 104–105, 226

College of William & Mary....212

Collinson, Peter..........89, 91, 102

colonial
   agent 32, 51, 53, 69, 74, 104, 107,
      125, 130, 143, 161, 166,
      169, 178, 197–198, 201,
      212, 216, 222, 229, 241,
      263, 274, 307, 315, 329, 338
   dismissal *(1774)*........53, 77, 220
   Ohio territory 59
   treason 117
   government...............................134
   postal service............146–147, 149
      See also postal service
   postmaster general..................168
   dismissal 169

colonies/colonists ... 114, 118, 139,
      171, 174, 178, 201, 204,
      238, 240, 263, 290, 332
   copper penny 150–153
   first insurance company.............280
   land speculation 58
   relations with UK *(1974)*...........69
   unification of....................146–149
   voluntary grants 134

Columbus, Christopher..........293

commerce.............3, 25, 31–32, 58,
   119, 139

commercial
   banking system............................32
   society..30

common consent.....................137

community...............................32

community service 51

competitor/competition 15, 28

compound interest 14, 38,
   47–50, 66, 69, 141.
   See also saving

conductor................................ 90

Confucius................ 204–205, 216

Congress 96, 128, 161, 164, 167,
   178, 180, 211, 213, 230,
   245, 285, 330, 332, 342
   delegate to...............................125
   first meeting.............................167
   first meeting *(1790)* 167
   opinion of pay...........................96

Connecticut 271

Connecticut Compromise 182

conscription 188, 333

conservative............................133

Constitution. *See* US Constitution

Constitutional Convention ....
   xxii, 106, 125, 134, 137, 139,
   161, 163–164, 166, 181, 184,
   192, 217, 233, 273, 276, 329

Constitution Day 180

consumption 143

contacts.................................... 18

Continental Congress............102,
   173, 191, 279
   Second *(1775)*..........178, 226, 230

Continental dollar.
   See Dollar: Continental

Cook, Captain James..............254

Copley Medal *(1753)*. *See* Britain/
   British: Royal Society: Copley
   Medal *(1753)*

copper penny. *See* colonies/colonists:
   copper penny

courtesy..................................298

court system 133

355

THE GREATEST AMERICAN

Covey, Stephen R. 9
  Leadership Center 9
creative disruption 129
credit cards 144
cricket 103
critics 210, 212, 232, 299, 328–344
croakers 72
C-SPAN 24
culture 235–268
  chess, sports and games 254–257
  wining friends and influence people
    258–261
cunning................................... 210
Currey, Cecil B........................ 334
Dashwood, Francis 316
Da Silva, Howard 249
daughter. *See* Franklin, Sally
daylight savings time 26, 87
dealmaker............................... 276
death xxii, 33, 211, 224, 227, 292
  wealth 144
debts 15, 61–64, 75, 77, 125,
    135, 143, 221. *See* personal
    finances; *See also* personal
    finances
debunking myths 87
deception 28
Declaration of Independence.. xxi,
    28, 161, 173, 177, 184, 224,
    226, 229–230, 266, 316,
    326, 329, 348. *See also* War of
    Independence *(1775-1783)*;
    See also American Revolution
    (1776)
  age   102
  first anniversary *(1777)* 178
  first draft 190

Frankling's single change .. 190–193
  grievances 173
  prophecy 219
  slavery 191
de Condorcet, Marquis............ 25
deflation 72
Defoe, Daniel.................. 76, 279
Deist 192, 271, 325, 339
de Lafayette, Marquis 291
de Ligniville, Anne-Catherine......
    318. *See* Helvétius, Madame
democracy/democratic....... 2, 130,
    173, 326
  meritocracy 122
  representation........................... 162
Democrats................................ 133
demography 99
Denham, Thomas.................... 63
Department of Government
    Efficiency (DOGE) 150
descendants .14, 218, 231, 266, 310
Destutt de Tracy, Comte......... 231
de Tocqueville, Alexis 242
devil 316
Dewey, John.................. 274, 275
Dickinson, John 249
Dick, Sir Alexander 115
diet 102–105
  meat 105
diplomat....3, 13, 70, 214, 218, 222
discipline 31
Discovery Channel.................... 234
diversification 12, 52, 69
dividends................. 38, 47, 49, 53
  compounding............................. 49
division 130

INDEX

Doctrine and Covenants.........293

Dollar 39, 72
  $100 bill 7, 113–114, 211,
    330, 346
  collpase of 39
  Continental..............................151
  eagle silver dollar 7, 176
doomsayers..................71–75, 156
  See also personal finances
double agent...........................335
Dow 71
draft. *See* conscription
Drucker, Peter 140
earning power..........................141
earnings recession 72
East India Company................. 57
economy/economics............... 39,
  111–158, 218, 220
  American Dream..............121–126
  connection with Adam Smith.........
    113–120
  downturns..........................77, 142
  first copper penny 150–153
  free trade.........................127–129
  inequality.........................130–132
  new 39
  optimism..........................156–158
  paper money and inflation154–155
  political economy.............137–140
  post office........................146–149
  post-war 157
  Smith, Adam...................113–120
  today's tax burden 133–136
  virtue of thrift 141–145
Edinburgh, University of........239
Edison, Thomas A. 26
education 28, 122, 237–241
  liberal arts 237, 239
ego 211

Egyptian pyramids. *See* Freemasons
elastic currency........................221
elderly years. *See* old age
elections 161
election years...........................134
electric/electricity 85–88, 275
  experiments...........................29, 89
  kisses 89
  parties 89
  shows 89
  terminology...............................90
electroshock therapy...............108
Elizabethan mores 316
Elysian Fields, The.......... 252, 324
Emerson, Ralph Waldo...........275
enemies 222–225, 287
England/English.........................
  xxi, 10, 27, 53, 63, 70, 81,
  85, 119, 135, 156, 163, 169,
  186–187, 191, 201, 214,
  241–242, 249, 256, 264,
  274, 307, 332, 335, 342
  banking crisis *(1772)*..................53
  Cornwall 274
  Ecton 307
  first voyage to *(1724)* 198
  London 15, 32, 53–54, 59,
    69, 77, 104, 107, 109, 117,
    123–124, 127, 130, 161,
    169, 178, 197, 198, 201,
    212, 216, 222, 229, 254,
    255, 306, 314–316, 335,
    337–338, 341
    banking crisis *(1772)*...............12
    Craven Street 264, 316, 323, 338
    journeyman printer *(1725-1726)*
    25
  parliament............................... xxi
Enlightenment, the 103, 115,
  190, 325
entrepreneur/entrepreneurship ....

357

24–26, 215, 278, 328, 340

EPA 79

epitaph 13, 221, 289

Euro 72

Europe/European 213, 271, 290

aristocracy 122

immigrants 342

exercise 102–105, 107–108

expenditures 144

See personal finances

experiments 88, 103, 275, 336

See also electic/electricity

fads 103

faith 2, 299, 339

false gods 316

fame 7, 209–213

family 322–324

tree 307–310

Familysearch.org 307

fast money 54–56

See also personal finances

Fast Money Alert 54

father 308. *See also* Franklin, Josiah

Father of America's Growth
Machine 32

Faÿ, Bernard ... 1, 89, 164, 197, 342

fear 205

mongering 71–75

See also personal finances

Feast of Tabernacles 282

federal deficit 61

Federal Drug Administration ..107

Federal Reserve 39, 151,
154–155, 347

feedback system 15

Fibonacci 101

financial crisis *(2008)*.

See Great Recession *(2008)*

financial independence 215

See personal: finances

financier 218

Finger, Stanley 102, 110

fire department, first.

See Union Fire Company

fire insurance 26

fireman's pole 310

Fischer, Bobby 254

Flanders 271

Fleming, Thomas 146,
315–316, 338

flirtatious 227

Florida

Winter Park 265

Folger, Abiah 308

foreign policy 138

See also international relations

foreign wars 3

forgiveness 209

Fortunate Richard 48

Fortune 500 9

Fothergill, John 102, 115

founding fathers ....
xxii, 1, 16, 27, 30, 32, 122,
165, 214, 258, 291, 293,
326. *See also* Washington,
George; *See also* Adams, John;
See also Jefferson, Thomas;
See also Madison, James; *See
also* Hamilton, Alexander; *See
also* Jay, John; *See also* Henry,
Patrick; *See also* Monroe,
James; *See also* Mason,
George; *See also* Hancock,

358

INDEX

John; *See also* Morris, Robert; *See also* Lee, Henry;

See also Paine, Thomas
in comparison to 1
land 58
land speculators...........................59
Fox Business............................... 76
France/French .. xxi, 15, 66, 68–69,
103, 105, 119, 124, 163,
170, 179, 187, 198, 201,
212, 219, 227, 241–242,
245–246, 250, 272, 291,
299, 301, 332, 335, 337, 341
devestating winter *(1783-1784)*..74
ladies 317–321, 341
language....................................123
Paris 25, 32, 53, 109, 198, 212,
227, 229, 243, 255, 305,
317, 341. *See also* Treaty of
Paris *(1783)*
bombing of *(2015)*...................68
Revolution *(1789)*....................219
trade 119
Versailles 246, 317
Frank, Dodd 79
franking privilege 147
Franklin Bache, Benjamin
(1839-1900)................310
Franklin Bache, Benjamin ("Benny") *(1769-1798)*........ 82,
170, 310
charged with libel and sedition
(1798)...............................82
death of.....................................82
FranklinCovey............................ 9
Franklin Custodian Funds.........9
Franklin Day Planner 9
Franklin, Francis
death 314
Franklin, Franky

death 104, 107, 337
Franklin Funds...........................9
Franklin House 308
Franklin Institute of Technology..
8, 13, 49
Franklin, James........................ 25
Franklin, Jane.......... 252, 276, 300
Franklin, Josiah 201, 308
Franklin Medal...................... 98
Franklin Public Library ....264. *See
also* Library Company *(1732)*
Franklin Quest 9
Franklin, Sally ..... xxii, 44, 81, 124,
168, 175, 284, 308, 314, 341
Franklin, Sarah. *See* Franklin, Sally
Franklin stove....26, 36, 86, 89, 93,
96, 104, 123, 220, 237, 275
Franklin, Temple 81, 170, 216,
272, 309, 310
Franklin Templeton............8, 126
Franklin, Thomas 308
Franklin, William ....
80, 116, 123, 130, 161, 168,
179, 186, 198, 202, 220,
222, 224, 301, 309–310,
312, 322, 335, 337
letter to *(August 16, 1784)*........301
postmaster of Philadelphia 169
royal governor of New Jersey ...169,
186
Franklin, William Temple203, 338
fraud 28
Frederick II, King...................250
FreedomFest...........................121
free education.........................330
free-market economics..... 17, 113.
See also economy/economics
Freemasons..................... 290–294

359

St. John's Lodge..........................291

free speech................................342

free thinker...................... 271, 311

free trade 2, 25, 32, 39, 118, 138, 221, 340
  benefits of 127–129

French and Indian War (1754-1763) 69, 188, 331

friends 258–261, 287

Friends Meeting House (Quakers) 272

frugality......... 9, 11, 15–16, 28, 43, 62, 66, 77, 126, 143, 204, 209, 220, 272, 298. See also personal finances; See thirteen virtues

Fugio cent 150

fundraising...................... 242–247
  matching funds 242

funeral 224, 261

Gadsden Flag 175

Galileo 90

gall stones................................105

Gates, Bill 215

GEICO 38

genealogy/genealogist 307
  See family tree

General Welfare.......................181

George Mason University........ 95

Georgia 167, 244

Germany/German 191, 198, 201, 241, 266
  language....................................123

Getty, J. Paul 74

Gibbon, Edward......................315

giving. See charity

glass armonica 87, 93, 203

globalization............................1, 2

God   2, 177, 179, 181, 191–192, 198, 210, 219, 221, 252, 271–273, 283, 287, 293, 339. See also religion

gold 72, 139, 154
  standard 3, 151–152

Goldman Sachs 72

golf 103

good apprentices 48

good citizens 48

gout   105, 109, 245, 256, 286, 321
  dialogue with 257

government
  abuse. See politics: government abuse
  big 140
  bonds...................................12, 57
  central supergovernment 331
  limited 140, 220–221, 342
  representative 2
  size of....................................3, 79

grandchildren ....xxii, 124, 170, 238, 287

Grand Ohio Company 56, 59

gratification
  deferring....................................28

gratitude.................................209

gravesite 150

Great Britain. See Britain/British

Great Compromise......... 163, 276

Great Depression (1929-1939)....34, 151

Great Recession (2008) 79, 154, 347

Great Seal
  designing of..............................230

Great Society...........................78

greed 28

360

INDEX

Greeley, Horace 125

Green, Alexander....................121

guitar 123

Gulf Stream........... 26, 87, 93, 275

Hale, Sarah Josepha................284

Hall, David 51, 89

Hamilton, Alexander...........3, 32, 154, 219

Hancock, John 291

hard work. *See* industry/industri-ousness

harp 123

HarperCollins 125

Harper, James.........................125

harpsichord 203

Harry, David 44

Harvard.......... 85–86, 91, 212, 238

haste 18

health 102, 105, 107

hedonist 210

Hellfire Club 316, 341

Helvétius, Madame 203, 227, 231, 251–252, 319, 324

Henry, Patrick 58

heretic 271, 339

Herschbach, Dudley............... 88

high finance............................140

Hill, Napoleon 123

Hillsborough, Lord.................. 59

history 102

hoaxer/hoaxes................. 311, 336

holidays........................... 304–306

Holland......................... 241, 271

home delivery..........................148

Home, Henry........................115

honesty...........................8, 17, 126

hope 2

horoscopes...............................108

hospital, first. *See* Pennsylvania: Hospital

hospitals 32, 102
air quality.................................104

Houdon, Jean-Antoine...........317

House 181–182, 259

Howe, Lord Richard....... 226, 256

humbleness 19

Hume, David 115–118, 326

humility 205, 210–211, 272

humor 248–253, 311

Hunter, William......................149

Hutchinson letters scandal.. 53, 77

Hutchinson, Thomas..............223

hygiene....................................102
aristocrats.................................104

illegitimate son ....123.
See Franklin, William

Illinois Company 59

illnesses 105, 220

immigration 221

import duties..........................135

incentive................................. 14

income 125

independence 64, 70, 78, 113–114, 161, 162, 179

Independence Day 177–179, 183, 348

Independence Hall. *See* Pennsylvania State House

India 254

Indiana Company 59

individualism ... 123, 279, 331, 343

THE GREATEST AMERICAN

individual retirement account (IRA) 56

industry/industriousness.............. 8, 11, 15–16, 28, 31, 39, 43–46, 55, 61–62, 65–66, 69, 76, 123, 126, 138, 143, 209–210, 215, 272–273, 298, 329, 340. *See* thirteen virtues

inequality. *See* economy/economics: inequality

inflation 3, 39, 58, 66, 70, 132, 139, 150–152
    effect on the penny.................... 151
    wartime virtue........................... 134

influence 14, 20–23, 258–261

Ingenhousz, Jan.......................102

innovation................................. 8

inoculation..................... 104, 107

insolent 210

insurance agency, first.............123

integrity 19

intellectual curiosity 126

intellectual property rights. *See* patents

interest rates 39, 141

Internal Revenue Service (IRS) 79, 172

international relations..... 195–206
    an international man........197–199
    China.......................................203
    travelling and vacations 200–202

internet misquotes.......... 265–267

inventor/inventions .... 2, 13, 24, 26, 32, 85–86, 92, 123, 218, 237, 274. *See also* lightning rod; *See also* bifocal lenses; *See also* Franklin stove

investing/investments ... 11, 41–82. *See also* personal finances
    industry...8
    succesful...............................51–53

IPO 56

Ireland 116, 130

Isaacson, Walter..... 25, 59, 98, 227

Islamic extremists 69

Italy/Italian..............................198
    language...................................123

Izard, Ralph............. 227, 318, 333

Jackson, James.........................167

James, Henry............................275

James, William 274

Jay, John.................................213

Jefferson, Thomas........... 1, 27–28, 30, 122, 134, 139, 165, 178, 190–191, 217, 226, 228, 229–231, 258, 267, 274, 284, 326, 332
    personality...............................258
    slavery 165

Jesus Christ 2, 205, 210, 272–273, 288, 339

Jewish synagogues 272

Johnson, Paul 248

Johnson Sr., Rupert................... 9

jokes. *See* humor

Jones, Colin.............................104

Jones, John Paul 291

Jordan, Teresa.........................327

journal 105

J. P. Morgan 74

Junto   15, 18, 20–23, 26, 122, 210, 212, 222, 240–241, 260, 263, 279, 290, 343
    list of questions 20–21

justice 204, 298. *See* thirteen virtues

INDEX

Kames, Lord 116. *See* Home, Henry

Kansas City Public Library 24

Kant, Immanuel 91

Kauffman Foundation 24

Keimer, Samuel 25

Kellow, Geoffrey C. 114

Kentucky
Louisville..................................310

keychain 310

Keynesians...........................78–79

Keynes, John Maynard 31, 78, 142

kidney stones.................. 109, 286

King (slave) 166

kite experiment .... 86, 336.
    See science;kite experiment

Knights Templar....................290.
    See also Freemasons

knowledge 20–23, 262–264

Knuth, Donald........................ 98

Koran 167

Krugman, Paul 78

Kuttner, Robert 76

La Comtesse d'Houdetot.
    See Helvétius, Madame

lady's man 311

Laffer curve 95

laissez-faire ... 32, 39, 119, 134, 340

languages learned 123

La Rochefoucauld, Duc de 317

last will and testament 13, 48,
    57, 80–82, 203, 286, 340
    addendum..................................80
    William Franklin......................169

Latin language.........................123

Latter-day Saints 292

Lawrence, D. H....................... 45

lead poisoning 109

Leather Apron Club 20

Lee, Arthur.................... 162, 213,
    222, 224, 227, 261, 301,
    318, 332–333, 335

Lee, Charles............................331

Lee, Henry 60

Lee, William............................227

left-handed 310

legislators
    religious test 2

Leicestershire...........................308

leisure 31, 254

Lepore, Jill..................... 170, 301

Le Roy, Jean-Baptiste..........3, 317

letters. *See* writer/writing

Leyden jar 89

liberal/libertarian 25, 45,
    94–96, 120, 135, 139, 213,
    229, 332–333, 343–344
    arts. *See* education
    immigration policies....................2

liberty 22, 29, 31, 176, 188,
    190, 331, 333

Liberty Bell 177

Liberty Coin Act 176

Liberty Forum conference 10

libido 3

library chair............................. 93

Library Company *(1732)* 26,
    29, 122–123, 162, 237, 263,
    279, 343

Library of Mistakes.................. 72

lifting weights.........................104

lightning rod 26, 36, 86,
    93, 123, 220, 237, 275, 279.
    See science;lightning rod

Lincoln, Abraham 285
local police 133
Locke, John 326
Logan, Dr. James....................118
London. *See* England/English:
London
long arm.......................... 94, 187
long walks 104
Lopez, Claude-Anne...... 316, 320,
323, 338
Louis XVI, King............. 251, 317
miniature 81
love 311–364
loyalist 335
lust 28
See personal: love, sex and
marraige
Lyons, Jonathan....................... 23
Machiavelli, Niccolo............... 17
Madeira port 105, 109, 266
Madison, James 176, 180, 182, 291
magic squares 100–101, 255
Malthus, Thomas 99
marketplace............................ 28
marraige 322–324. *See also* personal:
love, sex and marraige
Martin, Paul 79
Mason, George........................165
slavery 165
Masonic Lodges. *See* Freemasons
masons. *See* Freemasons
Massachusetts.......... 147, 201, 275
Boston.......... xxi, 8, 13, 25, 38, 48,
89, 123, 148, 198, 229, 238,
263, 340
Charlestown.................282–284
Exeter......................................264

mathematics.............. 98–101, 102
Mather, Cotton 241, 262, 279
Mathon de la Cour, Charles-
Joseph 48
maxims.................................... 17
Mayer, Henry.......................... 58
Mayflower 282
McAllister, John D. T. 293
McCarty, Helen Louise 309
McCormick, Blaine.....13, 14, 216
McCullough, David 303
Mecom, Jane 169, 306
Medicare 61, 107
medicine 2, 83–110
empirical testing.......................103
preventive..................................102
preventive care...........................107
meditation...............................205
Mellon, Andrew 215
Mellon, Thomas 14, 17, 31,
125, 340
mental attitude.
See optimist/optimism
mercury...................................105
Mesmer, Dr. Franz.....87, 103, 107
Mesmerism. *See* animal magnetism
Methodist................................278
Mickle, Samuel........................ 73
Middle East.................... 198, 347
Middlekauff, Robert....... 224, 339
military service 333
minorities................................1, 3
Mises Institute.........................329
mistress 313
mobs 205, 342
moderation........21, 204, 209, 272,

INDEX

298. *See* thirteen virtues

moneygrubbing 27, 30

moneymaking 27–29, 30–31

monopolies............................ 95

Monroe, James 291

Montesquieu, Charles 28

moon 7

morality.......................... 325–327

moral turpitude 31

Morellet, Abbé Andre............203, 252, 266

Mormons 290–294

    Constitution 293

morning routine......................108

Morris, Robert . 3, 57, 60, 131, 154

mother. *See* Folger, Abiah

Mozart 87

Mr. Wonderful. *See* O. Leary, Kevin

Munger, Charlie 14, 17, 31, 37, 39, 262

    death 38

musical instruments 123, 203

musician................................203

Musk, Elon 96, 150

mutual

    communication.......................129

    improvement............................20

national

    debt 3, 61, 64, 78

    defense 133

    healthcare...............................106

National Constitution Center 266

Native Americans 131, 162, 282

    disputes..3

    Paxton Boys crisis....................331

natural cures...........................105

natural liberty, system of.......... 32

natural rights doctrine 191

Nebraska 37

negotiator................................ 15

Negro School of Philadelphia . 29, 124, 166, 238, 242, 336, 343

nepotism 168–170, 309

networking..........................26, 29

New Brunswick.....................226

New England ... 131, 147, 283, 308

New Jersey 147, 169, 186, 224, 309

new Prometheus...................... 91

Newton, Sir Isaac 86, 90, 326

New York 9, 53, 77, 148, 169, 177, 201, 263

    Staten Island............................226

Nine Sisters ....291.

    See also Freemasons

Nixon, Richard.....................151

nongovernmental organizations (NGOs) 162

North American Free Trade Agreement...................129

northern peso 79

Notre Dame d'Auteuil..........318.

    See Helvétius, Madame

Nova Scotia 81

Nozick, Robert.......................274

nudist 311

Number 72 335

Number 206 335

Obama, Barack......................150

Obamacare.............................. 79

odometer.......................26, 87, 94

Ogline, Tim 113

Ohio 52, 56

old age 45, 105, 106–110,

365

134, 305, 324, 339

O. Leary, Kevin 145

Olive Branch Petition 226

one-liners. *See* humor

opium 109

opportunist 210

optimist/optimism 1, 15, 39,
52, 58, 74, 105, 109, 138,
156–158, 173, 229, 340, 348

Order of the Friars of St. Francis
of Wycombe.
See Hellfire Club

order/orderliness...... 209–210, 298
See thirteen virtues

overbearing.............................210

overindulging 109

overspending 62, 69

Oxford Club 122

Oxley, Sarbanes 79

pain
optimism..................................109

Paine, Thomas 178, 332

parents201. *See also* mother;
See also father

Parker, James 169

Parkinson's Second Law 62

parsimony 45

parties 305

partisan politics 4, 161

Pasles, Paul C. 98–99

patents 93–97
See also inventor/inventions

patience................................... 18

Patriot Act..............................347

patriot/patriotism 13, 16, 175

Patten, Simon N. 114

paving 281

Paxton Boys crisis 331

peace 120, 186–189

Peale, Norman Vincent 156

Pennsylvania.. 8, 60, 134, 139, 201,
212, 290
See also Philadelphia
Academy 123, 343
See also Pennsylvania: University
of
Constitution 333
Freemasons
grand master 291
General Assembly........23, 35, 100,
161, 243
Hospital 26, 107, 123, 162
militia 29, 162, 280, 343
president of 125
Society for Promoting the Abolition
of Slavery 166
State House...............................179
University of 26, 114,
237–238, 242, 280

Penn, Thomas.........................261

Penn, William 134
tax exemption.............................134

penny post 148
See also postal service

persistence...............................126

personal........................... 295–348
consumption 66, 77
family................................307–310
finances 41–82
austerity 76–79
budgeting..........................43–46
debt
getting out of 61–64
doomsayers and fear mongering ..
71–75
fast money 54–56
financial crisis....................65–67
investing 51–53

INDEX

real estate 57–60
wartime, protecting capital 68–70
love, sex and marraige 311–321
responsibility 126
personality/personalities 207–234, 235–268
fame and vanity 209–213
George Washington..........232–234
John Adams.......................226–228
making enemies.................222–225
seven discoveries...............218–221
Thomas Jefferson..............229–231
Peter (slave) 166
Phelps, Glenn A. 58
Philadelphia ....xxi, 2–3, 8, 11, 18, 22, 25, 28, 32, 38, 48, 53, 55, 57, 80, 91, 123, 124, 137, 148, 157, 165, 168, 177, 198, 201, 203, 215, 221, 223–224, 229, 258, 263, 266, 272, 278, 306, 311, 313, 327, 331, 335, 342
Constitution Society 183
Contributionship for the Insurance of Houses from Loss by Fire.. 280
first hospital 280
Market Street 124
militia 188
undercutting rules of military law (1755)..............................188
slavery 165–166
Society 337
philanthropy 32, 244
philosophy/philosopher.......... 27, 30, 102, 116, 218, 269–294, 274, 323
dying 286–289
practical 274–276
Physiocrats 137, 138, 340
Pilgrims..................................282
Pirie, Madsen 27, 274
playboy..................................311

Plutarch......................... 241, 262

Plymouth Rock 282
polemics.................................. 22
political economy. *See* economy/economics
political philosophy 27, 28
politics 51, 102, 159–193
4th of July, celebrating......177–179
change in Declaration of Independence 190–193
Constitution 180–182
See also Constitution
factions 163
government abuse 171–173
nepotism 168–170
racism 165–167
rising or setting sun 183–185
GDP 185
yearly growth 183
three symbols of America .174–176
war and peace...................186–189
polymath................. 102, 115, 248
poor laws................................. 31
Poor Richard 15, 36
See publications: Poor Richard's Almanac
population prediction.............. 99
Port of Los Angeles.................128
postage stamps ....7. *See* stamps
postal service.
See also US Postal Service
dead letter office 148
delivery time 148
milestones 147
postmaster general .... xxi, 51, 53, 69, 77, 146–147
dismissal..............................53, 77
potential customers 18
poverty 34

367

Powell, Jim 121, 123, 126

pragmatic/pragmatism... 191, 275, 326, 339

prankster 248

prejudices 166

Presbyterians 276

Price, Dr. Richard....................118

pride 210

Priestley, Sir Joseph68, 91, 102, 336

Princeton...............................238

principles. *See* thirteen virtues; *See* three principles

Pringle, Sir John 115, 201

printer xxi, 3, 11, 13, 15, 22, 24–25, 61, 89, 109, 123, 134, 157, 198, 201, 214

    franchising................................26

    retirement 26

profits

    eleven rules...........................18–19

progress 1–2

Prométhée 335

prosperity 142

protectionist measures 128

Proverbs 31

Providence.............................192

prudence 8, 9, 11, 16, 21, 31, 39, 55, 61, 65, 69, 76, 78, 123, 138, 215, 273, 329

Prussia 250

psoriasis.................................109

public affairs........................... 86

publications

    7 Habits of Highly Effective People .9

    101 Great Philosophers: Makers of Modern Thought 27, 274

    Advice to a Young Man on the Choice of a Mistress 313

Annals of Philadelphia................117

Art of Procuring Pleasant Dreams, The..................................108

Art of War, The..........................17

Aurora, The..............................170

Autobiography 9, 14, 17, 23, 25–26, 31, 34, 52, 63, 66, 72, 93, 96, 122–123, 125, 143, 155, 157, 198, 204–205, 209, 210, 211, 214–216, 218, 220, 222, 224, 238, 242, 259–260, 262, 272, 276, 286, 297, 301, 307, 312, 323, 327–328, 337, 340, 342–343

Ben Franklin, America's Original Entrepreneur: Franklin's Autobiography for Modern Times ... 14, 216

Ben Franklin's 12 Rules of Management....................................14

Benjamin Franklin 334

Bolt of Fate 336

Book of Ages: The Life and Opinions of Jane Franklin 170, 300

Book TV 24

Cambridge History of English and American Literature 137

Code Number 72, Ben Franklin: Patriot or Spy?..................334

Coming Deflation, The 72

Common Sense 178, 332

Completed Autobiography by Benjamin Franklin, The... 133, 199, 216, 218, 220, 303, 329, 343

Conceived in Liberty...................330

Confessions 209

Constitutions of the Free-Masons, The 291

Crisis Investing 72

Death of Inflation, The 72

Debtor's Prison: The Politics of Austerity Versus Possibility............76

Democracy in America 242

Doctor Franklin's Medicine 102, 110

End of America, The 72

Essays to Do Good..............241, 262

INDEX

Experiments and Observations on Electricity..............91
Fast Money..............54
Federal Gazette..............167
Federalist Paper..............180
Forbes : 400 Richest People in America..............54
Forecasts & Strategies..............9
Gazette..............275
Gentlemen's Magazine..............314
Good, An Essay Upon the..............279
Great Reckoning: How the World Will Change in the Great Depression of the 1990s, The..............72
History of the Decline and Fall of the Roman Empire, The..............315
How Innovation Works..............95
How to Prosper During the Coming Bad Years..............72
How to Win Friends and Influence People..............34, 123, 258
Importance of Living, The..............206
Journal de Paris..............99
Ladies' Magazine..............284
Life of Adam Smith..............117
Maxims of Wall Street, The..............38
Memoirs of the Life and Writings of Benjamin Franklin..............81
Modest Enquiry into the Nature and Necessity of a Paper-Currency, A..............139
Money Masters, The..............11
Moral Arc, The..............325
Morals of Chess, The..............255
Morals of Confucius, The...204–205, 240
National Treasure..............16
Nature and Necessity of a Paper-Currency, The..............154
New-England Courant, The..............263
New York Times..............172
New York Tribune..............125
Notes on the State of Virginia..............230
Observations Concerning the Increase of Mankind and the Peopling of Countries..............99

On a Life Well Spent..............275
Papers of Benjamin Franklin..............300, 329
Papers of Benjamin Franklin, The..............199, 216, 218, 266
Parallel Lives..............241, 262
Pennsylvania Gazette..............25, 148, 162, 166, 240, 243, 279
Pennsylvania Gazette, The..204, 212
Pennsylvania Journal..............174
Philadelphia Aurora..............82, 310
Philadelphia Gazette..............98
Pilgrim's Progress..............241, 262
Political Philosophy of Benjamin Franklin, The..............28
Poor Charlie's Almanack..............38
Poor Richard's Almanac....8, 10, 17, 27, 30, 51, 63, 65, 69, 77, 107, 138, 141, 143, 249, 267, 304, 310
Power of Positive Thinking?, The.156
Principle of Population, An Essay on the..............99
Projects, An Essay Upon..............279
Proposals Relating to the Education of Youth in Pennsylvania..............124, 237
Protestant Ethic and the Spirit of Capitalism, The..............215
Richest Man in Babylon, The..............11, 45, 47
Robinson Crusoe..............76
Runaway America..............336
Scientific American..............325
Self-Help Messiah: Dale Carnegie and Success in Modern America.34
Shark Tank..............94, 145
Skeptic..............325
Society of Useful Knowledge: How Benjamin Franklin and Friends Brought the Enlightenment to America, The..............23
Spectator, The..............263
Speech of Miss Polly Baker, The...314
Theory of Moral Sentiments..............116

Think and Grow Rich 123
Time 307
Times, The 172
Wall Street Journal 79
Way to Wealth, The 10, 25, 43,
    51, 54, 62, 113, 136, 143
Wealth of Nations, The 28, 32,
    39, 78, 113, 116–118, 138,
    315, 340
Wealthy 100, The 33
*Wiped Out: How I Lost a Fortune
    in the Stock Market While the
    Averages Were Making New
    Highs*..........................72
*Year of Living Virtuously (Weekends
    Off): A Meditation on the
    Search for Meaning in an
    Ordinary Life, The* 327

public library, first.
    See Library Company *(1732)*

public office............................. 32

public relations........................ 25

public servant.......................... 24

publisher ....xxi, 25

punctuality............................. 8

punishment
    power of................................17

puns. *See* humor

Puritans........ 3, 271, 282, 305, 311
    views 30

quantitative easing..................154

quiet 227

quotes 1
    advice...............................17
    arbitrary government................171
    arithmetic...........................98
    becoming rich 10
    business.............................13
    chess 256
    Constitution 135
    croakers.............................73
    cup of life..........................105

death 80
debt 65, 66
democracy..............................2
doomsayers........................52, 71
eating 107
England and war 70
fads and superstitions 103
faults 15
forming a government..............161
France 68–69
God 192
invention.............................93
labor 9
Laissez nous faire....................129
little expenses 15
love 221
opium 109
paper money 154
parties 109
penny saved...........................47
personal debt and credit 12
private initiatives 29
prosperity............................121
racial equality 337
rattlesnake.....................174–175
religion..............................272
retirement 106
slavery..............................166
tart words............................36
technology 85
trade with France 119
vanity...............................210
virtuous people......................120
war 187
war and peace.........................120

racism 165–167

radical revolutionary..............332

Rae, John 117

rags-to-riches 17, 33, 122–123,
    215, 220

rationality............................. 39

rattlesnake 174–175

Rawls, John 274

INDEX

Ray, Catharine..........................315

Read, Deborah .... xxi, 44, 62, 65, 124, 143, 197, 201, 252, 297, 300, 314, 337
death xxi, 124, 286, 315, 324, 338
marriage 123, 312, 322–324
relationship with William.........312

reading 262

Reagan, Ronald 72, 176

real bills doctrine 139

real estate............................ 57–60
market *(post 2008)* 74

reason 205

regulations................................ 79

religion.............. 1, 2, 30, 192, 221, 229, 269–294, 325
afterlife..............................286–289
masons and mormons 290–294
philosophy 193
usefulness 271–273

rental properties 12

Republicans.................... 128, 133

reputation 15, 17, 19, 25, 316

resolution 209, 298
See thirteen virtues

retirement ....xxi, 106–110

retrenching........................ 77, 143

reverence 298

Revere, Paul............................291

revolutionary 214, 329

Revolutionary War. *See* War of Independence *(1775-1783)*

reward
power of......................................17

rich
defense of..............................30–33

Ridley, Jasper...........................292

Ridley, Lord Matt.................... 95

Rights 171–173, 191, 326

rising sun.................................174

Robertson, Dr. William..........116

Roll, Eric................................137

Rollins College 265

Roman Catholic.....................198

Romans................................ 27

Roosevelt, Franklin Delano ...151, 285

Rotary Club 18

Rothbard, Murray 330–335, 341, 343

Rule of 72 49–50

Runaway America 336

Rush, Benjamin....... 102, 104, 211

Samuelson, Paul 142

satire. *See also* humor

saving .... 11, 43, 45, 47, 51, 56. *See also* compound interest
accounts.....................................47

savoir faire................................. 3

Savoy 105

Saxons 191

Say, Jean-Baptiste 24, 215

Say's law 215

science/scientific..8, 16, 26, 32, 51, 83–110, 92, 102, 123, 214, 218, 275. *See also* technology/ technologist
accomplishments......................212
achievements............................230
advances.......................................2
after retirement 86
experiments...........................85, 86
kite experiment *(1752)*...............91
lightning rod 88–92
method 325
portrait as a scientist *(1766)* 86

371

wonders of 85–87

Scotland 72, 115–116, 130, 169, 179, 198, 201–202

Edinburgh..................72, 115–116

Scottish Enlightenment..........115

Scout Law 298

scurff 105

secretive...................................210

secular humanism....................327

See's Candies 38

self-discipline........................... 28

self-help....... 34–36, 107, 122–123, 279, 343

self-reliance 123, 169

Senate 181–182, 224, 227

settlers 59, 184, 283

sexual exploits .... 312. *See* personal: love, sex and marraige

sexual revolution 1

Shakespeare, William..........61, 95

Shermer, Michael 325

shipwreck................................274

siblings ....xxi, 25, 44, 169, 201, 252, 276, 300

silence .... 204–205, 209–210, 297. *See* thirteen virtues

Silence Dogood letters............. 16

silver 139, 154

sincerity........................... 209, 298

See thirteen virtues

Skousen, Jo Ann......................329

Skousen, Mark 10, 345–349

slaves/slavery .... 3, 30, 165, 232, 336. *See also* Declaration of Independence; *See also* Peter (slave); *See also* King (slave)

abolition of 3

importation ban *(1808)*............166

slaveholder 221

sleeping 108

smallpox................. 104, 107, 170, 314, 322, 337

Smith, Adam 28, 32, 39, 78, 113–120, 137–138, 142, 158, 221, 297, 315, 340–341

America prediction...................118

death 115

Smith, Hyrum...........................9

Smith Pangle, Lorraine........... 28, 243, 333, 341

Smith, Wright & Grey............. 74

social libertarian 341

social life 109–110

Social Security.................. 61, 125

Society of the Cincinnati.......205, 233–234

Socrates 205, 210, 272

Solomon, King........................205

Solomon's Temple...................290

See also Freemasons

SpaceX 96

Spanish language 123

Spassky, Boris 254

spectacles........................... 86–87.

See also bifocal lenses

speculative opportunities......... 52

speech of reconciliation 182

Spence, Dr............................... 89

spy accusation 292

Stamp Act/Tax..........xxi, 134, 162, 200, 223, 250

stamps 149

commemorative 214

half-cent..................................153

one-cent..................................153

INDEX

St. Andrews, University of...... 86, 91, 115, 212

statesman 274

static electricity. *See also* electric/electricity

St. Augustine..........................209

steam engine 95

Stevenson, Margaret 316, 323, 338

Stevenson, Polly 306, 316, 323

St. George Utah Temple 292

Stiles, Ezra....................... 272, 288

St. John's University................204

stock market.......... 55, 57, 69, 144
    corrections 71
    crash 72
    crashes.................................65
    crash *(Oct 1987)*.........................71

stocks 53, 72, 220

Stoic philosophy.....................205

storytelling 3

Stossel, John 76

Strahan, William115–116, 223, 315

street lighting 93, 281

success 34, 36, 262–264

Sunday blue laws..................... 30

superfluous property...............132

superstitions 103

Sweden....................................150

Swift, Jonathan.......................250

swimming 103, 107, 254
    fins 93

Tabarrok, Alex......................... 95

tariffs 128

taxation .... 32, 172, 223.
    See also economy/economics
    corporate.....................................79
    evasion 132

technology/technologist .... 26, 83–110, 123.
    See also science/scientific
    patents 93–97
    revolution................................187

teenage years........ xxi, 55, 123, 241
    runaway 198

teeth 105

temperance.21, 209–210, 272, 297.
    See thirteen virtues

Templeton, John 9

terrorism 69

Tesla Motors............................. 96

Texas, University of 28

Thanksgiving.................. 282–285
    discontinued 284

The Band................................. 23

Theist 192

The Union............................... 23

The Vine 23

thirteen virtues 204–205, 209, 215, 272, 297–299, 312, 327
    See also three principles

Thomas, Dylan.......................286

Thompson, John 191

Thorpe, Francis 116

three hundredth birthday 214

three principles.......... 8, 39, 55, 65, 69, 123, 126.
    See also thirteen virtues

thrift 8, 11, 17, 31, 39, 55, 61, 65, 69, 76, 120, 123, 126, 138, 141–145, 210, 215, 273, 278, 329, 340
    paradox of........................142–144

Titanic 127

tolerant...................................227

Tory imperialist.............. 331, 332

THE GREATEST AMERICAN

total disunion 134

tourism.................................... 69

Townshend Acts 178

trade 138, 152, 154, 221

training 28

Train, John 11

tranquility 209, 298
    See thirteen virtues

transportation........................... 2

traveling 197–199, 200–202

treason/traitors 117, 334, 335

Treaty of Paris *(1783)* 70, 163

Trump, Donald 72, 128

trust 8

Tucker, Gideon J. 265

Tucker, Tom 336

Turgot, Anne-Robert-Jacques . 25, 86, 317, 324

turkey 174, 284

Twain, Mark..................... 45, 265

tyranny....................................333

Tzu, Sun................................. 17

Ultra Large Container Vessel ..127

undersaving............................. 62

Union Fire Company 29, 86, 123, 162, 279, 343

urinary catheter 94

US Constitution................xxii, 94, 96, 135, 162, 171, 180–182, 219, 224, 329
    Article I
      Section 8
        Clause 8 94
      Section 10 153
    father of 180
    signing *(1787)*...........................176

US military 3

US Mint
    production *(2024)*....................150

US Postal Service.... 146–149, 153, 214. *See also* postal service

US Treasury Department 146, 150

Utah 292, 327

vacations. *See* traveling

vain 210

Van Buren, Carl 149

Van Doren, Carl.90, 313, 334, 337

Vanguard Group.....................278

vanity 209–213

ventilation 104

Vergennes, Comte de...... 245, 251

vigilance 175

Viol de Gambo.......................203

violin 123

Virginia 58, 60, 165, 226, 230

Volney, Comte de....................231

volunteer work 29

Waldstreicher, David 336

Wall Street..................... 65, 122

Walmart 8

Walpole, Richard...................... 59

Walpole, Thomas...................... 59

Walton, Sam............................ 8

Wang, David 204

war 3, 68, 76, 85, 186–189, 220, 224

warmonger 331

War of 1812 151

War of Independence *(1775-1783)*...xxi, 58, 69, 92, 129, 134, 149, 156, 169, 178, 188, 229, 232, 334, 336, 340. *See also* Declaration of

INDEX

Independence; *See also* American Revolution *(1776)*
death toll.....................................186
French assistance 219
post thoughts 129
wartime...............................68–70
    See also personal finances

Washington, George...............1, 3, 7, 30, 58, 82, 106, 134, 149, 165, 176–177, 182, 188, 200, 205, 211, 217, 226, 232–234, 251, 258–259, 284, 291, 293, 310, 311, 331, 333, 335, 346
   critics 232
   farewell address *(1796)*.............188
   personality................................258
   quotes 57
   slavery 165

Watson, Dr. John Fanning......117

Watt, James 95

Watts, Steven............................ 34

wealth 10–12, 16, 19, 28, 31, 47, 57, 131. *See also* compounding interest

Webb, Benjamin....................... 63

Weber, Max...............31, 215, 340

Wedderburn, Alexander..........117

Welch harp..............................203

Wesley, John............................278

Wharton School......................114

wheelbarrow........................18, 26

Whitefield, George................205, 244–245, 344

Whitehall Palace.....................117

whites 3

William & Mary 86, 91

Willing Powel, Elizabeth 179

Wilson, James 60

wine 105, 109, 252, 266
   cellar 109

Wisconsin 8

Witherspoon, John................. 58

women's rights........................... 3

Woodruff, Wilford 292, 293

Woodstock of Capitalism 37

World War I 151

World War II............65, 151–153

writer/writing................... 32, 274
   letters 300–303

Yale University 86, 91, 212, 238, 266, 300

Yale University Press 199, 218, 329

Yen 72

Yorktown....................... 333, 336

Yutang, Lin 206

ACKNOWLEDGMENTS

Many of these chapters are original; others are an updated version of a series of columns I wrote from 2009 to 2016 for the *Franklin Prosperity Report*. I want to thank the publisher Christopher Ruddy and my editor Stephanie Gallagher for their help and support. During this seven-year period, only one submission was rejected as too risqué for their conservative readers: chapter 77 on "On Love and Sex: Franklin's Hard-to-Govern Passions."

I've also drawn from a fifty-page booklet I wrote in 1996 entitled, "The Wit and Wisdom of Benjamin Franklin," published by Pickering & Chatto Publishers in London, long out of print.

I'd also like to thank Al Regnery, the publisher of Republic Books, and Ja Racharaks for supporting the publication of this book and for their outstanding work in editing and improving the chapters.

Lastly, I'd like to thank my wife and sweetheart, Jo Ann, for her unwavering efforts to refine my writing style and her felicity of expression. She is the inspiration and partner behind my success.

Note: Throughout this book I cite frequent references to two books: my own edition of *The Autobiography of Benjamin Franklin* (Regnery Publishing, 2006) and *The Compleated Autobiography by Benjamin Franklin*, compiled and edited by my wife and I (Regnery Publishing, 2006). *A* refers to the original *Autobiography*, and *CA* refers to the *Compleated Autobiography*.

In reading these various themes, you will hopefully see the versatile genius that Benjamin Franklin was and why we can be proud of him as a founding father…and grandfather of our nation.

Be free, AEIOU,
Mark Skousen

ABOUT THE AUTHOR

Dr. Mark Skousen is "America's Economist" (www.americaseconomist.us). He holds the Doti-Spogli Endowed Chair in Free Enterprise at Chapman University. In 2019, he received the "My Favorite Professor" Award. He earned his PhD in monetary economics from George Washington University in 1977. In 2018, he was awarded the Triple Crown in Economics for his work in theory, history, and education. He has taught economics, business, and finance at Columbia Business School and Columbia University. He has worked for the government (CIA) and non-profits (president of the Foundation for Economic Education) and has been a consultant to IBM and other Fortune 500 companies. He has been a longtime columnist for Forbes magazine, a frequent contributor of the Wall Street Journal, and a regular panelist on CNBC's Kudlow & Company and Rick Santelli's Exchange. He is the author of over twenty-five books, including *The Making of*

THE GREATEST AMERICAN

Modern Economics and *The Maxims of Wall Street* (www.skousenbooks. com). He has been editor in chief of an award-winning investment newsletter, *Forecasts & Strategies*, since 1980. He produces Freedom-Fest, "the world's largest gathering of free minds," every July in Las Vegas and other cities (www.freedomfest.com). His personal website can be found at www.mskousen.com. Based on his work *The Structure of Production* (NYU Press, 1990), the federal government has begun publishing a broader, more accurate measure of the economy, "gross output" (GO), every quarter along with GDP (www.grossoutput.com).

As a sixth-generation grandson of Benjamin Franklin, Mark Skousen has had a lifelong interest in "Grampa Ben." In 2006, in honor of his three hundredth birthday, he, along with his wife Jo Ann, compiled and edited the Franklin papers to publish *The Compleated Autobiography by Benjamin Franklin* (Regnery Publishing).